Teaching Hemingway and Modernism

TEACHING HEMINGWAY

Mark P. Ott, Editor
Susan F. Beegel, Founding Editor

Teaching Hemingway's *The Sun Also Rises*
EDITED BY PETER L. HAYS

Teaching Hemingway's *A Farewell to Arms*
EDITED BY LISA TYLER

Teaching Hemingway and Modernism
EDITED BY JOSEPH FRUSCIONE

Teaching Hemingway and Modernism

Edited by Joseph Fruscione

The Kent State University Press   Kent, Ohio

Copyright © 2015 by The Kent State University Press, Kent, Ohio 44242
All rights reserved
Library of Congress Catalog Card Number 2014049079
ISBN 978-1-60635-246-5
Manufactured in the United States of America

Library of Congress Cataloging-in-Publication Data
Teaching Hemingway and Modernism / edited by Joseph Fruscione.
    pages cm. — (Teaching Hemingway)
  Includes bibliographical references and index.
  ISBN 978-1-60635-246-5 (pbk. : alk. paper) ∞
  1. Hemingway, Ernest, 1899–1961—Study and teaching. 2. Modernism (Literature)—Study and teaching. I. Fruscione, Joseph, 1974– editor.
  PS3515.E37Z8917 2015
  813'.52—dc23
                    2014049079

Contents

Foreword
MARK P. OTT   vii

Introduction
JOSEPH FRUSCIONE   1

Modernist Style, Identity Politics, and Trauma in Hemingway's "Big Two-Hearted River" and Stein's "Picasso"
JULIE GOODSPEED-CHADWICK   10

"Miss Stein Instructs": Revisiting the Paris Apprenticeship of 1922
KATIE OWENS-MURPHY   21

Hemingway, Stevens, and the Meditative Poetry of "Extraordinary Actuality"
PHILLIP BEARD   30

Our Greatest American Modernists: Teaching Hemingway and Faulkner Together
JAMES B. CAROTHERS   42

From Paris to Eatonville, Florida: Hemingway's *The Sun Also Rises* and Hurston's *Their Eyes Were Watching God*
ANNA LILLIOS   51

The Sun Also Rises and the "Stimulating Strangeness" of Paris
MEG GILLETTE   62

Teaching the Avant-Garde Hemingway: Early Modernism in Paris
ADAM R. MCKEE   72

Teaching Hemingway Beyond "The Lost Generation": European Politics and American Modernism
DAVID BARNES   82

Twentieth-Century Titans: Orwell and Hemingway's Convergence
through Place and Time
JEAN JESPERSEN BARTHOLOMEW   92

The Developing Modernism of Toomer, Hemingway, and Faulkner
MARGARET E. WRIGHT-CLEVELAND   105

The Futurist Origins of Hemingway's Modernism
BRADLEY BOWERS   117

Hemingway, His Contemporaries, and the South Carolina Corps
of Cadets: Exploring Veterans' Inner Worlds
LAUREN RULE MAXWELL   128

Teaching Hemingway's Modernism in Cultural Context:
Helping Students Connect His Time to Ours
SHARON HAMILTON   137

On Teaching "Homage to Switzerland" as an Introduction to
Postmodern Literature
JEFFREY HERLIHY-MERA   149

Chasing New Horizons: Considerations for Teaching Hemingway
and Modernism in a Digital Age
ANDREW FLETCHER   158

Appendixes   169

Works Cited   213

Selected Bibliography   220

Contributors   223

Index   228

Foreword

Mark P. Ott

How should the work of Ernest Hemingway be taught in the twenty-first century? Although the "culture wars" of the 1980s and 1990s have faded, Hemingway's place in the curriculum continues to inspire discussion among writers and scholars about the lasting value of his work. To readers of this volume, his life and writing remain vital, meaningful, and culturally resonant for today's students.

Books in the Teaching Hemingway Series build on the excellent work of founding series editor Susan F. Beegel, who guided into publication the first two volumes of this series, *Teaching Hemingway's* A Farewell to Arms, edited by Lisa Tyler (2008), and *Teaching Hemingway's* The Sun Also Rises, edited by Peter L. Hays (2008). To promote their usefulness to instructors and professors—from high schools, community colleges, and universities—the newest volumes in this series are organized thematically, rather than around a single text. This shift attempts to open up Hemingway's work to more interdisciplinary strategies of instruction through divergent theories, fresh juxtapositions, and ethical inquiries, and to the employment of emergent technology to explore media beyond the text.

Teaching Hemingway and Modernism, edited by Joseph Fruscione, speaks to issues that remain of intense interest to students and scholars today: the avant-garde, Paris, politics, war, race, and trauma. The expertise and insight Fruscione brought to his definitive work, *Faulkner and Hemingway: Biography of a Literary Rivalry* (2012), is manifest throughout this volume. These far-ranging essays explore Hemingway's biography, his experience in Paris, the role of the Great War, and the implications that all these intersections had for the shaping and evolution of American modernism. This volume demonstrates that in today's classrooms and lectures halls Hemingway's work is being taught in more thoughtful and innovative ways than ever before. Indeed, the essays showcase the creativity, wisdom, and insight of authors from varied backgrounds united in their passion for sharing Hemingway's work with a new generation of students.

Introduction

Joseph Fruscione

Before we were teachers of Hemingway, we were students of Hemingway. Before we began defining *modernism* for our students, we were taught a set of terms, concepts, and exemplars that help articulate what modernism is—or, perhaps, more accurately, what modernisms are. I intend for this collection to guide students and teacher-scholars in (re)defining what Hemingway and modernism(s) continue to mean, both individually and jointly.

Just as, in Rita Barnard's words, "[n]o one cause or project can be singled out as the defining feature of this diverse body of writing" (39), so too no one Hemingway text or theme can capture his multifaceted engagement with modernism in the postwar era. My goal for *Teaching Hemingway and Modernism* is to offer concrete, intertextual models for effectively using Hemingway's work in various classroom settings, so students can understand the pertinent works, definitions, and types of avant-gardism that inflected his art. I aim for this volume to advance an intertextual–contextual approach to teaching Hemingway's work in light of evolving theories and constructions of modernism, instead of a more traditional single-author or single-text approach. When soliciting essays for this collection in the summer and fall of 2012, I encouraged multiauthor, context-based approaches to Hemingway and/in modernism—specifically, approaches that balanced a focused, individual treatment of Hemingway's work(s) with a clear link to the era and a clear set of assignments, prompts, and other teaching tools. Since Hemingway worked in dialogue with authors, artists, and larger literary and political movements in the postwar scene, models for teaching his work in its modernist context should not only discuss but also practice this author–milieu dialogue. In this way, I'm seeking to operate within yet expand on the fine work my predecessors Peter Hays and Lisa Tyler have done, respectively, in *Teaching Hemingway's* The Sun Also Rises (2007) and *Teaching Hemingway's* A Farewell to Arms (2008).

I have chosen teacher-scholars from various levels of their careers who will discuss their ways of teaching Hemingway's connections to such authors as Wallace Stevens, Gertrude Stein, William Faulkner, Ezra Pound, F. Scott Fitzgerald, Thornton Wilder, Zora Neale Hurston, and George Orwell. This multiauthor approach is, I hope, both critically engaging and pedagogically applicable to teachers at various levels of secondary and university education. Teaching students ways of researching and evaluating information critically—from both born-print and born-digital sources—is a key step in teaching them to think and write critically. Readers can expect to find, among various interpretive approaches to Hemingway's modernist-era work, a series of writing, discussion, and research-based tasks for different kinds of students.

My central goal is for this collection to strengthen yet complicate Hemingway's position as a modernist—and perhaps as a proto-postmodernist, as Jeffrey Herlihy-Mera posits in chapter 14—while moving beyond established narratives of the "lost generation" and the like. The book's fifteen contributors address a variety of critically significant questions, among them:

- How can we view and then teach Hemingway's work along a spectrum of modernist avant-gardism?
- How can we teach his stylistic minimalism both on its own and in conjunction with the more expansive styles of Joyce, Faulkner, Woolf, and other modernists?
- What is, or should be, Hemingway's place in evolving critical conversations about Anglophone modernism? What is new about Hemingway and/in modernism?
- How can we see the influence of Stein, Pound, and others on Hemingway in terms of dialogue and shared exchange, rather than simply a mentor-mentee relationship?
- What is *post*modernist about an author so often discussed exclusively as a modernist, and how might we teach Hemingway's work vis-à-vis that of contemporary authors?
- How can teacher-scholars bridge twentieth- and twenty-first-century pedagogies for Hemingway studies and American literary studies in high

school, undergraduate, and/or graduate settings? What role, if any, should new media play in the classroom?

Although much less broadly, I intend *Teaching Hemingway and Modernism* to work within the kinds of interdisciplinary, multiartist constructs that Douglas Mao and Rebecca Walkowitz have advanced in their collection, *Bad Modernisms* (2006). "The new modernist studies," they note persuasively, have "moved toward a pluralism or fusion of theoretical commitments, as well as a heightened attention to continuities and intersections across the boundaries of artistic media ... and (especially) to the relationship between individual works of art and the larger cultures in which they emerged" (2).[1] Furthermore, they add, "this direction resonates with developments occurring throughout the humanities in recent years, of course, but it seems to accrue particular influence in the orbit of modernism, because early twentieth-century writers were themselves so preoccupied with border crossings such as cosmopolitanism, synesthesia, racial masquerade, collage, and translation" (2). Hemingway's work at various levels participates in this modernist project of engagement and exchange, for instance in the kinds of stylistic, structural, and gendered newness seen throughout *In Our Time* (1925). In these fifteen essays, I have encouraged a similar, though smaller-scale, "variousness of approach" (in Mao and Walkowitz's terms [2]) in the hope of meaningfully situating Hemingway's work in its modernist context for teacher-scholars and students at different levels.

"As we come to acknowledge the extraordinary compass of the work," Michael Levenson comments in his introduction to *The Cambridge Companion to Modernism* (2011), "it's likely that it will prove better to be a minimalist in our definitions of that conveniently limp term 'Modernist' and maximalist in our accounts of the diverse 'modernizing' works and movements, that are sometimes congruent with one another, and just as often opposed or even contradictory" (3). In Hemingway's case, his diverse avant-gardism, in the 1920s and 1930s especially, may be said to require an equally varied set of teaching approaches. The kinds of concrete, student-centered pedagogies that these fifteen contributors offer here add successfully—and, one hopes, influentially—to ongoing critical conversations about Hemingway and/in the modernist moment and promise to enrich our teaching and scholarship.

A presiding, yet intellectually welcome, difficulty in arranging this collection was the challenge of working with literary modernism as a concept. My contributors and I are, of course, dealing with a plural, fluid, and debatable model;

that modernism is not simply a checklist of attributes or a singularly defined critical construct helps *Teaching Hemingway and Modernism* work within the "extraordinary compass" that Levenson and other scholars address. Seeing modernism as an expansive series of approaches and actions, as Levenson, Mao and Walkowitz, and others do, will help teachers at all levels successfully contextualize Hemingway's work along a spectrum of avant-gardism. There's no single, neat definition of modernism, just as there's no single way to teach *In Our Time, The Sun Also Rises,* and other Hemingway works.

Situating Hemingway in his literary-social context vis-à-vis modernism also entails understanding his nuanced treatment of gender and sexual fluidity, among other cultural narratives. (For an even richer treatment of this issue, see Verna Kale's forthcoming collection in this same series, *Teaching Hemingway and Gender.*) Seen in its gender-inflected modernist context, much of Hemingway's work manifests what Janet Lyon has convincingly seen as "the complicated and shifting relations of among sexual difference, the identity and performance of gender, and the various practices and desires issuing from sexuality" in the era (227). At some level, the essays by Lauren Rule Maxwell, Katie Owens-Murphy, and Julie Goodspeed-Chadwick work within the narrative of modernist gender that Lyon explores. Both directly and symbolically, Hemingway experienced postwar "salon communities" as loci of "an unusual intersection of public discourses and interiority" and of the "various experiences of experimental art," as Lyon has observed more broadly (236).

Moreover, as Rita Barnard notes, modernist authors—such as Hemingway, Stein, Faulkner, Hurston, Toomer, and others examined in this collection—embodied and explored various dialectics between changes and origins. In particular, many of "the creators of modernist literature were often men and women who had been born in small villages, but who pursued their careers in large industrial cities: they were people who lived in two distinct worlds simultaneously. Though fascinated by the new and absorbed in it in their daily lives, they were also constantly aware of the old: of residual modes of production that they themselves witnessed or participated in" (Barnard 53). Such dual newness and (at some level) nostalgia illuminate the tensions between experiment and tradition—stylistically, structurally, in terms of gender, and so on—in Hemingway's work and in the larger modernist era. The essays here by Phillip Beard, James Carothers, Anna Lillios, and Margaret Wright-Cleveland illuminate this notion of modernists' places and pasts. Moreover, understanding Hemingway and/in Europe—a relationship here explored by David Barnes, Bradley Bowers, Meg Gillette, and Adam McKee—deepens the transatlantic connections between Hemingway's native and adopted countries, as well as between the late Victorian and the modern. The Hemingway–Orwell pairing that Jean Jespersen Bartholomew offers likewise situates Hemingway transnationally in ways that stress the exchange and border crossings identified by Mao and Walkowitz, Lyon, and other modernist scholars. Much of our teaching of Hemingway, especially but not exclusively within the modernist moment, might rest within these various tensions and exchanges. Jeffrey Herlihy-Mera explores similar tensions and creativity by considering Hemingway as protopostmodernist, specifically through the lens of "Homage to Switzerland" and contemporary notions of irony, disorientation, and narrative fluidity.

"It is worth speculating," Barnard continues later in conjunction with *The Sun Also Rises* (1926), "that the popularity of Hemingway's work might be tied to his attempt to salvage a certain masculine austerity (or moral solvency) in a world where the locus of value was rapidly shifting from the traditionally masculine sphere of production to the traditionally feminized sphere of consumption and leisure" (63). Sharon Hamilton and Andrew Fletcher present, in particular ways, a means of viewing Hemingway in his literary–cultural moment in terms of magazines, periodicals, correspondence, and reviews. Teaching Hemingway's work and/as modernism through such approaches stresses that analyzing context, cultural narratives, and various period texts can get students beyond the basic plot—that is to say, from asking "what happens" to asking "why something happens" or "what else is happening," approaches that can meaningfully improve critical reading, writing, and researching of author and era.

I have divided the fifteen essays comprising *Teaching Hemingway and Modernism* thematically into the people, places, and politics underpinning Hemingway's writing and milieu. As might be expected, discussions of *In Our Time* and *The Sun Also Rises* are prominent in this collection. Yet many other Hemingway works—such as the "Paris 1922" sketches that Adam McKee discusses in chapter 7, or *To Have and Have Not*, which Phillip Beard discusses in chapter 3—are also explored, revealing his experiments with, contributions to, and deepening of Anglophone modernism.

The first five chapters concentrate on the key people in Hemingway's professional and creative life. Julie Goodspeed-Chadwick's essay, "Modernist Style, Identity Politics, and Trauma in Hemingway's 'Big Two-Hearted River' and Stein's 'Picasso,'" clearly examines "the modernist moment to which these writers respond" and then argues that "Hemingway branches off Stein to fashion trauma literature, which speaks to the modern world and modernity—namely, a rapidly changing world that was reshaped by war" (10). Katie Owens-Murphy, in "'Miss Stein Instructs': Revisiting the Paris Apprenticeship of 1922," likewise examines the Stein–Hemingway link while nicely "address[ing] their use of repetition at the level of the word, the phrase, and the sentence, which generates a wide range of rhetorical effects, from the destabilization of meaning to the formal representation of sequential motion" (23), in such works as "Picasso," *Three Lives*, and "Soldier's Home." In "Hemingway, Stevens and the Meditative Poetry of 'Extraordinary Actuality,'" Phillip Beard interrogates Hemingway's and Stevens's works, based on the latter's claim in a letter about the former's poetry of "extraordinary actuality." In particular, Beard's assertion that "meditative and poetic aspects of Hemingway's actual fiction, as distinct from his biography and persona, are in thematic tension with rhetorics of force, resistance, or manful striving" (30–31) undergirds his teaching model. James Carothers's essay, "Our Greatest American Modernists: Teaching Hemingway and Faulkner Together," examines the authors who are arguably America's Ur-modernists. "Teaching these two great contemporaries and rivals together," Carothers posits, "allows students to read their fictions in a variety of ways, first requiring that they get a firm grasp on the obvious aspects of both writers' work" (42). As Carothers describes his own teaching, "I also promise them that Hemingway, as I read him, is not all that simple, and Faulkner, I hope, is not quite as difficult as he is often made out to be" (43). Anna Lillios, in "From Paris to Eatonville, Florida: Hemingway's *The Sun Also Rises* and Hurston's *Their Eyes Were Watching God*," offers what might seem an unlikely pairing of Hurston and Hemingway, yet she successfully examines how these authors explored modernist concerns with moral values, race, self-identity and otherness, and gender equality. For Lillios, "meaning is, in fact, frustrated because of a slippage through boundaries of race, gender, and class" in these two complementary yet distinct novels (52), from authors whose thematic and contextual links beg further study.

The middle four chapters focus on the rich geographical and cultural places of Hemingway's modernism—particularly Paris and Spain. Meg Gillette's "*The Sun Also Rises* and the 'Stimulating Strangeness' of Paris" discusses teaching Hemingway's work about Paris *in* Paris, through a study-abroad program. For Gillette, "studying expatriate literature while living in Paris allows students to see their own questions about the 'stimulating strangeness' of the city refracted back to them by the novel, and as they gain from literature new ways of thinking about their own encounters with difference in the modern metropolis, they experience literature as equipment for living" (70). In "Teaching the Avant-Garde Hemingway: Early Modernism in Paris," Adam McKee successfully takes a literary–contextual approach while just as successfully examining the early, experimental Hemingway of the "Paris 1922" sketches, *In Our Time*, "Up in Michigan," and "On Writing." These early writings, for McKee, are "particularly rich" in framing "the influences on Hemingway's early, experimental modernism" (72)—namely, Stein, Joyce, and Cezanne. David Barnes, in "Teaching Hemingway Beyond 'The Lost Generation': European Politics and American Modernism," usefully situates Hemingway's modernism in terms of American *and* European cultural history. "What would happen," he asks, "if we read Hemingway as part of an early twentieth-century cultural matrix, one in which the work of other writers, newspaper reports, and visual culture contributed equally to the picture?" (82). Jean Jespersen Bartholomew, in "Twentieth-Century Titans: Orwell and Hemingway's Convergence through Place and Time," pairs two authors who are mainstays in secondary school and college curricula. For Jespersen Bartholomew, the authors "had similar multigenred approaches to developing their crafts and acquiring materials by means of immersed experience. Their stylistic aims overlapped as well, with Hemingway working to achieve a clean, bold, new style and Orwell wanting to strip away all adjectives. Considered together, the two deserve a serious look not typically given them in juxtaposition within modernism" (92).

The final six chapters adopt various cultural and theoretical lenses for understanding Hemingway's modernism both in its own time and in ours. Margaret E. Wright-Cleveland's "The Developing Modernism of Toomer, Hemingway, and Faulkner" examines the intersections of aesthetics, structure, and race among these three key authors. "The development of modernism in America," she writes, "was pivotal to the development of twentieth-century culture, literature, and politics and continues to influence today's culture. Indeed, understanding the shift in worldview explored through early twentieth-century modernism enriches one's understanding of current culture, literature, and politics" (105). In "The Futurist Origins of Hemingway's Modernism," Bradley Bowers takes a welcome look at some political–artistic influences on Hemingway through the lens of futurism, specifically "the shared aesthetic and philosophical roots of futurism and modernism" (117). For Bowers, "the experimental aesthetic and attitudes Hemingway expressed in *In Our Time* (1925), the carefully nuanced philosophical stance of *The Sun Also Rises* (1926), and the ruthless yet romantic heroism of *A Farewell to Arms* (1929) especially illustrate the writer's place in the developing futurist movement" (118). Lauren Rule Maxwell, in "Hemingway, His Contemporaries, and the

South Carolina Corps of Cadets: Exploring Veterans' Inner Worlds," takes a fascinating approach to teaching cadets at the Citadel about Hemingway's veterans in conjunction with Fitzgerald's *The Great Gatsby*. For Rule Maxwell, the cadets' "analyses of these connections, which were facilitated in part by my asking the students to consider how all of the works we read over the course of the semester serve as meditations on American history, help explain how the cadets used Hemingway's portrayals of veterans in his short stories to develop an understanding of ways World War I experiences informed identity in modernist works on a broader scale" (129).

Sharon Hamilton anchors her dynamic, lively work in "Teaching Hemingway's Modernism in Cultural Context: Helping Students Connect His Time to Ours" to the cultural context of the era through music, media, and other venues. "I believe students will more profoundly connect with a literary work," she writes, "if its contents become—literally—tangible for them" (137), such as through in-class musical performances, a lesson on dancing the Charleston, and a virtual walking tour of 1920s Paris. Jeffrey Herlihy-Mera's "On Teaching 'Homage to Switzerland' as an Introduction to Postmodern Literature" offers a dual modernist–postmodernist view of a nuanced Hemingway story. For Herlihy-Mera, "the structures in the story are useful in making postmodern concepts—and their links to the physical sciences and psychology—accessible to students" (149); furthermore, this story "constitutes an excellent example of his use of postmodern mechanisms, and a close examination of its departure from standard literary tropes should reveal an ever-present and yet generally unstudied dimension of Hemingway's work" (150). Lastly, Andrew Fletcher, in "Chasing New Horizons: Considerations for Teaching Hemingway and Modernism in a Digital Age," links Hemingway to Thornton Wilder in offering a pedagogy that meaningfully advances the role of digital humanities in literary studies. For Fletcher, "juxtaposing the work of an Ur-modernist like Hemingway to that of a less celebrated but equally prolific writer such as Thornton Wilder could allow students to discover the more nuanced tendencies, techniques, and style associated with modernism, rather than just the literary figures and times" (160). While offering the close analysis, contextualization, and research that Fletcher does, teacher-scholars can employ different media and technologies to deepen students' understanding of Hemingway in both modernism and modernist studies.

The appendixes contain writing and discussion prompts for deepening students' work with Hemingway; I aim for these to be useful, constructive, yet adaptable for particular course needs and class sizes. Herein readers will find a series of specific classroom exercises and writing assignments that we hope will be useful for various high school, undergraduate, and graduate curricula. The contributors and I share a belief in the need to offer concrete classroom practices, writing prompts, and specific discussion questions in a teaching collection—all of which help us expand students' interpretations of Hemingway's work and context. We hope these tools will be applicable, accessible, and adaptable for various learning environments and types of students, while also highlighting the rich connections between the teaching of writing and the teaching of various literary texts and movements.

The fifteen essays and related appendixes of *Teaching Hemingway and Modernism* balance text, context, and classroom practice while considering a broad, student-centric audience. In many respects, we are ultimately gearing our work to the current generation of Hemingway and modernism students, some of whom will also comprise the next generation of teachers offering *their* students ways of thinking about what modernism is, should be, and can be. These same future teachers may also be thinking about where we will continue to locate Hemingway in such a diverse, expansive moment.

Note

1. See also Douglas Mao and Rebecca Walkowitz, "The New Modernist Studies," *PMLA* 123.3 (2008): 737–48. In this article, the authors usefully and persuasively outline how modernist studies have expanded temporally, spatially, and vertically.

Modernist Style, Identity Politics, and Trauma in Hemingway's "Big Two-Hearted River" and Stein's "Picasso"

Julie Goodspeed-Chadwick

In examining the similarities in modernist style in the acclaimed early work of Ernest Hemingway and Gertrude Stein, I will treat the modernist moment to which these writers respond while also contextualizing their works in relation to each other. I will then consider how Hemingway branches off Stein to fashion trauma literature, which speaks to the modern world and modernity—namely a rapidly changing world that was reshaped by war. Such an examination should be of aid in teaching these works to lower-level undergraduate students, although the points I present could be extrapolated and refashioned easily for use in high school or upper-level college courses. Each year, I teach Hemingway and Stein in tandem in an undergraduate Introduction to Fiction course that focuses on modernist prose. At the end of the unit that includes Hemingway, students effectively demonstrate close reading skills that are sharpened by their experience in reading his work for implications and subtext. They also can showcase their knowledge of representative characteristics of modernist literature, as well as their ability to produce responsible interpretations of Hemingway's oft-anthologized story (and the longest one in the celebrated collection *In Our Time*) "Big Two-Hearted River" (1925).

As one would expect in an introduction to fiction course, students study the components of fiction and learn to identify and analyze them before articulating the significance of doing so and/or the significance of the text itself. This approach to "Big Two-Hearted River" is traditional. However, what I have found to be additionally effective—in the American literature course, a course on modernism, or one on introductory fiction—is pairing Hemingway with Stein, so students can tease out the similarities and differences in their writing and add additional interpretive strategies, especially critical close reading skills, to their arsenal.[1] When students understand what Stein is doing with her cubist portraits, then they can more successfully read Hemingway's cubist *In Our Time* with sensitivity and discernment.[2] In my experience, it is useful to first teach something of Stein's that is relatively short and easy, like her prose portrait "Picasso," because a story like "Big Two-Hearted River" looks deceptively simple and also functions as a kind of prose portrait of Nick Adams, locating him in the modernist moment in the same way that Stein so places Picasso. Moreover, Stein's style (primarily her use of repetition), her modernist experimentation in form, and her simple diction, are qualities that Hemingway borrows yet refines for his own purposes.

In "Picasso," first published in Alfred Stieglitz's journal *Camera Work* in 1912 and collected in Stein's *Selected Writings*, Stein presents her opinion of the painter and of his new style, cubism. By extension, we can discern reflexive commentary: in other words, we see Stein valorizing the new artistic style, by transposing the painterly elements of cubism to literature and, in fact, mirroring what Picasso is doing in her own work. In "Picasso," she marries form with content. As Stein herself asserts, "I was alone at this time in understanding [Picasso], perhaps because I was expressing the same thing in literature" (qtd. in Bridgman, *Gertrude Stein in Pieces* 118). On the first day of our study of Stein, we list on the whiteboard what the students observe about her writing, focusing on her language and style. To bolster their observations, I ask students to give me examples from "Picasso," a text short enough that they can revisit and reread parts of it closely in class. If the students are hesitant to offer their thoughts or ideas (typically, Stein's writing strikes them as bizarre and unreadable), I prompt them by selecting passages that highlight her use of repetition and cubist perspective and asking different students to read those passages aloud. Then I ask them what they notice and how those elements function in the text. (In my experience, students are never quiet at this point in the class.) Any paragraph in "Picasso" achieves our purpose of foregrounding Stein's modernist, cubist aesthetic. With this guidance, students will note that repetition in "Picasso" is employed to emphasize that the subject of the piece, Pablo Picasso, is an artistic pioneer who produces "a real meaning" (Stein, "Picasso" 294). His art is "a solid thing, a charming thing, a lovely thing, a perplexing thing, a disconcerting thing, a simple thing, a clear thing, a complicated thing, an interesting thing, a disturbing thing, a repellant thing, a very pretty thing" (Stein, "Picasso" 294). In mimicking a cubist approach, albeit in writing, Stein offers us different perspectives, ideas, and positions on cubism and on Picasso's work in particular. The adjectives in this passage point to different opinions on Picasso's art. We know the denotation of every word in this portrait: that does not confuse our students or us. What is so startlingly experimental and strikingly odd is *how* the words are linked together and the portrait organized. We are not treated to a biographical explanation: Picasso's characteristics are to be inferred (i.e., he is a hard and productive worker and a genius). We know that he is charming because Stein insists on it in whimsical repetition: "One whom some were certainly following was one who was completely charming. One whom some were certainly following was one who was charming. One whom some were following was one who was completely charming. One whom some were following was one who was *certainly* completely charming" (Stein, "Picasso" 293; emphasis added). What we can infer is that not everyone found Picasso and/or his work to be charming, and in this portrait, Stein insists on her point of view while also alluding to a range of other responses to Picasso. If I have not already introduced the students to cubism when we begin our unit on modernism, I do show images of Picasso's work to them, and I have discovered that the best examples of Picasso's art for my pedagogical purposes are ones that have titles that reportedly tell us what the paintings are depicting, as, for instance, Picasso's 1912–14 *Guitar* series.[3]

When students move patiently through Stein's portrait of Picasso and are prompted to explain what it is telling us, they get it right. But they have to slow down and read closely: they have to concentrate on what we are being told and consider what is left out and why that matters. Because I want to show students that they can approach and interpret Stein's work (and, later, Hemingway's), I remind them that they know what the denotations of the words are. On a very literal level, I ask them to tell me what we know about Picasso and his art from Stein: after all, this text is a prose portrait, and we are told some very concrete things about him. We then proceed to see what we can make of the text in terms of interpretation. We discuss how Stein's writing calls attention to itself and, how, by extension, she is calling our attention to our very own reading strategies. We might have to read differently from the ways in which we have read other literary texts: we need to read attentively, patiently, and creatively so that we can determine how to engage the text to make meaning(s). Simply reading out loud—having the students take turns—helps tremendously in putting into relief the modernist and cubist techniques, because the compression, excision, fracturing, and reassembling inherent in the language and style of the piece become more readily apparent. I make it a point of calling on every student in the class, and I ask one or two students to comment on what another student has read, making it clear that they can say anything at all. Picasso pioneered a new style of painting and became a tastemaker, much as Stein and Hemingway would become the literary pioneers and tastemakers of modernist literature, and their contemporaries did not find them easy to understand.[4]

It might help students to know that, as a friend and inspiration, Picasso was to Stein someone worthy of championing; by replicating his style in her piece about him, she offers a kind (of) homage. Hence her experimental portrait, by its very cubist nature, bypasses conventional expectations of biographical details, but it intentionally gives us Stein's take and impression of Picasso and his work (as well as the impressions of others). In that vein, "Picasso" is very much a subjective portrait that pivots on cubist style. It delivers an impression of Picasso through an approach informed by a fragmented modern world that attempts to put the pieces together to form a coherent and seemingly unified and whole narrative.

The careful attention to detail and close reading required in interpreting Stein likewise must be activated in interpreting Hemingway's work. These two writers present us with literary artifacts that speak to and capture the modernist moment, one marked by—as reductive as this list might seem to veteran scholars and readers of modernism—experimentation, fragmentation, disillusionment (the "lost generation"), opaqueness, subjectivity and foregrounding of perception, and an aesthetic of intellectualism and difficulty. The most defining events in the modern world were World War I and World War II, two forces of modernity that ushered in the contemporary world as we know it. The fast pace of technological innovation informed warfare to such an extent that it drastically altered the nature of war: those engaged in it no longer needed to see the enemy at close range, and they could wreak devastation more quickly and efficiently than ever before. Even as early as 1947, Robert Penn Warren argues in his essay on Hemingway that "the shadow of ruin [read: trauma] is behind the typical Hemingway [literary] situation" (444). Both Stein and Hemingway were writing in a very specific place in terms of culture and literary and sociohistory; their work responds to their time accordingly. Yet Hemingway's work arguably surpasses Stein in its treatment of war trauma and the modern response to traumatization.

Hemingway's two-part short story "Big Two-Hearted River" was first published in the little magazine *This Quarter* before being included in *In Our Time*. While I do not teach *In Our Time* in its entirety—in fact, for my 200-level Introduction to Fiction course, I teach this text as a representative one from

Hemingway—I do explain to my students that *In Our Time* is a modernist collection of violent narratives that reverberates with traumatic representations and speaks to the world in which Hemingway and his contemporaries lived. Because Stein influenced Hemingway—and because their work exhibits cubist qualities—I ask students to consider how Hemingway's early prose evokes Stein's and how what we have learned about cubist literature from Stein's "Picasso" allows us a metaphorical segue into Hemingway's "Big Two-Hearted River."[5] As Linda Wagner-Martin observes, by combining Ezra Pound's relentless editing (and terseness) "with Gertrude Stein's larger imperatives that usually dealt with capturing emotional states, Hemingway could pare away some parts of the conventional story and leave the stark bones that comprise his best works" (35). Wagner-Martin also believes that it is most productive to read Nick Adams from *In Our Time* as "a returning veteran" because she makes a compelling case that Hemingway's writing may be "more autobiographical than reviewers wanted to see it as being" (40-41). I find this feature important to note, but I must admit that I was teaching "Big Two-Hearted River" as a story about a veteran, a man who had some experience of war, *before* I knew that it could, in fact, be read as autobiographical. One reaches the same conclusion as biographers by isolating the traditional components of fiction, analyzing each, and reassembling them in relation to each other. (I have not yet assigned a biographical essay or chapter for students to read in my Introduction to Fiction class, mostly because we are focused on developing close reading skills of primary texts.)

Considering to what extent Hemingway adheres to and deviates from conventional prose expectations affords students the opportunity to become better close readers and astute readers of sophisticated texts. It is certainly possible to generate multiple strong readings of "Big Two-Hearted River," but the reading I am presenting here has been sanctioned as arguably the most persuasive one. Indeed, Frederic J. Svoboda classifies "Big Two-Hearted River" as exhibiting the "great themes in Hemingway," specifically in connection with wilderness and innocence (or the lack thereof). According to him, "Big Two-Hearted River" is "where Nick as a young man finds a refuge from war and responsibility in a fishing trip to a burned-over wilderness" (Svoboda 168–69). As Hemingway himself writes tellingly, "'Big Two-Hearted River' is about a boy coming home beat to the wide [sic] from a war. Beat to the wide as an earlier and possibly more severe form of beat, since those who had it were unable to comment on this condition and could not suffer that it be mentioned in their presence. So the war, all mention of the war, anything about the war, is omitted. . . . [T]he war was in the story" ("Art of the Short Story" 88).

One of the basic strategies in analyzing fiction requires us to consider the setting. In Hemingway's work, as in Stein's, every detail matters, including the organization and presentation of material. That "Big Two-Hearted River" opens with "burnt timber" tells us that this is a world that has been damaged (*IOT* 133),[6] and one that has been damaged at every level: at the microcosmic level by a recent fire and at the macrocosmic level by war. Nick desires to hike into the Michigan hills because from the top he can see that the "burned country stopped off at the left with the range of hills" and "ahead islands of dark pine rose out of the plain" as far as his eye can see (135). He is retreating into nature to heal, and his motivations can be gleaned throughout the story, which leads us into characterization and what is, for me, the most powerful element of the story.[7]

In fleshing out who Nick is, we focus on what he says and what he does. I mark passages that I think are key, but I also ask students to offer examples that illuminate Nick's character. With our selected passages, we engage in close reading and discuss what we know about Nick and why it might be important for us to know what we do. Normally, we would also be in a position to consider what other characters say to or about our protagonist, but, in reading this experimental fiction, we are not privy to other perspectives. Even Nick's thoughts are masked from us; we are ostensibly being treated to a limited or selective omniscient point of view. The reader is given access to the thoughts and actions of a single character, but there is a compromise between first-person narration and third-person narration. This narrative point of view keeps us centered on Nick's (compulsive) concentration on pragmatic concerns, tasks related to hiking, making a camp, and fishing. With only one notable exception, he does not delve into his psyche, does not reflect on his identity, past, or motivations. Nick aligns himself with what we now recognize as the archetypal Hemingway hero whose masculinity finds expression in a love for the outdoors, a rugged individualism, and adherence to a code of strength and independence that keeps weakness at bay on most occasions.

The gaps in "Big Two-Hearted River" result in a startling lack of full character development and thwart the reader's expectations regarding plot. Yet paradoxically, since the story revolves around Nick, he is among the keys to unlocking the complexities of the plot and characterization. We are thus forced to figure out who Nick is based on what little we know. I do this in the classroom by first asking students to outline the plot and then listing what we know about Nick from the outset. To begin to apprehend and comprehend him (and, by extension, his world), we can engage in detective work in the realm of identity politics. Dominick LaCapra conceptualizes identity politics as "a grid of subject positions," and adds that a great problem in research is that, "through processes of identification or excessive objectification, one remains [caught] within that grid" (175). In hindsight, relevant questions pertaining to Nick's identity politics (what it means to be an "I") include: What does it mean to be a man? What does it feel like to be shell-shocked? How does one recover and heal from trauma according to a Hemingway-sanctioned code of honor?

The "I" of "Big Two-Hearted River" emphasizes the present while engaging, stoically, in masculine-coded activities and behavior. (Note: My students enjoy identifying the qualities of the Hemingway hero as embodied by Nick and elaborating by unpacking their examples.) In the story, the painful recent past is elided, as is any serious, long-term consideration of the future. Students can conjecture why this is the case, and most of the time they will cite trauma as the determining force that motivates Nick. In light of this discussion, a prose refrain, with slight variations, should be noted in the story: "this was good" (*IOT* 140). Considering Hemingway's understated, minimalist style and the quintessential gaps present in modernist literature at large, we know that the refrain is a signal that this good place is counterbalanced by what is, or has been, *not* good. The narrator's linear relation of events and intense concentration on mundane detail may prompt an unwary reader to interpret the story as a mere travelogue. But if we are to mine or cull a theme from the text, we have to pay attention both to what is said and to what is not said. Why is Nick camping and fishing by himself, especially when he recalls male bonding with Hopkins so fondly? (In this regard, Nick comments that he "did not like to fish with other men on the river. Unless they were of your party they spoiled it" (149), which implies conversely that it is enjoyable to fish with friends.) He decides to make coffee the way that Hop would, thinking "Hop deserved that" (141). However, Nick's sentimentalism—what amounts to a nostalgic reflection, strange for him—devolves into the harsh realization of the present day, though he laughs good-naturedly at the outcome: "The coffee was bitter," yet that "made a good ending to the story" (142). The postwar world differed sharply from the prewar one, and Nick's life is not as it was, especially for someone who needs to recover and heal from trauma. My reading of "Big Two-Hearted River" is informed by my research specialty, which is trauma studies in conjunction with twentieth-century American literature. When I teach this piece, I unfold it by guiding students in analyzing traditional components of fiction; I ask them to consider the contexts of the story, illustrating them and providing examples, as I have attempted to do here. As a class, we examine and discuss the following in terms of conventional expectations of prose: plot and dramatic structure, characterization, point of view, setting, symbolism, style and tone, and themes. Those components I have not yet treated in this chapter, I will touch on shortly, but I have found asking students to locate (and analyze) examples from the text to be very effective strategy in fostering active participation, student ownership of learning, and lively discussion. My students and I ask the following questions related to context: What was the world like in 1925? What are the moods and themes of *In Our Time*'s other stories? What are the hallmarks of modernist (American) literature, as exemplified in Stein's "Picasso" and Hemingway's "Big Two-Hearted River"? How might the ways we were able to approach and open up Stein's work apply to Hemingway's?

Hemingway's painstaking romanticization of the natural world in his work and the lack of any obvious conflict in "Big Two-Hearted River" (required in the plot trajectory of traditional fiction) show students that something is amiss—that something is *there*, but not directly. Our narrator tells us that the pine chip is fresh and the wood is clean—all pristine and idyllic—and that the soggy onion sandwiches that he has carried and dipped in the stream, along with the water he is drinking out of his hat, presumably soiled from hiking and camping, are delicious and to be desired (*IOT* 146, 154). And students will rightly point out that the only overt conflict in this story is when the leader breaks on the fishing pole in part 2. Clearly, by breaking down the story into its formal components, we can see what is left out and what is emphasized. Characterization and setting supersede plot development and the emergence of obvious themes. Hemingway's deceptively simple language is indebted to Stein, and his disregard for fleshing out conventional structures and narratives (also influenced by Stein) means that we need to attend to what is repeated (foregrounded) and what is elided or left out, which I see as metaphorical red flags in this story. The symbols and symbolic acts in Hemingway's texts contain and detain meanings until students (and professors) are patient enough to begin to tease out the meanings in light of the rest of the story and what we know about related contexts. Stein's prose portrait "Picasso" can serve as such a context, preparing us to enter into Hemingway's "Big Two-Hearted River."

The carefully crafted symbols and symbolic acts in "Big Two-Hearted River" offer us, if we read from a perspective informed by Stein, a subtext that drives or activates the main ideas of the story. In the beginning, Nick symbolically removes himself from civilization: he intentionally retreats from the scarred ground where grasshoppers are soot-blackened and seeks out communion with nature, where he can take refuge in tranquility and individualistic pastimes. In his own scarred personal world, Nick does what other trauma survivors do:

he copes as best he can. In order to heal, according to the dominant paradigm in trauma studies, trauma survivors must secure a safe place to regroup, learn to tell their trauma story, and reconnect to communities (Herman 3). Nick has succeeded in the first step and appears to be working on the second in the form of this story/testimony as he tries to make sense of it. Unfortunately, he appears to be a long way from reconnecting to a community and establishing a sense of belonging. Indeed, the narrative ends as follows: "He was going back to [his solitary] camp. . . . There were plenty of days coming when he could fish the swamp" (*IOT* 156). While he may not be fully recovered and healed from a presumable trauma that animates his actions and haunts his behavior, Nick retreats from tragedy both at the macrocosmic and microcosmic levels. Students can map conceptually (or graphically on a traditional map or a digital document) where Nick physically goes in the story: he retreats from a wider world to a more private one. But he also retreats from anything with the potential to be traumatic: "In the fast deep water, in the half light, the fishing would be tragic. In the swamp fishing was a tragic adventure. Nick did not want it. He did not want to go down the stream any further today" (*IOT* 155). Employing Stein's favorite technique, repetition, to call readers' attention to something vitally important to the message of the story, Hemingway shows us that Nick refrains from seeking out the traumatic: his purpose in fishing is to heal himself, not to inflict or take on anything that invites or smacks of tragedy, because trauma has marked Nick and caught him in its grip; in the words of Dori Laub, "[trauma survivors] live not with memories of the past, but with an event that could not and did not proceed through to its completion, has no ending, attained no closure, and therefore, as far as its survivors are concerned, continues into the present and is current in every respect" (69). In response to what has wounded him, Nick's body acts out and retreats from any potential threats or triggers. The violent imagery of Nick gutting his fish correlates to the violent world he has experienced—and, at some level, Hemingway's readers may have known—during the war.

I am drawn to this story partly because of its sensitive treatment of a traumatized character endeavoring to heal, to not only survive but thrive in the modern world. And we must remember that Nick's postwar world is a brutal one. As Susan Sontag poignantly states to those of us who are civilians, "We don't get it. We truly can't imagine what it was like. We can't imagine how dreadful, how terrifying war is; and how normal it becomes. Can't understand, can't imagine. That's what every soldier, and every journalist and aid worker and independent observer who has put in time under fire, and had the luck to elude death that struck down others nearby, stubbornly feels. And they are right" (126). In Nick Adams, Hemingway gives us the gift of a courageous and enduring personality: one who endeavors to roll with the punches and right wrongs. From the perspectives of the students I have taught, the joy they might discover in studying Hemingway and "Big Two-Hearted River" lies in their ability to open up a story that is rich in complexity and that still resonates for readers in the twenty-first century in its treatment of masculinity and trauma.

Notes

1. According to Michael North, Hemingway dubbed himself "Hemingstein" to pay homage to Stein as his mentor: "Stein was, then, in the most complicated way possible, Hemingway's aesthetic proxy" (North 195). In delineating their similarities and differences, North remarks, "The chief characteristic of the Anderson-Stein-Hemingway brand of modernism was to be its restoration of direct, colloquial language. For Hemingway more purely than for any other male modernist this was a masculinist project, and clarity of reference was to be a masculine virtue. Here, however, directness of reference leads straight to a gap . . ." (North 198-99).

2. Jacqueline V. Brogan stresses that "Stein's importance as an author and influence is not limited to the impact of cubism on the literature of her time. Her profound influence on Ernest Hemingway, who in most instances should not be called a cubist writer (*In Our Time* being a notable exception if one regards it, as I do, as a 'cubist anatomy' rather than a collection of short stories) is illimitable, as it is on others. [H]er stylistic presence . . . is clear from his first successful short stories throughout his novels" (260).

3. It may be useful to show Picasso's portrait *Gertrude Stein* (1905-6), which was painted before Picasso's cubist period, alongside one of his cubist works as an instructive juxtaposition on what cubism is not and what it is.

4. In "On Writing," Hemingway has Nick Adams (the main character in "Big Two-Hearted River") declare, "He wanted to write like Cezanne [sic] painted." Nick adds, "He could see the Cezannes. The portrait at Gertrude Stein's. She'd know if he ever got things right" ("On Writing" 239). In reference to this manuscript, Stein writes, "He had added to his stories a little story of meditations. . . . It was then that Gertrude Stein said, Hemingway, remarks are not literature" (Stein, *Alice B. Toklas* 207).

5. Students can respond to Daniel Joseph Singal's following synopsis of cubism and consider the ways in which Hemingway maximizes the utility of a cubist style in relating a narrative about trauma and recovery (a scenario in which the subject feels broken and strives toward healing and wholeness) in "Big Two-Hearted River": "Picasso and his colleagues maintained [that] all objects would have to be seen in shifting relation to each other. The painter's task was thus to break up forms into component parts and have those parts continuously overlap, conveying not so much a sense of fragmentation as of wholeness. Sharp outlines were always to be avoided; rather, colors and textures were to bleed from one object into another, with subdued colors usually employed to

enhance the sense of unity. Whenever possible, both the interior and the exterior of a form were to be rendered alongside each other; likewise the background was to have the same value and prominence as the main subject of the painting, and the two were to interpenetrate" (Singal, "American Modernism" 118-19).

6. Citations to Ernest Hemingway's "Big Two-Hearted River" refer to the 2003 Scribner's edition of *In Our Time:* Hemingway, *In Our Time* (New York: Scribner, 2003). *In Our Time* was originally published in 1925.

7. Another interpretation that elaborates on this one posits that Nick is escaping "the twin evils" of modern war and modern civilization. It takes into account that Nick leaves his books, artifacts of civilization, behind him. See Sean McCann, "Teaching *In Our Time* in Our Time: An Online Professional Development Seminar," America in Class, sponsored by the National Humanities Center, accessed 13 Dec. 2012, <http://americainclass.org/seminars/teaching-in-our-time-in-our-time/>. For McCann, "Big Two-Hearted River" is Hemingway's response to the problem of how to act honorably in a dishonorable world: a man should get out, go into nature (preferably the Upper Peninsula of Michigan), and fish, which presents itself as a desirable antidote because nature does not let one down. See the following passage from the beginning of "Big Two-Hearted River": "Nick felt happy. He felt he had left everything behind, the need for thinking, the need to write, other needs. It was all back of him" (*IOT* 134). Another passage toward the end presents a caveat, however: "He wished he had brought something to read. He felt like reading" (*IOT* 155).

"Miss Stein Instructs"

Revisiting the Paris Apprenticeship of 1922

Katie Owens-Murphy

For those outside Hemingway studies, it seems unlikely that the author's prose, so apparently simple in its style that it is used to teach English as a second language, should have much in common with the impenetrable prose style of Gertrude Stein; that a twenty-three-year-old from the Midwest should have much to discuss with a seasoned forty-eight-year-old expatriate who had already been living in Paris for nineteen years; and that the future author of "The Short, Happy Life of Francis Macomber," in which a man who fails to kill a lion on a big-game-hunting expedition is shamed and cuckolded by his wife, should glean much of anything from the feminist, lesbian critic of "Patriarchal Poetry." Within the circles of Hemingway scholarship, however, the so-called Paris apprenticeship of 1922—Hemingway's initiation by Stein into the literary expatriate scene during his stint in Paris as foreign correspondent for the *Toronto Star*—is well-documented, although the relationship between the two writers is often cast in psychoanalytic terms. Michael Reynolds has argued that Stein, bearing a resemblance to Grace Hall Hemingway in both character and stature, effectively became Hemingway's "Paris mother" (*Paris Years* 35). Much attention has also been given to the public feud that later erupted between Hemingway and Stein over who most shaped the other's writing, an "anxiety of influence" quarrel that was conducted chiefly in print throughout the 1930s.

Hemingway's bitter, retrospective disavowals of Stein's influence in such works as *Green Hills of Africa* and *A Moveable Feast* have been taken to heart by some critics and biographers, who have not always given due attention to Stein's role in shaping Hemingway's iconic prose style. "She had . . . discovered many truths about rhythms and the uses of words in repetition that were valid and valuable and she talked well about them," Hemingway writes in *A Moveable Feast* (*MF* 17). Here, I examine Stein's influence on Hemingway's prose, focusing on those "rhythms" and "repetitions" that made her writing nearly impenetrable but that helped Hemingway to develop a prose style more self-consciously literary than his earlier journalistic attempts at writing. What is more, the rhetorical structures and tropes that Hemingway adopted from Stein—repetitions of phrases and word patterns, the proliferation of conjunctions—challenge our commonplace characterizations of Hemingway's prose as plain, compact, and minimalist. Examining Hemingway's debt to Stein not only reveals one of the major sources for his famous style but also draws our attention to important elements of Hemingway's prose that might be easily overlooked: his repetition of key words and phrases; his protracted sentences, lengthened through the repetitive use of coordinating conjunctions; and the lyrical cadence that pulses behind his most moving passages.

Teaching Hemingway and Gertrude Stein offers a dual pedagogical advantage in the modern American undergraduate literature classroom. Read one way, Stein's prose becomes more transparent as students trace her strategies throughout Hemingway's more narrative-oriented prose. Read another way, Hemingway's seemingly facile style becomes richly multidimensional when placed in conversation with Stein's more deliberately experimental repetitions. If Hemingway and Stein represent clarity and opacity respectively—two stylistic extremes of American modernism—then a comparative study reveals just how intimately connected these poles may be.

Hemingway's style is often attributed to his early work as a journalist for the *Kansas City Star*, whose prescriptive house rules for journalistic writing were documented on a now-famous single-page style sheet: "Use short sentences. Use short first paragraphs. Use vigorous English."[1] In *The Autobiography of Alice B. Toklas*, however, Stein credits herself with having encouraged Hemingway to move *beyond* his training as a novice journalist: "If you keep on doing newspaper work you will never see things, you will only see words and that will not do, that is of course if you intend to be a writer," she advised (217).[2] In 1923, Hemingway—still employed by the *Toronto Star*—returned to North America with his wife Hadley for the birth of their son, and his letters to Stein indicate that he was taking her advice indeed: "I am going to chuck journalism I think," he wrote in a letter to Stein and Alice B. Toklas dated 9 November 1923. "You ruined me as a journalist last winter. Have been no good since" (*SL* 101). Other letters to Stein in the same year likewise betray her influence. Relying on one of Stein's favorite grammatical constructions, the gerund, he wrote her (c. 18 February 1923), "I've been working hard and have two things done. I've thought a lot about the things you said about working and am starting that way at the beginning. If you think of anything else I wish you'd write it to me. Am working hard about creating and keep my mind going about it all the time. Mind seems to be working better" (*SL* 79). The Paris apprenticeship had certainly made an impact on the young Hemingway: during his regular visits to Stein's famous rue de Fleurus apartment, Stein gave Hemingway practical advice about writing, critiqued his works in progress, and even shared her own work with the burgeoning writer, commissioning Hemingway's help in copying and correcting the proofs for her massive manuscript, *The Making of Americans*. With her characteristic immodesty, Stein declared that "correcting proofs is . . . like dusting, you learn the values of the thing as no reading suffices to teach it to you. In correcting these proofs Hemingway learned a great deal and he admired all that he learned" (*Alice B. Toklas* 217). So he had "learned a great deal"—but what exactly did he take away from Stein's tutelage?

Though Hemingway's literary legacy has been his universal accessibility, in contradistinction to Stein's inaccessibility, both stylists demonstrate that simple diction and syntax structures can yield varied and intricate literary effects. Neither writer will ever send a reader running to a dictionary, as Faulkner once quipped of Hemingway; Stein herself declares, in "The Gradual Making of The Making of Americans," that "English grammar is interesting because it is so simple . . . any child thirteen years old properly taught can by that time have learned everything there is to learn about English grammar. . . . It is this that makes the English language such a vital language that the grammar of it is so simple" (*Writings 1932–1946* 277). In my teaching of Stein and Hemingway, I demonstrate the ways in which simplicity can yield such complexity by unearthing the grammatical structures that constitute each writer's narrative prose. In particular, I address their use of repetition at the level of the word, the phrase, and the sentence, which generates a wide range of rhetorical effects, from the destabilization of meaning to the formal representation of sequential motion.

Stein was adamant that there is no such thing as repetition—only insistence—but one of the hallmarks of her writing style is its relentless repetition of simple words and phrases, which are reworked into different patterns and combinations. The most extreme examples of her experiments with repetition and syntax appear in her prose portraits, particularly that of Picasso (1912): "One whom some were certainly following was one who was completely charming. One whom some were certainly following was one who was charming.

One whom some were following was one who was completely charming. One whom some were following was one who was certainly completely charming. . . . One whom some were certainly following and some were certainly following him, one whom some were certainly following was one certainly working" (*Selections* 104–5). Paragraphs like these force teachers and students to pay close attention to syntax: while the general structure of each sentence remains the same, the arrangement of the words—especially the placement of modifiers like *certainly* and *completely*—can alter the meaning of a sentence. In this case, *certainly* is alternately attached to Picasso's charm, to his work ethic, and to his influence as "one whom some were certainly following," shifting Picasso's characterization from debonair socialite to laboring artist to charismatic genius. One technique teachers might encourage students to use in navigating Stein's byzantine writing, then, is to track these modifiers and the ways in which they signal shifts in meaning. Because Stein tends to rely on plain and repetitive structures, the slightest grammatical deviations can effect profound hermeneutical changes.

These repetitions and variations, coupled with Stein's short, staccato sentences, can produce some interesting tensions and ambiguities; the close resemblance between certain passages from Hemingway's short fiction and Stein's prose poems show that this lesson that was not lost on him. In the story "Soldier's Home," Hemingway captures Harold Krebs's fraught mental state upon returning home from the war through frenetic repetitions that evoke Stein's syntactical wordplay:

> Nothing was changed in the town except that the young girls had grown up. But they lived in such a complicated world of already defined alliances and shifting feuds that Krebs did not feel the energy or the courage to break into it. . . . Most of them had their hair cut short. . . . They all wore sweaters and shirt waists with round Dutch collars. It was a pattern. He liked to look at them from the front porch as they walked on the other side of the street. He liked to watch them walking under the shade of the trees. He liked the round Dutch collars above their sweaters. He liked their silk stockings and flat shoes. He liked their bobbed hair and the way they walked. . . . He liked the girls that were walking along the other side of the street. He liked the look of them much better than the French girls or the German girls. But the world they were in was not the world he was in. He would like to have one of them. But it was not worth it. They were such a nice pattern. He liked the pattern. It was exciting. But he would not go through with all the talking. He did not want one badly enough. He liked to

look at them all, though. It was not worth it. Not now when things were getting good again. (SS 147-48)

Hemingway articulates Krebs's ambivalence toward women and toward his position at the margins of his own community through the narrative's repetitive vacillation between pleasure ("he liked") and proviso ("but"). The result is a chaotic string of non sequiturs in which Krebs denies himself the pleasures of romance: "He liked to look at them all, though. It was not worth it" (SS 148).

Stein's use of repetition, of course, can also cause a term to take on an unstable or even ironic meaning, especially those repetitive epithets that are affixed to the female protagonists of *Three Lives* (1909). Just how "good" is Anna in "The Good Anna," with her martyr complex and her control issues? Certain lines seem particularly ironic, as when the officious Anna tries in vain to discipline her dogs: "The good Anna had high ideals for canine chastity and discipline," the narrator remarks sarcastically (*Three Lives* and *Q.E.D.* 8). The same goes for "The Gentle Lena," in which Lena's "gentleness" initially appears to be a flattering quality, though it quickly becomes a euphemism for her passivity and helplessness. I often ask my students to track Stein's epithets, like her modifiers, across the text to chart their changing meanings and their implications for the characters to which they are attached.

Hemingway likewise exploits repetition's potential for irony. Much like Stein, he uses it to gently mock his characters for their arrogance, naïveté, or general obtuseness. Take, for example, his story "Mr. and Mrs. Elliot," in which each successive line, by way of repetition, qualifies or even undermines the previous line:

> Mr. and Mrs. Elliot tried very hard to have a baby. They tried as often as Mrs. Elliot could stand it. They tried in Boston after they were married and they tried coming over on the boat. They did not try very often on the boat because Mrs. Elliot was quite sick. She was sick and when she was sick she was sick as Southern women are sick. That is women from the Southern part of the United States. Like all Southern women Mrs. Elliot disintegrated very quickly under sea sickness, travelling at night, and getting up too early in the morning. (SS 161)

What begins as a joint effort to conceive a child—"Mr. and Mrs. Elliot tried very hard to have a baby"—is gradually undermined as Mrs. Elliot, who could hardly "stand" intercourse, feigns (or at least exaggerates) illness in order to avoid it. By the end of the story, we learn that Mrs. Elliot is not really interested in having babies with Mr. Elliot at all because she is interested in her girl friend, instead: "Mrs. Elliot and the girl friend now slept together in the big mediaeval bed. They had many a good cry together. In the evening they all sat at dinner together in the garden under a plane tree and the hot evening wind blew and Elliot drank white wine and Mrs. Elliot and the girl friend made conversation and they were all quite happy" (*SS* 164). This final phrase—"they were all quite happy"—highlights once more the dysfunction of the marriage.

In addition to her repetition of words and phrases, Stein employs repetition on a syntactic level, protracting her sentences through strings of coordinating conjunctions until they swell to the size of paragraphs. In her essay "Poetry and Grammar," she writes that the conjunction "is not varied but it has a force that need not make any one feel that they are dull . . . Conjunctions have made themselves live by their work. They work and as they work they live" (*Writings 1932–1946* 315-16). Stein, like Hemingway after her, relies on coordinating conjunctions to convey heated emotion with more immediacy than traditional syntax would allow, as when Jeff Campbell expresses his emotional frustration with Melanctha in *Three Lives*: "And then when I got rich with such a feeling, comes all that other girl, and then that seems more likely that that is really you what's honest, and then I certainly do get awful afraid to come to you, and I certainly never do feel I could be very trusting with you" (*Three Lives* and *Q.E.D.* 87). Stein also uses conjunctions in order to convey her sense of the "continuous present," a concept she adapted to fiction from *her* mentor, philosopher and psychologist William James. Stein's effort to capture the essence of human beings, not only in her portraits but also in her extensive novel, *The Making of Americans*, relies on conjunctions in order to convey a sense of sequence, on the one hand, and immediacy on the other. The result is a prose that is deeply rhythmic, since conjunctions penetrate the passage at fairly even intervals:

> Miss Charles was then one having general moral and special moral aspirations and general unmoral desires and ambitious and special unmoral ways of carrying them into realisation and there was never inside her any contradiction and this is very common in very many kinds of them of men and women and later in the living of Alfred Hersland there will be so very much discussion of this matter and now there will be a little explanation of the way it acts in the kind of men and women of which Miss Charles was one. (*Making of Americans* 462)

In order to capture this continuity, I ask my students to read passages like these aloud. Invariably, their affect is rather flat, since these coordinations eliminate the hierarchical relationships that are typically generated by subordinating conjunctions within regular prose; invariably, too, students run out of breath, which enables them to experience the sheer exhaustion effected by this grammatical structure, which itself has a cumulative component as each new clause is simply appended to the last without qualification. Stein's grammar is also, however, linked to time, as her fascination with the continuous present suggests. In "Portraits and Repetition," she explains her efforts to link formal structure with sequence and motion in a way that mimics the visual effects of film: "I was doing what the cinema was doing, I was making a continuous succession of the statement of what that person was until I had not many things but one thing.... [a few pages later] I had to find out what was inside any one ... I had to find it out by the intensity of movement that there was inside any one of them" (*Writings 1932–1946* 294).

Stein's insistence that the essence of a person is best articulated through the "succession" that the continuous present affords sounds an awful lot like Hemingway's articulation of true writing, which places a similar emphasis on sequential action and the surprising affective response it can generate. Many students are familiar with Hemingway's emphasis on showing versus telling in relation to the famous "iceberg theory" he expounds in *Death in the Afternoon* (1932), but in another passage from the same book he delivers an alternate version of this concept while recounting what he learned from the Paris apprenticeship. His statements here bear a telling similarity to Stein's comments on "continuous succession": "I was trying to write then and I found the greatest difficulty, aside from knowing what you really felt, rather than what you were supposed to feel, and had been taught to feel, was to put down what really happened in action: what the actual things were which produced the emotion that you experienced ... the real thing, the *sequence of motion* and fact which made the emotion" (*DIA* 12).[3] Despite his reputation as a literary minimalist, Hemingway too proliferates coordinating conjunctions during moments of intensity in order to dramatize this "sequence of motion" that he sees as essential to representations of action and feeling, be it bullfighting or lovemaking. In fact, this method of writing yields some of the most memorable passages within Hemingway's oeuvre: richly touching, incantatory, and emotionally vivid, they are rendered through the very syntactical structure that underpins Stein's cinematic prose. Consider, for example, the iterative love scene between Frederic Henry and Catherine Barkley in *A Farewell to Arms* (1929): "I loved to take her hair down and she sat on the bed and kept very still, except suddenly she would dip down to kiss me while I was doing it, and I would take out the pins and lay them on the sheet and it would be loose and I would watch her while she kept very still and then take out the last two pins and it would all come down and she would drop her head and we would both be inside of it, and it was the feeling of inside a tent or behind a falls" (*FTA* 114).[4] These conjunctions appear at regular intervals, creating a rhythmic, lyrical cadence that simulates the smoothness of their body movements and that transforms this passage into something like a prose poem. Hemingway seems to have indeed learned much about "rhythms and the uses of words in repetition."

Because their reputations precede them, Hemingway and Stein can pose special, albeit contrary, challenges to the modern American literature classroom. I find that students are predisposed to like Hemingway for his "straightforwardness" and to dismiss Stein for her "impenetrability" before they have explored and learned to appreciate their stylistic kinships, which are best evidenced by the Paris apprenticeship. By focusing on the structural similarities that underpin their prose techniques, I work hard to disabuse students of these caricatured depictions of Hemingway and Stein as stylistic contraries. In fact, I tell them, Hemingway is no more transparent than Stein is inscrutable. A comparative analysis of these two writers reveals just how scrambled Hemingway's narrative becomes when it is paired with the dizzying repetitions that Stein made so famous, while Stein's elliptical word games are thrown into sharp relief when placed within the sparse syntax structure for which Hemingway is best known. Each writer illuminates the other.

Considering these two writers together also highlights stylistic nuances that are diminished or obscured by their somewhat distorted literary reputations. Reading Hemingway in the context of Stein enables us to see those intricate features of his writing that are overlooked because of his international reputation as a minimalist who writes simply and clearly. In fact Hemingway, like Stein, is deeply invested in the complex rhetorical effects that plain diction and simple syntax structures can produce, and examining his writing alongside that of an avant-garde modernist helps us to appreciate just how difficult his writing can be. Conversely, Hemingway renders Stein's syntactical calisthenics with greater transparency in his fiction, which is more obviously narrative than Stein's prose-lyric hybrids. Students who are intimidated by Stein's experiments with prose can approach them through Hemingway's writing, which packages many of the same grammatical and rhetorical strategies in a more accessible, though no less avant-garde, format.

Teachers might consider placing passages from the two writers side by side on a handout so that students can see, in concrete form, the stylistic consistencies that run through these works. (See Appendix A: Stylistic Consistencies Between Stein's *The Making of Americans* and Hemingway's *A Farewell to Arms* for one such handout, based on the passages I examine here.) The pairing of Hemingway and Stein in the classroom enables students to reread and reinterpret the work of each in light of the other. Moreover, this juxtaposition provides a framework for understanding clarity and opacity in complementary ways. Difficulty, it turns out, can be achieved through surprisingly simple rhetorical techniques: the repetition and placement of a single word, the recontextualization of a term or epithet, or the rhythm created by a series of successive coordinating conjunctions. Viewed this way, the legacy of the Paris apprenticeship might be read not simply as a story of agonistic competition but as one of nuanced stylistic cooperation by two of the most influential prose stylists of American modernism.

Notes

1. To view the whole sheet, see *The Kansas City Star*, <www.kansascity.com/static/pdfs/Hemingway_style_sheet.pdf>; accessed 6 March 2013.

2. Citations to Stein's *Autobiography of Alice B. Toklas* refer to the following edition: Gertrude Stein, *The Autobiography of Alice B. Toklas* (New York: Vintage Books, 1990).

3. Citations to Hemingway's *Death in the Afternoon* refer to the following edition: Ernest Hemingway, *Death in the Afternoon* (New York: Scribner, 1999).

4. Citations to Hemingway's *A Farewell to Arms* refer to the following edition: Ernest Hemingway, *A Farewell to Arms* (New York: Scribner, 2003).

Hemingway, Stevens, and the Meditative Poetry of "Extraordinary Actuality"

Phillip Beard

In 1942, Wallace Stevens made an unusual claim regarding the writing of Ernest Hemingway: he asserted that Hemingway was not only a poet, but a poet of "extraordinary actuality." I aim to show that Stevens's claim illuminates a repressed and crucial aspect of Hemingway's work. Stevens made this claim in a letter to Henry Church dated 2 July 1942 (*Letters* 411), presenting Hemingway as a poet who could describe certain kinds of reality without coloring the perceived objects with the imagination, implicitly because certain kinds of natural reality command a meditative attention, not a projecting or mastering style of thinking. While rather complex discussions could ensue from this claim concerning how, or even if, it is possible to withdraw the imagination or even the ego participation from written descriptions, Stevens does provide simple tools for making sharp and interesting distinctions in Hemingway's work: Stevens's claim, explored in the classroom alongside readings of some of his accessible poems, helps show that an attitude of meditative attention is frequently important to Hemingway, and that this passive, observing stance is a crucial alternative in his work to any imperative to be active, forceful, or violent.

A lively consideration of Stevens, Hemingway, and the poetry of "extraordinary actuality" can get students to expand their awareness of Hemingway, especially the man of rumor and biography often discussed as a connoisseur of violence, an enthusiast of spectacular shows of force, or someone who equated heroism with might. I do not repudiate that macho image of Hemingway: he promoted it himself (as in his 1932 study of bullfighting, *Death in the Afternoon*), and it is observable in the fiction. However, meditative and poetic aspects of

Hemingway's actual fiction, as distinct from his biography and persona, are in thematic tension with rhetorics of force, resistance, or manful striving.

Putting Hemingway and Stevens in dialogue not only corrects an oversimple view of Hemingway through a consideration of meditative attitudes within his work, it also distills some of Stevens's key concerns for undergraduates to whom this poet may appear abstruse or arcane. Another virtue of the analysis is that it gets students to think about Hemingway's fiction in terms of how his sentences work, rather than—as students too often do—only in terms of plot summary or a cursory list of themes. Conjoining Stevens and Hemingway on the subject of what constitutes an "extraordinary actuality" can encourage students—who often feel compelled to rush through prose of any kind to glean "key ideas"—to slow down and scrutinize Hemingway's prose and (perhaps) participate in the meditative intensity of his descriptions. (See Appendix B: Sample Assignments and In-Class Prompts.)

In conjoining Stevens and Hemingway, I first review Stevens's letter to Henry Church and then examine how Stevens's poetry itself may illuminate a concern with "extraordinary actuality."[1] From this point, my lesson highlights two ways in which Hemingway promotes a detachment from the concerns of an impulse to master or from a contentious mind. First, Hemingway occasionally shows his *protagonists* in meditative attitudes, as he does with Nick Adams in "Big Two-Hearted River" (1925). Second, Hemingway's *narration* may suggest or even promote meditative reflection; sometimes this style of narration works in counterpoint to the action or dialogue, which may be conflictual or even violent, as in *To Have and Have Not* (1937).

In 1942, Stevens corresponded with his friend Henry Church concerning a lecture on poetry and actuality that Church was trying to arrange at Princeton University. In a letter from Hartford, Connecticut, dated 2 July 1942, Stevens wrote that he thought Church's "subject is not really POETRY AND ACTUALITY, but POETRY AND THE EXTRAORDINARY ACTUALITY OF OUR TIME." For Stevens, when an actuality is "extraordinary enough, it has a vitality all its own which makes it independent of . . . the imagination" (*Letters* 411). Stevens then recommends Ernest Hemingway as the ideal person to lecture on this subject, explaining, "Most people don't think of Hemingway as a poet, but obviously he is a poet . . . the most significant of living poets, so far as the subject of EXTRAORDINARY ACTUALITY is concerned" (*Letters* 412). In using the word *extraordinary* here, Stevens is probably distinguishing such experience from ordinary experience in that, by his own definition, he means to isolate objects that allegedly have stability and meaning apart from any input of imagination. In his *Adagia,* a collection of epigrams and aphorisms, Stevens focuses and amplifies the ideas found in his letter to Church by saying, "In the presence of extraordinary actuality, consciousness takes the place of imagination" (191, qtd. in Hollander 212). The philosopher Immanuel Kant described an epistemology, or theory of knowing, in which all knowledge was mediated by impressions and ideas: the full reality of a "thing" was an ultimate unknowable (42). But the experience that Stevens describes as "extraordinary" in Hemingway may be the experience Stevens describes in the title of the ultimate poem in his *Collected Poems:* "Not Ideas About the Thing but the Thing Itself" (534)—that is, allowing a neutral awareness to behold a circumstance rather than projecting imaginative color, feeling, or interpretation onto the circumstance. The role of meditation envisioned by Stevens is described compellingly by William Bevis in his book *Mind of Winter: Wallace Stevens, Meditation, and Literature.* Bevis argues that the readers often misconstrue, or have a hard time discerning, the meditative qualities in Stevens's work for at least two reasons. First, meditation involves mental inactivity, or a surrendering of mastering intelligence to a kind of neutral beholding. This inaction is unconventional in the West and in much of the critical rhetoric of romanticism, which lauds the active projecting qualities of "imagination." Second, meditative states of mere being, mere beholding, or other kinds of mental neutrality in the face of objects or nature are often seen, even apart from a rhetoric of romanticism, as negative states. Often, Bevis argues, states of mental inaction in Stevens's work are not negative opposites of imaginative states, but dialectical assistants of more active states of mind (25–28).[2]

When one carefully reads Hemingway's fiction with Stevens's definition in mind, the prose writer may also be understood, on significant occasions, as a meditative poet of objects and natural forms, not as one who only (or even ultimately) promotes the mastering of reality with force. These objects and natural forms in Hemingway's work seem (as Stevens says) to exist independent of the imagination and command a caring respect. Stevens's assertion can help bring to light several aspects of Hemingway's work that have often been overlooked through an emphasis on Hemingway's personal interest in boxing, hunting, and war. Again, Stevens's provocative (yet utterly accurate) definition of Hemingway as a "poet of extraordinary actuality" affords opportunities to show a kinship between the fiction writer and the poet that is both stylistic and philosophical. Hemingway's effects, even his moral effects, often reside in lyrical compressions rather than didactic narratives; an understanding of him as a meditative poet writing in prose allows a more complex view of him than the stock image of a cartoonish he-man. Hemingway's fiction—for example, the ends of "Indian Camp" and *To Have and Have Not*—often achieves its overall effect by putting a receptive, meditative (and occasionally *caring*) attitude in lyrical counterpoint to episodes of strife or violence.

In addition to his 2 July 1942 letter to Church, Stevens's poems may be used in the undergraduate classroom to model and illuminate his attitude toward an "extraordinary actuality," suggesting a trustworthy fundament of experience that rewards the fidelity of contemplative attention. These include "Nuances of a Theme by Williams," which seeks to describe a star beyond metaphor (*Collected Poems* 18), and "On the Road Home," in which nature is "freshest" when received apart from conventional myth (*Collected Poems* 203). Stevens also models a meditative attitude that involves a detachment from self-awareness, a passive observing of the object of meditation. I'll show clear examples of this detachment in Stevens's poetry and in Hemingway's "Big Two-Hearted River."

Prototypical of Stevens's own meditative poetry is "Nuances of a Theme by Williams," in which he takes a four-line poem about a star by William Carlos Williams, "El Hombre" (31), and expounds on its implications in ten more lines. In a somewhat ambiguous contradiction of the traditional tendency of poets to personify and allegorize stars, Stevens urges the star to "shine nakedly," to shine "like bronze, / that reflects neither my face nor any inner part / of my being" (*Collected Poems* 18). In the poem's second stanza, he tries to strip his sight of all anthropomorphic projection, and he asks that the star "Be not chimera of morning, / Half-man, half star" (18). While giving these mandates to the star, he also instructs himself in how to behold the star as a uniquely extra-human reality, whose otherness may become a model of composure and a stoical sign of order. Students see that Stevens's vision of the star resembles Hemingway's view of physical objects that command attention with little or no effort of metaphor. Once sensitized to this possibility, students begin to notice this tendency not only in obviously meditative passages concerning nature, such Nick's observance of the trout in "Big Two-Hearted River," but also in Hemingway's incidental descriptions of physical objects or even of food and drink. Students may confront and comment on the commanding physicality of the "bacon fat hardening on [the] plate" in "Soldier's Home" (*IOT* 75) or the "icy cold and ... faintly rusty" wine in *The Sun Also Rises* (126) and ask how, and with what value, these realities intrude on the hectic surroundings of domestic (Krebs's family drama) or global (post–First World War Europe) life.

Stevens, meanwhile, also empties the self of prejudicial reflections or projections in the "face" of a natural object, a key movement in many meditative disciplines. Stevens's poem "On the Road Home" describes a conversation between two people walking "in a wood" (*Collected Poems* 203), who (fairly agreeably) debate the nature of metaphysical truth. At issue seems to be the existence of a total truth that would be true for humans and true cosmically; one of the sojourners asserts that "there is no such thing as the truth" and the other that "there are many truths, / But they are not parts of a truth"; the first then adds that "words are not forms of a single word . . . / The world must be measured by eye" (*Collected Poems* 203-4). The poem is in some sense a record of disillusion, but the tone is calm and eventually comfortable. In confrontation with each potentially anxiety-provoking, skeptical maxim, the natural world about these two becomes vibrant ("the grapes seemed fatter. / The fox ran out of his hole"), magical ("the tree, at night, began to change, / Smoking through green and smoking blue"), or welcoming:

> It was at that time, that the silence was largest
> And longest, the night was roundest,
> The fragrance of the autumn warmest,
> Closest and strongest. (*Collected Poems* 204)

The fewer human demands the travelers make on their environment, the more they become aware of its domestic particularity: the fragrance of autumn becomes, effectively, an object of meditation to which they surrender their potential demand to project human truth onto the woods.

This pattern of skepticism and reception in Stevens's "Nuances of a Theme by Williams" and "On the Road Home" resembles the cultural and philosophical drama of Hemingway's *In Our Time*. Confronting the loss of stable truths—sometimes literally associated with the father (as in "Indian Camp," when the heroic scene of childbirthing surgery planned by father Henry Adams goes badly awry) or sometimes with the world of fathers or traditional patriotic verities (as in the droll or grim interchapters associated with the Great War, or in "Soldier's Home," which features another veteran, Harold Krebs)—Nick Adams ultimately finds consolation in the meditative observation or work in nature in "Big Two-Hearted River."

In Our Time details a broad skepticism not only of traditional orders of truth and security, such as patriotism, religion, and romantic love, but also of physical force as a means of controlling an unruly world. *In Our Time* rarely, if ever, celebrates violent force. Rather, violence victimizes innocent refugees ("On the Quai at Smyrna") or results in self-destruction ("Indian Camp," "The

Battler") or in absurd, unheroic battle scenes (the italicized interchapters relating to the First World War in France and Italy). Only in "Soldier's Home" is violence briefly accepted, less as an opportunity for heroic triumph than as a kind of natural storm to be endured in certain moments; Krebs's triumphs over fear and his battlefield enemies are described only as him having "done the one thing, the only thing for a man to do, easily and naturally, when he might have done something else" (*IOT* 70). In "Soldier's Home," it is Krebs's fidelity to the facts of what happened in the war, rather than the acts of violence he committed during it, that becomes the ground of a stoical, heroic composure.[3]

In counterpoint to such grim warnings about a life lived too forcefully, the ultimate story of *In Our Time*, "Big Two-Hearted River" (divided into two parts), stresses a receptive attitude in the face of nature. This text's moments of reassurance and composure often rely on a poetry of objects and nature that resembles Stevens's. "Big Two-Hearted River," with its Zen-like meditation on trout holding themselves steadily in the river, counterpoises receptive, observant moments (not only of nature and but of objects like cups of coffee) with the descriptions of violence elsewhere in the story collection that are typically more absurd or grotesque than heroic.

In "Big Two-Hearted River," the landscape Nick first encounters is ravaged by fire in ways that suggest not only T. S. Eliot's *The Waste Land*, but also the First World War zones described in the book's interchapters, or any place stripped of conventional structures of dwelling or meaning: "There was no town, nothing but the rails and the burned-over country. The thirteen saloons that had lined the one street of Seney had not left a trace. The foundations of the Mansion House hotel stuck up above the ground. The stone was chipped and split by the fire. It was all that was left of the town of Seney. Even the surface had been burned off the ground" (*IOT* 133). The law of nature implied by the alternately burned over and vernal lands is undulation; Hemingway uses a variant of this word to describe the land itself at the point where the line of the fire ends: "Then it was sweet fern, growing ankle high, to walk through, and clumps of jack pines; a long undulating country with frequent rises and descents, sandy underfoot and the country alive again" (*IOT* 136). Here, as in Stevens's "On the Road Home," the world is "measured by eye" in language rich in visual images: "The river was there. It swirled against the log piles of the bridge. Nick looked down into the clear, brown water, colored from the pebbly bottom, and watched the trout keeping themselves steady in the current with wavering fins. As he watched them they changed their positions by quick angles, only to hold steady in the fast water again. Nick watched them a long time" (*IOT* 133).

The language is not only visual, but free from obvious subjective coloration: substantives carry an extraordinary amount of meaning: *the river* was there; *the trout* kept themselves steady in *the current* with wavering *fins*. The ordinary language that Hemingway uses here creates an artifact that resembles the ordinary reality of objects, while remaining extraordinary; Hemingway's words do not incarnate the objects they describe, but by using simple, direct language, familiar language, he creates verbal objects that in their stylistic character resemble the objects he describes: if he is describing a simple meal, he will use simple terms; if he is describing the enduring reality of a river, he may say, "the river was there." And the steadfastness of the language and the sentences or images becomes a sign, like Stevens's star or woods, for steadiness, or for reliability.

On the other side of the blasted landscape he first encounters, Nick finds, first, the river, and then, near the piles of a bridge, the trout in the water. Hemingway's rendering of the trout may be seen to embody Stevens's "extraordinary actuality"—"a vitality all its own which makes it independent of . . . the imagination" (*Letters* 411). Like the star in "Nuances of a Theme by Williams," Hemingway's trout represent both an extra-human reality that has nothing to do with the human subject and a natural reality that is fundamental to human life; further, the fish possess a style that may be, when observed properly, a model of composure. When the fish "hold themselves steady," they model a kind of stoic virtue, a proper balance of surrender and force.

In the writing of Stevens and Hemingway, the ordinary survives skepticism and is even aided by skepticism, as in Stanley Cavell's account *In Quest of the Ordinary*. Cavell says that philosophy's business has become "the recovery of . . . the ordinary from skepticism," the "overcoming" of metaphysics, and, in "literature[,] the domestication of the fantastic and the transcendentalizing of the domestic" (27). This "transcendentalizing" of the domestic occurs in many of Stevens's poems; in "The Emperor of Ice Cream," for instance, the comforts of ice cream take on a metaphysical dimension in the face of death ("Let the lamp affix its beam / the only emperor is the emperor of ice cream") (*Collected Poems* 64), while in "Large Red Man Reading," ghosts, having dwelled in an afterlife, return with nostalgia for the physical world and find an oracular poet of the ordinary speaking vatic (i.e., priestly) lines about "the pots on the stove, and the tulips among them" (*Collected Poems* 423).

With a less vatic emphasis, the ordinary becomes transcendental in Hemingway's "Big Two-Hearted River" not only in Nick's meditative sight of the fish but also as a mouthful of beans heated on a campfire prompts an echo of saving tradition. "'Chrise,' Nick said. 'Geezus Chrise,' he said happily" (*IOT* 140).

Such ceremonies of food, made privately, recall the meal Bugs prepared and shared with Nick in "The Battler," suggesting that one order of the ordinary is ceremonial, or that which can be reliably nourishing and comforting. Like his contemplation of the fish "holding themselves steady," Nick's contemplation of coffee (made according to an old friend's method) becomes another opportunity for him to surrender a striving mind to the ordinary: "Nick drank the coffee, the coffee according to Hopkins. The coffee was bitter. Nick laughed. [Because Nick's own, unused recipe was potentially superior to Hopkins's method.] It made a good ending to the story. His mind was starting to work. He knew he could choke it because he was tired enough" (*IOT* 142).

But the larger order of the ordinary, containing this ceremonial category, is the given of nature, the epistemological sturdiness of objects, or, otherwise, the reliable if undulatory reality of nature. Before Hemingway, William Wordsworth evoked this undulatory characteristic of nature. In "A Slumber Did My Spirit Seal," he did so on a large scale by stating that "earth's diurnal course" conditions everything (*Poems and Prefaces* 115), while in "The Tables Turned," he noted it at work on a small scale, commenting of the breathing life of a forest that "one impulse from a vernal wood / May teach [more] than all the sages can" (*Poems and Prefaces* 107). Fundamental cyclical realities include the sun, the seasons, and the daily oscillations of light and dark. In Hemingway's *In Our Time*, the ceremonial ordinary is housed in the given ordinary of nature; thus Nick thinks of his camp as "the good place" (*IOT* 139). The process of knowing or of observation in "Big Two-Hearted River" is more trusting than forceful, less a matter of mastering reality than of finding expressions of reception and care.

The claim that receptivity and observation are often as important as violence in Hemingway's work, demonstrated by the model of composure found in *In Our Time*, becomes especially provocative when applied to Hemingway's third major novel, *To Have and Have Not*, a text ostensibly about crime, punishment, and literal class warfare. Yet this work too has crucial moments of meditative focus on natural and/or object realities that suggest that the greatest category of alienation is not between social classes, but between humanity and the sustaining "other" of nature. This is plain in the extended description of a marlin as (in Stevens's phrase) an "extraordinary actuality," as well as in the narrator's concluding meditation on commerce moving against the grain of ordinary life and against the Gulf Stream. Hemingway's style in this novel holds out the prospect of a meditative detachment but often obscures it with chaotic action, a drama by characters who are in brutal competition with each other.

In *To Have and Have Not*, Harry Morgan is a former policeman who now makes a tenuous livelihood as a charter fisherman. The novel is often regarded as one of Hemingway's lesser works, partly because it is often seen as an awkward blend of hard-boiled crime fiction and social activist polemics. Nonetheless, it contains many passages of typically strong lyricism and an attitude toward nature and the ordinary that, while less obvious than in the earlier fiction, is crucial to the novel. Since the natural themes are marginal to the main, class-warfare action, it can be a fruitful text for students to interpret; as a preliminary activity to discussion, students can be prompted to briefly annotate scenes in the novel involving people and nature. Key questions students may then consider are 1) are there objects of nature (or of other, built environments) in the novel that *could* be objects of meditative attention? and 2) what is it about the world of the novel that inhibits the characters from having the kind of relationship with (natural) objects that Nick Adams has in "Big Two-Hearted River"?

The opening pages of *To Have and Have Not* describe a placid Havana morning that is about to break into a storm of gang warfare. The first paragraph, told in Harry Morgan's voice, renders the street scene with the clarity and disquieting calm of a Hopper painting, with hints of class struggle within the picturesque vista (*THHN* 14). The descriptions have the heft of a crystal mug and nearly make the plain view of the street scene ring with the clarity of a meditative insight. Thus, among the detriments of the grimly competitive world of the novel is the lost opportunity for the kind of composure that Nick Adams, for example, gains in "Big Two-Hearted River."

A key early scene in *To Have and Have Not* involves Morgan, his African-American assistant Wesley, the alcoholic boat hand Eddy, and a tourist, Mr. Johnson. The scene has been set up with Morgan making observations about the weather and the sea which suggest that successful fishing requires both observation and an artistry fit to the rhythms of nature: "The moon is right. There's a good stream and we're going to have a good breeze" (*THHN* 20-21). Morgan tries to teach Johnson how to use his reel with the proper drag-setting, as Johnson apparently has had little experience of any sort of fishing and expects to purchase the feeling of success in this trip. Johnson, hardheadedly persisting in using too much resistance in the machine of the reel, loses the fish. The lesson seems to be that too much force and human-induced friction in the event will be counterproductive. The marlin is potentially an object of meditation, but has become a particular object of desire, a natural opponent to be overcome, or a trophy to be captured: "I saw a splash like a depth bomb, and the sword, and eye, and open lower-jaw and huge purple-black head of a black marlin" (*THHN* 21). A rhetoric of force that humans must respect is more apparent in this novel than in *In Our Time:* the fish makes a splash like a "depth bomb," and the fish's sail looks like a "full-rigged ship." In *To Have and Have Not,* the rhetoric of force and mastery that inflects Morgan's view of nature seems not simply a commercial or even sporting necessity but to some degree a compromise (if not corruption) of the fish, whose eye stares back at the men in a profound reminder that nature can be an interlocutor, a bold "thou" to the "I" of human consciousness.

In the narration of the fish's eye, there is a moment of recognition that this fish, like the trout in "Big Two-Hearted River," is also a sublime representative of the otherness of nature. The action of the novel is often combative, but the lyrical description of the fish emphasizes its physical mass and colossal otherness. Despite Morgan's application of war metaphors to the marlin, the fish must be respected for its innate, majestic power, not simply valued as a trophy, and Johnson fails to accord it this respect. Here, to catch the fish, one must not only exert considerable effort but also align oneself with the rhythms of nature and have cooperative support: "That's what you wanted to fight all by yourself.... A fish like that would kill you" (*THHN* 21). The balance needed here is very like that which nature offers Nick in "Big Two-Hearted River," with fish substantially smaller than the marlin. In trying to catch an especially large trout, he loses the fish and feels unbalanced by the urge to be in contest with the fish: "He had never seen so big a trout. There was a heaviness, a power not to be held, and then the bulk of him, as he jumped" (*IOT* 150). The key phrase relating the trout in the story to the marlin in the novel is "a power not to be held"—that is, not to be possessed by a human. The power is to be observed, but ultimately not to be completely owned or commodified. Almost every character in the novel is in the service of an alienating, competitive commodity culture. This is true not only of Morgan but also of the lawyers (e.g., Bee Lips), the writers (e.g., Richard Gordon), and the various financiers (e.g., the grain broker) in the novel. In the context of this alienation, the novel's consistently racist rhetoric ("chinks," "niggers," "wops," and "limeys") becomes less a gratuitous sensationalism than a sign of the dehumanizing effects of a competition for limited goods. The concluding meditation in the novel, after Morgan has been killed trying to rob and kill some Cuban revolutionaries (whom he had judged would kill him if he didn't get them first), shows ships at sea trying to navigate "the stream." In this ending, the narrator becomes a significant character, as he suggests the largest category of alienation to be the alienation of meditative awareness from a natural ordinary:

> In the big yard of the house across the street a peacock squawked. Through the window you could see the sea looking hard and new and blue in the winter light.
>
> A large white yacht was coming into the harbor and seven miles out on the horizon you could see a tanker small and neat in profile against the blue sea hugging the reef as she made to the westward to keep from wasting fuel against the stream. (*THHN* 262)

The stream is here the ordinary of life itself: the ocean is "hard and new," as if independent of the human catastrophes the novel has just detailed, especially the individual tragedy of Morgan's life and death. The tanker, as a symbol of commerce, interrupts the blue context of the stream and thus seems another indicator of human enterprise struggling to master, rather than respect, the given reality of nature. Harry Morgan was diverted from the ordinary calm he experienced with his wife and daughters and from the aptitude of contemplative composure he demonstrated in his respectful description of the marlin. In the world of *To Have and Have Not,* the loss or devaluation of meditative emptiness, the loss of the category of "surrender" of a human demand to own or command nature, becomes a crucial part of Hemingway's depiction of tragedy.

Putting Stevens's affirmation of a "consciousness [that] takes the place of imagination," "in the presence of an extraordinary actuality" (*Adagia* 191, qtd. in Hollander 212), alongside these moments in Hemingway can promote student consideration of the category of meditative attention that is repressed in studies of romanticism at large (in favor of an interest in imaginative projections) and of Hemingway in particular. His characters occasionally enact such a detached consciousness, but Hemingway's style may also demonstrate a meditative attention that is in philosophical tension with the kinetic, contentious realities of the characters. When students evaluate the various qualities of respect, commitment, and detachment with which Hemingway confronts certain circumstances, especially natural circumstances, they may read one of the most influential prose artists of the twentieth century not only with an alertness to complexity in an apparently straightforward writer but also with a new attentiveness to verbal detail, as his sentences often enact, but do not incarnate, the stability they describe.

Notes

1. John Hollander brought to light this letter of Stevens's in his brief 1985 essay "Hemingway's Extraordinary Actuality," but Hollander focused on Hemingway's rendering of dialogue in "Hills Like White Elephants" rather than on his meditative relation to a given reality. See Hollander, "Hemingway's Extraordinary Actuality," in *Modern Critical Views: Ernest Hemingway*, ed. Harold Bloom (New York: Chelsea House Publishers, 1985).

2. Bevis offers a compelling reading of Stevens's "The Snow Man" that interpret's the Snow Man's emptying of consciousness as a meditative "conquering" of subjectivity rather than as a senseless evasion of imaginative work, as the poem has been often read (by Helen Vendler and Harold Bloom, for example).

3. See also "The Battler," in which Nick Adams has hopped a ride on a freight train and is punched by a brakeman, who expels him from the train. Nick is flush with fantasies of revenge, but life soon suggests that he pick his battles carefully, that he define his use of force artfully. Nick meets an ex-prizefighter who has taken too many blows to the head; his fights, far from being ennobling, have amounted to deranging punishments. Ad Francis is a kind of adult travesty of Huck Finn, the adventurer living on the run, managed by a Jim-like African American character called Bugs, who swats Ad Francis with a blackjack if he becomes too uncontrolled and enraged (*IOT* 53–62).

Our Greatest American Modernists

Teaching Hemingway and Faulkner Together

James B. Carothers

Although Hemingway and Faulkner are, without a doubt, the greatest American fiction writers of their generation and probably of their century, their rather obvious differences have often obscured their extraordinarily similar experiments with modernism and responses to the modern dilemma. When this commonality becomes clear, their differences in style, in setting in place and time, and in presentation of their central characters can be understood as radically different ways of treating this protean subject. Teaching these two great contemporaries and rivals together allows students to read their fictions in a variety of ways, first requiring that they get a firm grasp on the obvious aspects of both writers' work. Almost all of Faulkner's best fiction is set in his Yoknapatawpha County, Mississippi; he writes long sentences, often with a challenging syntax and vocabulary; and he seldom, if ever, gives his central characters clear renderings of his own experience. Hemingway, in contrast, takes the whole world for his province, except for the Oak Park in which he grew up; he writes an often-imitated "minimalist" style with clear diction and grammar; and he almost always seems to present discoverable parallels to his own rich and well-documented life.

With these differences in mind, it is eventually possible to read many of their several masterworks (whatever that term may mean) as extraordinarily demanding and rewarding novels and short stories that ask how we should live in the modern world and reward us with genuinely profound answers. At the undergraduate level, I typically select four novels and a generous group of short stories by each for a semester's readings and arrange the course with a bloc of Hemingway followed by a bloc of Faulkner. We begin by examining their common assumptions that Hemingway and Faulkner are very different writers and that Hemingway is "easy" and Faulkner, "difficult." Which author a student judges the better depends on whether he or she likes "easy" or "difficult," but I try to explain to my students that I am much less interested in which of the two they prefer than in their reasons for that judgment. I also promise them that Hemingway, as I read him, is not all that simple, and Faulkner, I hope, is not quite as difficult as he is often made out to be.

To get the conversation going, I ask them to read "The Short Happy Life of Francis Macomber" and "A Rose for Emily," and complete a take-home quiz listing points of comparison between the two stories. To start discussion, I ask whether Margot Macomber shoots Francis on purpose—and then the arguments begin. After fifteen or twenty minutes of this, I despair of reaching an answer to this question and instead ask them to explain why Miss Emily kills Homer Barron. More arguments inevitably follow, including (for the last twenty years or so) the notion that Homer Barron is gay. Well, I conclude, we haven't done much in the way of comparing these two stories, but it does seem that neither story gives us an unequivocal answer to the seemingly elementary question: what happened?

Next I usually ask the students to read *In Our Time*, as printed in the Finca Vigía edition of *The Complete Short Stories*. This gives occasion for a description of Hemingway's journalistic experience, his service in World War I, how he came to be in Paris, and how he came to write and publish *In Our Time*. I give an in-class quiz on the book, along the following lines: "Is *In Our Time* best described as a novel, as a cycle of related short stories, or as a collection of independent short stories? The best discussions will include particulars of character, plot, and scene, with apt brief quotations." I use their various answers to this question as the basis for further class discussion, looking particularly at the interconnectedness of the Nick Adams material and the apparent disconnectedness of the other pieces in the book. As with the Macomber-Emily task, I am not especially concerned with what the students conclude, but I focus a good deal of attention on the textual evidence they choose to employ and the evidence they choose to ignore. Many of my students still seem to believe that all questions can be answered in the traditional five-paragraph essay format, in which they announce a thesis in the introduction, make three points of some sort, and restate those points and the thesis in the concluding paragraph. This kind of writing substitutes apparent form for genuine critical thought, and is, in my opinion, totally unsuitable for commenting on Hemingway's and Faulkner's fictions. I then pose the questions that I hope will guide our subsequent readings in Hemingway: Are his stories and novels fundamentally consistent with one another? If so, how? If not, why not? We go on to read the remainder of the Nick Adams stories in *The Complete Short Stories,* and one of the topics for the first paper I assign is a detailed analysis of all the Nick material, with reference to Young's arrangement of *The Nick Adams Stories.*

Additionally, we read several of the best known stories beyond the scope of *In Our Time* and Nick Adams, always including "The Snows of Kilimanjaro," "Hills Like White Elephants," "A Clean, Well-Lighted Place," "The Gambler, the Nun, and the Radio," and "An African Story." At this stage, I introduce the late unlamented code of behavior wrongly attributed to Hemingway, but I try to do so in such a way that the students will not misunderstand and misuse it (see Appendix C: Hemingway and "The Code"). I give some background on the origin of the code, taken from Philip Young's 1952 book, *Ernest Hemingway,* about which Hemingway had serious questions and objections. Of course, referring to the code is a risky business, and I am well aware that for the last twenty-five years or so it has been deliberately omitted from the vocabulary of Hemingway scholars and critics, who have found it arbitrary, limited, and reductive. There is danger in even mentioning the code, and I strongly advise against assigning papers or asking exam questions based on the misleading assumption that Hemingway approved of the code and judged his characters by its supposed constituent elements. What you can do is ask students to consider the differences between the hero, the protagonist, and the central character, since the modern world that Hemingway and Faulkner confronted did not offer the heroic opportunity.

Modernism, as I use that protean term in teaching Hemingway and Faulkner, is both an attitude and a literary movement, and the term has been applied to various periods, authors, and texts in Western literature since the Renaissance. The version with which we are concerned here became prominent in Anglo-American literature among others, from at least World War I, and probably earlier. Modernism is concerned with time—specifically with the present—which I assumed to be separate from the past, and to differ radically from it. The modernist writer articulates his/her consciousness of the differences between the present and the past, and makes art of those differences. The modern dilemma may be described in terms of biological, economic, psychological and social determinism, which lead to individual alienation, loss of religious faith, lack of love, and fragmentation along the lines of social class, gender, and race, as well as fragmentation *within* the boundaries of social class, gender, and race. In this condition, many traditional literary subjects, forms, and themes (the hero, the sonnet, the happy ending) no longer seem plausible or possible. Modernist texts are often formally fragmented, both spatially and temporally, from the individual word, phrase, or sentence, through point of view and chronology, to the totality of *genre*. Modernist texts, furthermore, are often ambivalent, ambiguous, or pessimistic about whether there are genuine solutions to this dilemma. To the extent that modernist texts offer possible solutions, art itself is prominent among them.

This, then, is the modern world that Nick Adams faces, and he is followed by Jake Barnes in *The Sun Also Rises,* and then by Frederic Henry in *A Farewell to Arms,* among many others. As Jake and Frederic tell their own stories, they become artists, craftsmen who shore these fragments against their possible ruin, to borrow a phrase from T. S. Eliot. They are both extraordinarily candid, and I stress that their candor is not only a statement of what they have done and not done, said and not said, but also a kind of tacit confession of their failures.

Students often resist a consideration of Hemingway's protagonists as flawed. In looking at *The Sun Also Rises,* they want to believe that Jake is a true aficionado of the bullfights, and they do not like to have pointed out to them not only that Jake is considerably less knowledgeable about the corrida than he and his friends would like to believe but also that he jeopardizes Pedro Romero by putting him in harm's way, in the form of the temptations of Brett Ashley and the fists of Robert Cohn—and Jake himself feels the scorn of Montoya. Jake is no hero, and nor are Robert Cohn or Pedro Romero, though all three have, in some sense, "the usual medals," as Mike Campbell puts it (*SAR* 140).[1] In exploring *A Farewell to Arms,* students likewise consider the confessional aspect with reluctance and some suspicion. Frederic, to them, seems simply unfortunate. He and Catherine and their child are victims of the war, or caught in "the biological trap" (*FTA* 14).[2] Yet Frederic makes unwise choices, from the time he refuses to heed the Major's advice to stay in the safety of the field hospital during the bombardment to the moment he abandons the retreat along the road from Caporetto, and all of these choices and their possible consequences are prefigured by his choice to spend his leave drinking and acting irresponsibly rather than visiting the priest's family in the Abruzzi. Like H. R. Stoneback, I have for years asked my students to explain the elusive passage early in the novel in which Frederic asserts that the priest "had always known what I did not know and what, when I learned it, I was always able to forget. But I did not know that then, though I learned it later" (*FTA* 139). The students typically want what the priest "had always known" to be something about love, but what he actually knows is that Frederic chose to take his leave among the fleshpots of wartime Italy, and that such choices have consequences. Hemingway's subtlety on this point, as on so many others, is easy to ignore but highly significant when studied.

Often I finish the Hemingway assignments with either *For Whom the Bell Tolls* (1940) or *The Old Man and the Sea* (1952), pointing out that both of these texts give us older, more reflective, prudent, and knowledgeable protagonists than Nick, Jake, or Frederic, who are nonetheless ambitious, determined, courageous, and more nearly engaged in heroic endeavors. Neither Robert Jordan nor Santiago, however, is a fully realized hero. Jordan manages to blow the bridge, but he breaks his leg and chooses to remain and face death rather than jeopardize the escape of his beloved Maria. Santiago can return home with only the grotesque skeleton of the once magnificent marlin he has battled so valiantly and so well, and he, too, may be dying. Both show what intelligent and brave men may do, and both seem to me to be worthy of our admiration, but neither merits our unqualified approbation. Both of them, as Santiago puts it, have gone "out too far" (*OMS* 120). Neither of these texts, perhaps in part because of the unusual length of the former and the unusual brevity of the latter, has been favored with the kind of critical attention granted *In Our Time*, *The Sun Also Rises*, and *A Farewell to Arms*, but they stand, I think, as masterful narratives of what an individual may do in response to the modern dilemma.

After a midterm examination on Hemingway, I give out a list of Faulkner's novels and ask which titles they have read previously. Far fewer have read a novel by Faulkner than a novel by Hemingway, and few have read any of Faulkner's short stories beyond the predictable anthology selections. I begin with short stories, specifically "Barn Burning" and "Shingles for the Lord," to introduce Yoknapatawpha County, to show Faulkner's range from violence to comedy and folk humor, and to highlight the deliberate ambiguity of death in "Barn Burning." We also discuss the students' sympathies and judgments of the characters in that story. For years, it was read as an encomium on Sarty Snopes, along the lines laid out by an early critic who argued that the Sartorises "act with an ethically responsible will," while the Snopeses are "amoral" (O'Donnell 285–99). But some present students do not join with Sarty in his awe of the planter de Spain's achievement and methods, and the preferred reading of the story now maintains that Sarty wishes to accomplish two antithetical acts, to save de Spain's barn from his father's arson and to save his father from de Spain's possibly deadly retribution. He fails, probably at both, although his father and brother survive to figure in other fictions.

Thus, we have introduced the same question for Faulkner that we asked about Hemingway: How far are his characters "the same" from one text to the next? How closely do the central figures of his fiction respond to their own versions of the modern dilemma? As with Hemingway, the students are asked to read in Faulkner's short fiction (especially in "The Country" and "The Village" sections of his *Collected Stories*) to accustom themselves to the geography and climate of Jefferson and Yoknapatawpha County; the question "What is the name of Faulkner's mythical county?" appears on every reading quiz. The first Faulkner novel I assign the students, *As I Lay Dying* (1930), introduces them to a tumultuous and threatening world, in which pleasure, dignity, life, and traditional values may be destroyed in an instant, whether through human agency, flood, or fire, and not even discipline and determination can prevent catastrophe. One of the great differences between Hemingway and Faulkner becomes evident in considering "the heroic question" in *As I Lay Dying*: Faulkner refuses to settle on a single unequivocal protagonist, choosing instead to present the myriad distinctive voices of the Bundren family and their observers. After their mock-epic struggles, the Bundrens finally manage to reach Jefferson and bury Addie. Anse Bundren, the feckless paterfamilias, muddles through and acquires a new wife, a new set of store teeth, and a new "graphophone." The diminished family returns to their poor rural home, apparently ready to go on, taking pleasure in what they can. I ask the students, is this a happy ending, a funny one, a grotesque one? Even when I provide working definitions of comedy and humor, Faulkner's intention here remains deliberately ambiguous, rather than a matter of objective, demonstrable truth.

Light in August (1932), the next novel usually assigned, provides material for discussions both of comedy and humor and of tragedy and alienation. The narratives of Lena Grove, Joe Christmas, and Gail Hightower are brought to separable endings—respectively open, closed, and ambiguous—in separate but related concluding chapters. The quiz on this novel should prompt detailed and lively discussion: "Choose one: For chapter 19, evaluate Gavin Stevens's 'white blood, black blood' reading of the death of Joe Christmas. For chapter 20, describe the changes that have taken place in Gail Hightower over the course of the novel. And for chapter 21, explain why Faulkner provides the unusual perspective of the furniture dealer and his wife to "round off" the story of Lena Grove, Byron Bunch, and Lena's child?" Most students will address Gavin Stevens's racial binary, and although I announce at the beginning of our reading of the novel that textual evidence and Faulkner's own analysis of his creation indicate that no one, especially Christmas, can know the "true" story of his racial makeup, it is remarkable how many contemporary readers continue to assume that Christmas is a mulatto. My own practice in responding to these readings is to credit imaginative, original, and responsible use of textual evidence, rather than simply evaluating whether the student has given the "right" answer, although an unquestioned acceptance of the Gavin Stevens thesis requires, I think, a detailed qualifying response. Similarly, a simple, unequivocal explanation of such Hemingway stories as "A Clean, Well-Lighted Place" and "Hills Like White Elephants" (or of any of the novels) deserves a similar analysis in response. We do not read Faulkner or Hemingway to reduce their narratives to mottoes or ideologies, or we ought not to. Their fictions are difficult, demanding our best attention and respect.

Nowhere in Faulkner's work is this more evident than in *The Sound and the Fury* (1929), the novel that he said he loved the most because it failed the most. Many students have tried to read the Benjy section and given it up, and I think we need to help them to understand that in order to read this novel—or *The Sun Also Rises*—in anything like the spirit in which we know it was written, we need to get over the notion that a narrative worthy of reading must yield up whatever meanings it has to the reader the first time around. I introduce *The Sound and the Fury* as a thousand-piece puzzle without straight edges, without four right-angled corners, and without a picture on the box to guide us. Having said that, I offer them some corners and edges and a kind of picture in the form of a four-page handout that I think may be of some help (see Appendix D: Chronology and Lineage, *The Sound and the Fury*). I also tell them about students in an honors class I taught many years ago who assumed Faulkner would be "easy" after reading Shakespeare. I told them to read the Benjy section over the weekend and said I would take any questions they had the following week. When I asked for questions on Monday, the response was a very long silence. Finally, the best of the students asked: "Are there two Quentins?"

"Yes," I said.

"Is one of them female?" another asked.

"Yes," I said.

"Oh!" a third student volunteered. After that, we could begin.

The Sound and the Fury must be Faulkner's most difficult text, although arguments can be made for both *Absalom, Absalom!* (1936) and *Go Down, Moses* (1942), one of which usually concludes the assigned readings. With the four-page handout, or something like it, we can make some progress, and most students take pride in gaining at least a partial understanding of this formidable text, just as we might approach *Ulysses* with Gifford and Seidman's *Ulysses*

Annotated. Such materials provide students with a way into the texts, rather than with a substitute for the exquisite pleasures of reading texts themselves.

As with Hemingway, I ask students to read Faulkner with a sense of chronology, in part so that I can expose them to and warn them away from the fifty-year-old notion that Faulkner became a genius in 1929, enjoyed thirteen remarkable years of excellence, and lost his genius in or after 1942. To this end, I have sometimes assigned *The Reivers* (1962), and asked them on the final examination to compare this journey with that of the Bundrens' adventures in *As I Lay Dying*, as I earlier asked them for a comparison of Nick, Jake, or Frederic with Robert Jordan or Santiago.

The final examination also includes a question on Hemingway and Faulkner together. In my early days of teaching the two together, I would ask something like the following: "Suppose the last library in the world were on fire this morning, and you had time to save the works of Hemingway *or* Faulkner, but not both. Make your choice and justify it." The results, however, were not encouraging. It did not matter which choice they made, because they tended to write one-sided polemics that did gross injustice to the writer whose works they had consigned to the flames, and little honor to the one whose books they had chosen to rescue. So I eventually replaced that invitation to a five-paragraph recitation of the obvious with a new question: "Why Hemingway *and* Faulkner?"

If I were to answer this question myself now, I would start with the assertion that they have both given us the best fictions that we have had. Both had long and productive careers, giving us, repeatedly, profoundly engaging novels and short stories. The works of both show variety, and, over time, development and change, and they both require our bifocal vision, encompassing not only an understanding of the immediate circumstances of their composition and publication but also an understanding of how these works continue to speak to us. Both writers gave us brilliant maps of their fictional landscape, with Hemingway saying "This is country!" all over the United States, Europe, and Africa, while Faulkner gave us the universe in his Yoknapatawpha microcosm. Both writers were innovators in style and narrative form, and both gave us their lifelong meditations on how we might live in this modern world. Above all, both writers filled their stories, and our minds, with hundreds of unforgettable characters, scenes, moments, phrases, sentences, and paragraphs of extraordinary individual prose. We are fortunate to have had them, and we are fortunate that we are able to continue to read and teach their texts.

I would, of course, ask myself to provide examples.

Notes

1. Citations to Hemingway's *The Sun Also Rises* refer to the following edition: Ernest Hemingway, *The Sun Also Rises* (New York: Scribner, 1954).

2. Citations to Hemingway's *A Farewell to Arms* refer to the following edition: Ernest Hemingway, *A Farewell to Arms* (New York: Scribner, 2003).

From Paris to Eatonville, Florida

Hemingway's *The Sun Also Rises* and Hurston's
Their Eyes Were Watching God

Anna Lillios

At first glance, *The Sun Also Rises* (1926) and *Their Eyes Were Watching God* (1937) are radically different modernist texts. Ernest Hemingway writes about jaded sophisticates in decadent Paris and war-ravaged Europe, whereas Zora Neale Hurston depicts the "Negro farthest down" in her all–African American hometown of Eatonville, Florida. Yet because the novels were published within twelve years of each other, they often appear side by side on American literature syllabi. Teaching them in succession has its advantages, because they can provide opportunities to discuss modernist concerns with race, self-identity and otherness, and gender equality. Ann Douglas, in *Terrible Honesty: Mongrel Manhattan in the 1920s* (1995), highlights the value of juxtaposing different texts, noting that 1920s culture was one of doubleness, most notably with white-black forays across the color line. According to Douglas, "cross-race analogies fostered by cultural proximity and creative rivalry proliferated" in the Harlem Renaissance (82). In comparing F. Scott Fitzgerald's *The Great Gatsby* (1925) with Hurston's *Their Eyes Were Watching God*, for example, she finds that both authors combine an "expressive mix of romantic imagination and shrewd observation" (86). Such discoveries stimulate new readings of supposedly fixed canonical texts. A similar comparison between *The Sun Also Rises* and *Their Eyes Were Watching God* can likewise yield new interpretations for students.

Hemingway and Hurston may have had widely divergent careers—Hemingway was highly famous in the period from the 1930s through the 1950s, while Hurston made less than $1,000 on her books during her whole career and always struggled financially—but their lives intersected in several areas. Both were Scribner's authors and they may have met each other, although there is no record that they did so. They shared the same editor, Maxwell Perkins, for the two months before Perkins's sudden death in 1947, and Perkins presumably told each of the other's work, as he was wont to do with all of his authors. Also, both writers lived in Florida at various periods in their lifetimes, although Hurston was living elsewhere, mainly in New York City, during Hemingway's famous residence in Key West between 1928 and 1940. Despite these commonalities, though, the only record of a personal connection between them comes in a letter that Hurston wrote to her ex-husband, Herbert Sheen, on 28 June 1957: "Ernest Hemmingway [sic], also a Scribners author beats me hopping around and living informally. He suggested that I run over to the Isles of Pines [sic], an island belonging to Cuba and buy a spot. It is not so well built up an[d] one can find quiet there to work" (*A Life in Letters* 755). It is unknown whether Hemingway gave this advice to Hurston in person or through a Scribner's editor, but it suggests his empathy for her situation, his willingness to offer a solution, and his assumption that they are fellow authors in need of a quiet place to write. Even up to several years before their deaths—the two authors died within sixteen months of each other—Hemingway and Hurston were devoted writers, who felt literature mattered in people's lives.

On the first day of the Hemingway-Hurston unit, I review the tenets of modernism, ultimately with an eye toward familiarizing the students with the values and characters. This unit is part of the modernist section of the course, which includes T. S. Eliot's *The Waste Land*, F. Scott Fitzgerald's *The Great Gatsby*, and William Faulkner's "A Rose for Emily" and "Barn Burning." The students are assigned two short chapters, "American Versions of Modernism" and "Modernism Abroad and on Native Grounds," in *1865 to the Present*, volume 2 of *The Norton Anthology of American Literature* (663–68). We discuss the usual characteristics of modernism, such as fragmentation, interpretative omissions, juxtapositions, symbolism, allusions, and the use of mythology as a structuring device. I then draw the students' attention to the element I consider most important, which is the modernist search for meaning. In *The Postmodern Turn* (1987), Ihab Hassan concurs that the ending of a novel functions as the locus of meaning in the work.

I next alert the students to the fact that the endings of *The Sun Also Rises* and *Their Eyes Were Watching God* do not yield clear-cut meanings or give a satisfactory sense of closure. Meaning is, in fact, frustrated because of a slippage through boundaries of race, gender, and class. The novels may end in a similar fashion—each featuring a female (and male) survivor, a pilgrimage journey, meditations on the primitive, and a highly symbolic landscape—but they also illustrate the problematic nature of each of these elements and, ultimately, of defining modernism.

After we finish discussing the novels' contextual and modernist background, I then turn to character and setting. Since *The Waste Land* appears on the syllabus before *The Sun Also Rises*, I challenge students to find wasteland aspects in the debilitated hero and desiccated landscape of *The Sun Also Rises*. I request that the students frame their discussion in terms of the hero paradigm presented in Joseph Campbell's *The Hero with a Thousand Faces* (245–46). I shy away from the stereotype of the Hemingway wounded hero, as introduced by Philip Young, because I'm more interested in placing *The Sun Also Rises* in its historical position as a work published after *The Waste Land* rather than as a psychological study of Hemingway's psyche. I ask the students to consider the trajectory of the typical hero's journey and compare it to the journey that Jake and Brett have taken from the battlefields of World War I to the bars of Paris. Students will note that the land and its people are devastated by war: the characters have finally emerged from the Underworld (the trenches); they seek water to replenish their souls (but only find alcohol); they engage in nonprocreative sex; there is an interrogation of masculinity and femininity; they go fishing, which has symbolic overtones, and view bullfighting, an activity suggestive of ancient fertility rites; and the work ends with allusions to the timeless world of Eastern religions. *Their Eyes Were Watching God* also has its points of comparison to *The Waste Land*: after slavery has seared the land and its people, the hurricane brings a sense of restoration and renewal.

On the second day of discussion, I continue to explore the topic of heroes, ask if the students can name any female heroines who go on adventures and return with boons to save their worlds. I wonder why the hero paradigm is almost always male-oriented (actually, there was one heroine text, *Inanna*, about the goddess of ancient Sumer, who was also called Ishtar by the Semites; see Wolkstein and Kramer). At this point, I divide the students into groups and ask each group to analyze a different character in *The Sun Also Rises* in terms of his or her heroic qualities. Students note that Jake Barnes is not a typical male hero, because of his emasculating war wound; that Robert Cohn is lost in his romanticism; and that Brett Ashley did not follow a traditional female role, instead leaving the domestic sphere to undertake a significant journey to the front in World War I, thus complicating the notion of "hero" and typical gender roles. Brett's descent to the Underworld occurs outside the novel's parameters, when she served as a V.A.D. nurse during the war. During her journey, which eventually takes her to Paris after the war, she finds a mentor in Count Mippipopolous, who assists in her transformation. Later, when I am discussing *Their Eyes Were Watching God,* I will remind the students of Brett's role reversal and note that Janie Crawford follows a similar pattern: rejecting her traditional domestic role, journeying to the Underground during the hurricane when her world is disrupted in its fury, and finding a mentor in Tea Cake, who assists in her transformation. Like Brett, she too will stand alone at the end of her journey.

On the third day of discussion, I zero in on the search for meaning in the novel, which comes during a key scene when Brett and Jake are enjoying the Parisian nightlife with Count Mippipopolous. The count has many lessons to teach Brett and Jake. He is the only person in the novel who can show them by his example how to recover from their psychological wounds. In the "presentation-of-the-bill" scene in chapter 14, Jake complains: "All I wanted to know was how to live in it" (*SAR* 148).[1] *It* is one of those tiny, yet highly meaningful, Hemingway words, which I challenge students to define (*pretty,* used at the end of the novel, is another). In this case, I want them to realize that *it* symbolizes existential angst, epistemological gloom, and the "nada" that permeates the atmosphere of such stories as "A Clean, Well-Lighted Place" (1933). Jake is tortured by Brett's presence and his inability to consummate their relationship. When he recalls how much he longs for her, he laments to her, "'There's not a damn thing we could do'" (*SAR* 26). She sums up their situation by saying, "'I think it's hell on earth'" (27). Later, alone in bed, with his "mind jumping around," he admits, "Then all of a sudden I started to cry" (31). At this point, we probe into Jake's psychology as I explain the effects of World War I shell shock. Students, of course, are familiar with PTSD and can connect Jake's mental state to that of friends or family who have been to war in Iraq or Afghanistan.

Like Jake, the count is a war veteran, who has been in "seven wars and four revolutions" (*SAR* 60), whereas Jake has been in only one. The count, too, has wounds: arrows have passed through his chest near his heart. "'It is because I have lived very much that now I can enjoy everything so well,' he tells Jake. "... 'That is the secret. You must get to know the values'" (60). The count, a bon vivant who at first glance appears to play only a minor role in the story, is a key figure because he embodies and articulates the values that Hemingway most wishes to convey. According to H. R. Stoneback, in *Reading Hemingway's* The Sun Also Rises, "he has assumed the role of one of the novel's most important exemplary characters" (59).

The count's values are numerous, as listed in chapter 7: "'don't... mix emotions up with a wine like that'" (60), he tells Brett and Jake; "'never joke people'" (59); tip the concierge for the bad behavior of your friends; support the son of your father's great friend; and so on. But the primary value he embodies and can teach Jake is how to live in the present by fully enjoying each moment as it presents itself. Jake is tortured by his past and agonizes over the future. The count's appreciation of the simple things in life, such as sharing good wine and food with friends, reminds the reader that all anyone possesses, in reality, is the present moment.

Yet pinning the count down is a challenge, as his dialog with Brett shows:

> "Doesn't anything ever happen to your values?" Brett asked.
> "No. Not any more."
> "Never fall in love?"
> "Always," said the count. "I am always in love."
> "What does that do to your values?"
> "That, too, has got a place in my values."
> "You haven't any values. You're dead, that's all."
> "No, my dear. You're not right. I'm not dead at all." (*SAR* 61)

Perhaps Brett cannot see the count's values because she herself does not have any; according to Stoneback, "although Brett claims her place in the inner circle of those who know the values, her conduct—flicking ashes on Jake's rug, disregarding ceremony in her will to drunkenness, and misunderstanding entirely what the count says about values and love—argues her exclusion from the company of Jake and the count" (103). Brett largely sees love in erotic terms and other people in terms of her self, whereas the love the count feels and extends is *agape,* an all-embracing joy in all of God's creation. In fact, the imagery surrounding the count suggests that he represents "Christian virtues and values," according to Stoneback: "his good manners, his generosity, his highly ritualized (even sacramental) sense of experience, his joie de vivre, and above all the doctrine of love that he [espouses] in this key scene are exemplar[il]y Christian" (103-4). The arrow scars he exhibits to Brett and Jake can be seen in a Christian context as allusions to the Roman martyr Saint Sebastian.

On the other hand, in an early draft of the novel, the count is described in terms that suggest an eastern religion. When Jake looks at him, "He was sitting there like Buddhah [sic]" (qtd. in Svoboda, *Hemingway and* The Sun Also Rises 27). This mixture of Christian and Buddhist elements connotes Eliot's *The*

Waste Land, which ends on the banks of the Ganges River in India. Returning to Campbell and the hero's journey, I ask students to define the Hemingway hero—is he Western and Christian or Eastern and Buddhist? And what about the heroine? Is Brett more than just a man-hating Circe?

After establishing the characters and their values, we turn to a discussion of the setting. I require students to read the following two essays, which I post online: Allen Josephs's "Toreo: The Moral Axis of *The Sun Also Rises*" and H. R. Stoneback's *Hemingway's Paris: Our Paris?* The Stoneback essay gives students the sense that Hemingway is writing about a real place. I follow up by showing them a map of Paris, pointing out Hemingway's residences and hangouts, which a tourist can visit. I next turn to the walk, in chapter 8, that Jake and Bill take through the streets of Paris after their evening out with the count, noting particularly that they walk along "the rigid north and south of the Rue Saint Jacques" (*SAR* 78). Stoneback points out that the Rue Saint Jacques was the start of an ancient pilgrimage route to Santiago de Compostela, the shrine of St. James, in Spain. Thus, at its deepest levels, Stoneback argues, the novel is a "quest, the pilgrimage undertaken in order to grow in grace"; he also claims that the "deepest thrust of this novel is radically spiritual" (Stoneback, *Hemingway's Paris* 156). Josephs also sees *The Sun Also Rises* as spiritual, but interprets that spirituality in terms of the toreo and explains how the bullfight ritual symbolizes a world that stops profane time (158). Ritualistic activities, such as hunting, fishing, fighting in war, eating, making love, and working at an art, were Hemingway's Ur-subjects.

Jake judges all the characters by how they regard the bullfight (Josephs 154). Pedro has the greatness: "Hemingway would equate [his performance in the ring] with religious ecstasy," according to Josephs (157). It is a feeling that "takes a man out of himself and makes him feel immortal" (Stoneback, *Hemingway's Paris* 157). Montoya recognizes how fragile Pedro is and how he must be protected. Cohn is oblivious to the bullfight's power, even bored by it. Brett receives the highest bullfighting prize from Pedro—the ear he has cut off from the bull—but she forgetfully leaves it behind in a drawer in her hotel room.

On the fifth and final day of discussion, with an eye toward a macrocosmic view of Hemingway's moral outlook, I introduce the writing assignment, which requires students examine the ending of either *The Sun Also Rises* or *Their Eyes Were Watching God*. Their assignment is to write a five-page (1,250-word) essay showing how the ending of the novel illustrates the author's worldview (bringing in such elements as gender relations, self-empowerment, and setting). Since I often teach American Literature II as an online course, I give students the option of creating an electronic archive of materials related to the assignment. They post their projects either on blogspot or as a web page, which helps them merge traditional textual analysis with technology. (See Appendix E: Discussion Questions and Writing Assignment.)

In preparation for the paper, the class and I try to "'get to know the values,'" as the count says, that are at the core of *The Sun Also Rises*. The characters are struggling to redefine themselves in face of their experiences in the Great War. Bill has the most pragmatic set of values, as illustrated in the scene with the stuffed dogs: "'You give them money. They give you a stuffed dog'" (*SAR* 78). His value is to "'never be daunted'" (79). The worst thing is not to live at all, like the Dayton, Ohio, pilgrims, who pay exorbitant prices for nothing. The count's simple values have led him to strip his illusions to the barest minimum. He "can enjoy everything so well" because ample life experience has taught him to live in the moment (60), by which he makes himself strong and invulnerable to the vicissitudes of life. This is the lesson Jake has to learn. Because of his injury, Jake lacks the luxury of being emotional and sentimental, like Robert. Robert can journey to the imaginary Purple Land of his favorite book, but Jake will lose his mind if he lets himself go. Jake already has trouble sleeping at night and has many symptoms of what would later come to be called PTSD, as mentioned previously.

Brett too exhibits symptoms of stress and, in this regard, is Jake's soul mate, even his double. They met while he was in the hospital and, presumably, fell in love while she was caring for him. As I point out to my students, Brett's job as a nurse is crucial. She is associated with the magical healing powers of the medicine-woman. It can be argued that she is the perverse catalyst that heals Jake's soul by means of a searing, unrequited—and presumably unconsummated—love affair. Jake and Brett are inextricably linked, because they understand what each other has gone through during the war. The count is the only other character who can relate to them in this respect. Thus, he is significant as someone who has endured the rite of passage of seeing—and surviving—the hellish aspects of life and gaining a viable philosophy of life that enables him to survive. These characters' main goal is to learn how to survive and live in "it"—that is, the existential angst of those who have seen the dark side of existence.

The narrative, then, is a journey toward salvation. In "The Snows of Kilimanjaro," Hemingway writes that it is essential to "work the fat off [the] soul" (*SS* 63). Hemingway was a convert to Catholicism and was attending mass daily when he was writing *The Sun Also Rises*; he wrote part of the novel at Chartres, which has a medieval cathedral. An early title was "A New Slain Knight." Jake is a pilgrim who goes south for renewal. Each of his stops, at San Sebastian, Pamplona, and Roncevaux, are also stops on the pilgrimage route to Santiago de Compostela. He moves from the "brown, heat-baked mountains" to the "sudden green valley" and the fertile, lush "rolling green plain" (*SAR* 114, 111, 114). Fishing is also symbolic of life and renewal. The trout are "beautifully colored and firm and hard from the cold water," he observes. Compare this setting to the dark, smoky cafes in Paris. He cannot pray in churches, but out of doors he realizes that the mountain forests are, as Bill calls them, "God's first temples" (127).

When Brett summons Jake to Madrid at the end, he realizes that "the Norte station in Madrid is the end of the line" (*SAR* 244). The question is, have Jake and Brett achieved any self-enlightenment, the goal of any pilgrimage? Jake's response to Brett's invitation to fantasize once again about their relationship—"'Isn't it pretty to think so?'" (251)—suggests that he has acquired a sense of irony about her intentions and is unlikely to fixate on their would-be erotic relationship. In fact, he may have begun his transformation during his encounter with the count. On that night, he kissed Brett in a passionate, sexual way for the last time.

When we move on to Hurston's *Their Eyes Were Watching God*, to keep continuity with Hemingway I ask the students to comment on the values that they find in the Hurston novel. Of course, they notice that values deriving from an African-American context are radically different from those arising from an expatriate context. Janie Crawford, as the heroine of *Their Eyes Were Watching God*, must be concerned first with handling her basic survival needs and then with disentangling herself from the legacy of slavery. Henry Louis Gates Jr., in *The Signifying Monkey*, suggests a deeper concern: "On the broadest level, *Their Eyes* depicts the search for identity and self-understanding of an Afro-American woman" (184). But Janie's grandmother, Nanny, a former slave who still has a slave's mentality, does not care about the development of Janie's self. She warns Janie against the typical fate of the black woman in the post-slavery era: "'De nigger woman is de mule uh de world'" (Hurston, *Watching God* 14). Instead, Nanny wants Janie to aspire to a better life, and she sees the acquisition of land and property—"sittin' on high"—as the means of accomplishing this goal: "'Ah wanted to preach a great sermon about colored women sittin' on high, but they wasn't no pulpit for me'" (15).

Shifting the discussion to a comparison between the values of Brett Ashley and Janie highlights that American literature (up to this time) had focused almost exclusively on the values and fates of white characters. I ask the students if they can recall any black females in American novels before the 1930s. A few students may have read the poetry of Phillis Wheatley, or Harriet Jacobs's

Incidents in the Life of a Slave Girl. They are struck by the fact that a black female presence is lacking in American literature. I then tell them that Toni Morrison has written about this very idea in *Playing in the Dark*, in which she complains that the African-American perspective is missing in our early American literature and that, furthermore, a "black presence is central to any understanding of our national literature" (5). I also briefly tell the students about the Harlem Renaissance and Hurston's integral part in it. This movement celebrating black music, literature, dance, theatre, and art during the 1920s and 1930s was in part a reaction to the earlier American renaissance of the 1850s, which featured almost exclusively the literature of white males, such as Henry David Thoreau, Ralph Waldo Emerson, Nathaniel Hawthorne, Herman Melville, and Walt Whitman. I draw the students' attention to *Hemingway and the Black Renaissance*, an essay collection edited by Gary Edward Holcomb and Charles Scruggs (2012), which discusses Hemingway's close connection with the black writers of the Harlem Renaissance. According to Holcomb and Scruggs in their introduction, Ralph Ellison, particularly, felt that "Hemingway's prose expresses . . . the sort of courage in face of modern existential alienation that the blues voices" (5). The blues is a quality that Houston Baker, in *Blues, Ideology, and the Harlem Renaissance* (1987), finds in Janie. He sees her as a blues singer as she goes through her life's journey.

Janie's journey begins as she learns about love, a value that emerges during her three love affairs. Like Brett Ashley, Janie attempts to find her identity through her relationships with men; students easily find the flaws in these affairs. In time, however, she realizes that she must find her own purpose in life. Janie's first two marriages are based on economic factors, with men who do not appreciate her individuality: the first husband wants her to work in the fields like a "mule," and the second wants her to loll on the porch as a trophy wife. The latter tells the townspeople, "'She's uh woman and her place is in de home'" (Hurston, *Watching God* 41). Her life changes when she meets her third lover, Tea Cake. He is a nuanced American hero because of his playfulness, a quality not usually attributed to the hero with a thousand faces. When he teaches Janie how to play checkers, she finds herself "glowing inside." She's thrilled because: "Somebody wanted her to play. Somebody thought it natural for her to play" (91). According to Gates, "Play, finally, is the irresistible love potion that Tea Cake administers to Janie. . . . Janie and Tea Cake teach each other to become 'good players' in what the text depicts as a game of love" (Gates 195). Unlike her first husband, who wants her to work like a mule, and her second husband, who feels she is above work, Tea Cake opens a new dimension in

Janie's life. Like the count in *The Sun Also Rises,* he is a mentor, teaching her the right way to live, but it has nothing to do with the Protestant work ethic. According to Gates, "the text opposes bourgeois notions of progress" (186). He eventually takes her to the Muck, the rich farmland on the south end of Lake Okeechobee in the Everglades. She begins to speak out, tell stories to the farm workers (word play), and gain a sense of self: "Only here, she could listen and laugh and even talk some herself if she wanted to. She got so she could tell big stories herself from listening to the rest" (Hurston, *Watching God* 128).

Our more macrocosmic view of Hurston brings us to the ending of *Their Eyes Were Watching God* to determine her worldview. I ask the students to compare the force of the hurricane with World War I, which Jake experienced in *The Sun Also Rises*. A hurricane, like war, upsets the balance in characters' lives and forever changes them. The storm is a common metaphor for creation, destruction, and regeneration, because it involves the mingling together of the four elements. As I have noted elsewhere, by uniting air (wind), water (rain), and fire (rays of light in the eye of the storm), all of which disturb the fourth element, earth, the hurricane symbolizes cosmic synergy ("'Monstropolous Beast'" 89–93).

I explain to the students that Hurston's hurricane was also real. Her portrait of the hurricane as a "monstropolous beast" in *Their Eyes Were Watching God* was based on three specific hurricanes occurring in 1928, 1929, and 1935. The 1928 hurricane, which most closely resembles the storm in the novel, was one of the most powerful on record and one of the worst natural disasters in U.S. history. The Red Cross reported in 1929 that 1,810 people died; three-quarters of those were black, many of them undocumented Bahaman transient workers. This Category 4 hurricane had sustained winds of 155 miles per hour. It created a tidal-wave effect in Lake Okeechobee, sweeping over its soft mud dikes, which could not hold back the waters. The transient workers, such as Janie and Tea Cake, were doomed. Janie feels the presence of God as she and Tea Cake wait out the storm's fury: "The wind came back with triple fury, and put out the light for the last time. They sat in company with the others in other shanties, their eyes straining against crude walls and their souls asking if He meant to measure their puny might against His. They seemed to be staring at the dark, but their eyes were watching God" (Hurston, *Watching God* 151).

The storm also destroys Janie's way of life with Tea Cake when a rabid dog bites him after the storm and Janie is forced to shoot him before he kills her. When I ask the students to interpret the ending, they recognize that its symbolism creates open-endedness. Janie's memories of Tea Cake, which "commenced to sing a sobbing sigh out of every corner in the room," stimulate her imagination until Tea Cake's image comes "prancing around her" (184). When she tells herself, "Of course he wasn't dead," she begins to fantasize about him, while "his memory made pictures of love and light against the wall" (184). These good memories and even bad ones—of the "day of the gun, and the bloody body"—now inspire her to be an artist, perhaps. The statement "Here was peace" suggests that Janie has found herself (184). When she tells her friend, "'Ah done been tuh de horizon and back'" (183), she knows that her journey is over. She has accomplished what Hurston feels every human must do: "Two things everybody's got tuh do fuh theyselves. They got tuh go tuh God, and they got tuh find out about livin' fuh theyselves" (183).

Finally, both *Their Eyes Were Watching God* and *The Sun Also Rises* end with moments of transcendence, when the characters have the opportunity to transform. As modernists, Hemingway and Hurston took great care with these endings, believing them to be, in Ihab Hassan's terms, the "locus of meaning." In a letter dated 16 May 1943 praising the novel *Cross Creek* (1942) by her friend, Marjorie Kinnan Rawlings, Hurston comes closest to describing her goal as a writer. She is writing to Rawlings, but she could also be referring to her other Florida friend, Hemingway: "You are conscious of the three layers of life, instead of the obvious thing before your nose. You see and feel the immense past, what is now, and feel inside you something of what is to come. Therefore, you are not pacing the cell of the current hour. You are free because you have made your peace with the universe and its laws. You are deep and fine" (*A Life in Letters* 486).

Note

1. All citations to *The Sun Also Rises* are to the following edition: Ernest Hemingway, *The Sun Also Rises* (New York: Scribner Classic/Collier Edition, 1986).

The Sun Also Rises and the "Stimulating Strangeness" of Paris

Meg Gillette

It's two weeks before we leave for our summer study abroad program in Paris, and my students are sprawled across my living room floor watching *Midnight in Paris*, Woody Allen's 2011 film about a nostalgic screenwriter (played by Owen Wilson) who finds himself magically transported each night to Paris in the 1920s. With one expatriate cameo after the next ("Oh, hi Mr. Hemingway"), the film introduces students to many of the writers on our reading list, and with its beautiful scenery (expansive gardens of flowering trees, Haussmann-era boulevards and buildings) and paeans to Paris ("This is unbelievable. Look at this. There's no city like this in the world"), the film generates excitement among the students for our upcoming trip. When the film ends, I ask them why they have chosen to go to Paris and why they think so much great writing came out of Paris in the 1920s. "There's just something about the beauty of the city," they tell me, echoing the film's romantic clichés. "I think it was the friendships," suggests another, echoing the film's interest in the artists' personal lives. Indeed, it is hard to imagine any other answer after watching *Midnight in Paris*. Because Owen Wilson travels to the 1920s only at midnight and then spends his time there at private parties, residences, and deserted cafés, modern Paris disappears from sight, and all that is left is an otherworldly community of artists who seem to exist in a private world unto themselves.

When I teach my three-week American writers in Paris class (which attracts both undergraduate general education students and English majors alike), I try to challenge this popular view of literature as being somehow outside history by offering an alternative view: Raymond Williams's thesis, expounded in "The Metropolis and the Emergence of Modernism" (1992), that "there *are* decisive links between the practices and ideas of the avant-garde movements of the twentieth century and the specific conditions and relationships of the twentieth-century metropolis" (83). For Williams, "the most important general element of [modernism's] innovations in form is the fact of immigration to the metropolis, and it cannot too often be emphasized how many of the major innovators were, in this precise sense, immigrants" (91). As Williams argues, not only did immigration create elements of "liberation and alienation, contact and strangeness" (93), "which so regularly form part of [modernism's] repertory" (91), but it also fostered contact with different languages that denaturalized their conventions and stimulated artistic experiment: "Thus language was perceived quite differently. It was no longer, in the old sense, customary and naturalised, but in many ways arbitrary and conventional. To the immigrants especially, with their new second common language, language was more evident as a medium—a medium that could be shaped and reshaped—than as a social custom" (92). For Williams, it is the "stimulating strangeness" of Paris (93), its differences and discontinuities, and not its extraordinary romantic beauty or assemblage of genius (as *Midnight in Paris* would suggest), that gave rise to the achievements of modern literature.

Our first class in Paris begins with a discussion of Williams's essay. Students tell me everything they remember from the essay, and I act as secretary, writing their recollections on the board and sprinkling in questions to help them see how the ideas fit together (e.g., "But why does he talk about Wordsworth? What does he discover in Wordsworth's poetry?"). Then, for examples of the "stimulating strangeness" Williams describes, I ask students to tell me about their time in Paris thus far: "Have you had interactions in Paris with people who are different from you?" I ask. "What new languages and customs have you experienced? Have you felt disoriented in the city?" Students grow animated as they recall the differences that surprised them ("The computer keyboards here don't use QWERTY!" "Remember the two women kissing at the restaurant?"), and as they reflect on their experiences, they begin questioning their own assumptions about language ("Why do our keyboards use QWERTY anyway?) and exhibit the kind of liberation and alienation which Williams identifies with the modern metropolis (e.g., "It didn't bother me that the women were kissing," one student boasts. "I just wish they hadn't been standing so close"). Drawing connections between the essay and their own time in the city, students gain not only a greater understanding of Williams's argument but also a new perspective by which to view their experiences studying abroad.

That afternoon, we continue our work with Williams by heading to two museums—the Musée d'art et d'histoire du Judaïsme (Museum of Jewish Art and History) and the Musée du quai Branly (Anthropology Museum)—so students can see evidence of the early twentieth-century "melting pot" Williams describes. At the Museum of Jewish Art and History,[1] students spend time in the Dreyfus Affair exhibit examining the era's anti-Semitic cartoons: "How do these cartoons negotiate difference?" I ask. "What specific stereotypes do they promote?" At the Anthropology Museum, students attend the exhibit entitled "Human Zoos: The Invention of the Savage,"[2] where they learn about the late-nineteenth- and early twentieth-century practice of putting "primitive" peoples on display as a form of popular entertainment. "Why do you think people attended these 'human zoos'?" I ask. "What do these exhibits reveal about the fears and fantasies of the people who produced them?" Touring these museums, students learn about modern strategies for negotiating difference (e.g., othering, projection, scapegoating, exoticism, primitivism, and escapism) and begin building the critical vocabulary we'll use in our discussions of *The Sun Also Rises*.

The next day begins our discussion of Hemingway's novel. Prior to the class, students read chapters 1–8 and write a short (one- to two-page) journal response, examining the novel in light of the issues raised in the previous class:

> Journal 1: In "The Metropolis and the Emergence of Modernism," Raymond Williams uses the term *melting pot* to describe twentieth-century metropolises like Paris. In what ways is the Paris of *The Sun Also Rises* a melting pot? How does *The Sun Also Rises* represent "the vitality, the variety, the liberating diversity and mobility of the city"? (R. Williams 89).
>
> To think about this question, make a list of the different people Jake comes into contact with during the first eight chapters of the novel. Then choose one of these contacts and write a paragraph describing how the encounter affects Jake. How might Williams's essay or the museums we visited help you make sense of his response?

The next class begins with a discussion of their journal responses. Making a list on the board of all the different people Jake encounters (e.g., a prostitute, a lady, a Jew, gay men, and a count), we note how disconnected they are from the people and places from which they came. When I ask students about Jake's responses to these encounters with difference, they note his alienation with Georgette ("It was a long time since I had dined with a *poule,* and I had forgotten how dull it could be" [*SAR* 24][3]), his anti-Semitic digs at Cohn (boxing only "improved his nose" [11], "He had a hard, Jewish, stubborn streak" [18]), and his othering of the gay men at the bal musette ("Somehow *they* always made me angry. . . . I knew then *they* would all dance with her. *They* are like that" [28; emphasis added]). By foregrounding the diversity within these early chapters, and Jake's uncomfortable responses, the discussion alerts students to the novel's engagement with the dynamics of the melting pot and so complicates the popular view of the "lost generation" as a homogenous, isolated set.

Turning our attention from characters to setting, we look next at the novel's representation of the city. First, though, I tell them what anthropologist Dean MacCannell said about modern metropolises in his landmark work *The Tourist* (1976): namely, that they are riddled with discontinuities (e.g., "Modern battleships are berthed near *Old Ironsides;* high-rise apartments stand next to restored eighteenth-century townhouses; 'Old Faithful' geyser is surrounded by bleacher seats"), and that the modern subject, living in this world of differentiations, "striv[es] for a transcendence of the modern totality, a way of attempting to overcome the discontinuity of modernity, of incorporating its fragments into unified experience" (13). Students' own experiences in the city again help us explore the theory we are considering: "What have you noticed in Paris that struck you as out of place?" I ask. "Have you encountered the sort of discontinuities that MacCannell describes?" As students swap stories about the juxtapositions that surprised them (e.g., a Moroccan couscous restaurant tucked within a classic Parisian limestone building, an Egyptian obelisk in the middle of the Place de la Concorde), they also offer tentative explanations: one student tries to ease our confusion about the obelisk by looking it up in her *Essential Guide to Paris* ("The pink granite obelisk from Luxor [was] offered to the French nation by the viceroy of Egypt in 1836" [45]), but when her explanation invites more questions from the class ("Why was it presented to France? And what was here before?"), we again experience the collective striving for meaning, the struggle "to overcome the discontinuity of modernity" that MacCannell describes. At this point, I direct them back to the novel, and, reviewing Jake's descriptions of the city, students discover catalogues of displaced forms (e.g., fifteenth-century churches juxtaposed with modern road workers [*SAR* 33], statues of Napoleonic generals in front of expatriate cafés [37]) and come to consider Jake as a fellow tourist, tangled in the fragments and discontinuities of the modern metropolis.

But as Allyson Nadia Field argues, in "Expatriate Lifestyle as Tourist Destination: *The Sun Also Rises* and Experiential Travelogues of the Twenties," Jake is more than a fellow tourist; he is also our travel guide. An in-class activity using 1920s travel books alerts students to the tourist framework of *The Sun Also Rises* and helps them think about how the novel speaks back to the city by providing strategies for navigating it. To help students place the novel in the tradition of 1920s travelogues, I give them chapters of popular 1920s Paris travel guides—*Paris on Parade, How to Be Happy in Paris,* and *Paris with the Lid Off*,[4] which I have cut apart with a razor—and ask them if they see similarities between these guidebook chapters and chapter 5 of *The Sun Also Rises*. Accustomed to the monuments-and-museums approach of their own twenty-first-century Paris guidebooks, students are startled by 1920s versions, with their irreverent tone ("But remember, this trip is not for Goody-goods, or crepe-hangers, or hard-shells, or nose-tossers. This will be a chummy, clubby party" [B. Reynolds 7]) and alcohol-fueled subject matter (containing chapter upon chapter about cafes, bars, and music halls). Flipping between the 1920s guidebooks and *The Sun Also Rises*, students discover not only a shared interest in the expatriate lifestyle but also shared genre conventions: daily itineraries ("In the morning I walked down the Boulevard to the Rue Soufflot for coffee and brioche" [*SAR* 43]), advice on when to travel ("The horse-chestnut trees in the Luxembourg gardens were in bloom" [43]), walking directions ("I got on an S bus and rode down to the Madeleine, standing on the back platform. From the Madeleine I walked along the Boulevard des Capucines to the Opéra, and up to my office" [43]), even café recommendations ("How about Wetzel's? They've got good hors d'oeuvres" [45]). To underscore Jake's role as a narrator *qua* tour guide, we grab our bags and follow Jake on a tour of Montparnasse ("Where should we go first?" one student asks. "The Select," another volunteers, remembering Jake's preference for it over the Rotonde [*SAR* 43]).

And yet despite the novel's reassuring promise of an expatriate experience, following Jake through the city brings only more uncertainty. Sitting down at the Select to order coffees, we begin measuring not only the authenticity of our visit ("Oh my gosh, this is where Jake hung out!"; "Look, they have pictures of Hemingway over the bar") but also the differences between our experiences and Jake's; as it turns out, the building has been remodeled (the pictures of Hemingway are a new addition), there are no writers or artists in sight (at 11:00 A.M. we are the only customers in the café), and, of course, Jake Barnes never *actually* sat here (since he is fictional, after all). Assessing the differences between our experiences and Jake's, we experience again the changes between the Paris Hemingway knew and our modern metropolis, and as I read to them another passage from MacCannell's *The Tourist*, we reflect on our own investment in the café's authenticity:

Increasingly enough, the generalized anxiety about the authenticity of interpersonal relationships in modern society is matched by certainty about the authenticity of touristic sights. The rhetoric of tourism is full of manifestations of the importance of the authenticity of the relationship between tourists and what they see: this is a *typical* native house; this is the *very* place the leader fell; this is the *actual* pen used to sign the law; this is the *original* manuscript; this an *authentic* Tlingit fish club; this is a *real* piece of the *true* Crown of Thorns. (MacCannell 14)

For MacCannell, the sightseer's investment in authenticity is a kind of coping mechanism in modernity, a way to momentarily set aside its uncertainties and get a handle on its discontinuities and fragments. From this perspective, our own anxiety about the authenticity of the modern café seems like the most authentic part of our visit.

To prepare students for our next class, which will shift our focus from what the novel says about Paris to how the novel says it, I give them their second journal assignment to complete while finishing their coffees at the Select:

Journal 2: According to Williams, the experience of immigration underlies the experiments of modern writing since "to the immigrants . . . language was more evident as a medium—a medium that could be shaped and reshaped" (R. Williams 92). This assignment invites you to think about what is experimental in Hemingway's style. To discover the complexity in Hemingway's seemingly straightforward prose, try writing a description of what you see in the café using one of Hemingway's cafe descriptions (e.g., of the Napolitain [*SAR* 22] or of the Café des Amateurs [*MF* 5]) as a template. Afterward, write a paragraph explaining which Hemingway characteristics you adopted. In what ways might Hemingway's style be called experimental?

The next class, they share their descriptions, and we note Hemingway's use of small adjectives ("warm," "red," "solid" [*SAR* 23]), understatement ("I watched a good-looking girl walk past the table" [23]), and accumulative sentences ("It was a warm spring night *and* I sat at a table on the terrace of the Napolitain after Robert had gone, watching it get dark *and* the electric signs come on, *and* the red and green stop-and-go traffic signal, *and* the crowd going by, *and* the horse-cabs clippety-clopping along at the edge of the solid taxi traffic, *and* the poules going by" [23; emphasis added]).

To enable the students to consider what is experimental about Hemingway's style, I tell them about Hemingway's admiration of Paul Cézanne, often called the father of modern painting, and how Hemingway credited Cézanne as a major influence on his writing: "I was learning something from the painting of Cézanne that made writing true simple sentences far from enough to make the stories have the dimensions that I was trying to put in them" (*MF* 13). Using my computer to display the three Cézanne painting that were on exhibit at the Luxembourg Museum ("L'Estaque, vue du golfe de Marseille," "Farmyard at Auvers-sur-Oise," and "The Poplars") when Hemingway would visit,[5] I lecture about how Cézanne broke from the traditions of representational art by foregoing documentary accuracy for a style characterized by short brushstrokes and mosaic patches, bold planes of color, repetition of colors and motifs, elimination of nonessential details, and the reduction of landscapes to simplified shapes (cylinders, cones, spheres).

Of course, looking at these paintings on my computer is a weak substitute for the real thing, so with this working knowledge of Cézanne, we pack up our copies of *The Sun Also Rises* and head to the Musée d'Orsay, where the students continue to study Hemingway's experiments with language while working on their next journal assignment:

> Journal 3: "Cézanne is my painter," Hemingway told Lillian Ross in a 1949 interview. "I can make a landscape like Mr. Paul Cézanne" (Ross 136). Today, we visit the Musée d'Orsay to compare Hemingway's landscapes with Cézanne's. First, tour the exhibit and choose one of Cézanne's paintings to analyze. Which characteristics of Cézanne's style do you see in the painting? (Note: if the gift shop has a postcard of your painting, you might buy one and tape it into your journal.) Next, select one of Hemingway's landscape descriptions (e.g., "We passed some lovely gardens" [SAR 97], "For a while the country" [99], or "The bus climbed steadily up the road" [113-14]) and write a second paragraph explaining the elements of Cézanne's style you see in Hemingway landscape. How does Hemingway do with words what Cézanne does with paint?

Sitting outside the museum a few hours later, students report back on their journaling and their discoveries that Cézanne's geometric shapes, bold planes of color, and omitted details appear in Hemingway's landscapes too; one student even likens Hemingway's use of short words to Cézanne's use of small brush strokes. To help them think more historically about these stylistic experiments, I ask them if they see any connections between the natural landscapes they have been analyzing and yesterday's discussion of the metropolitan melting pot. At first they note only differences, but, as they talk, some find more provocative contrasts ("It's like he is trying to escape the contact, strangeness, and fragmentation of the city"), while others discover unexpected similarities ("Look at the fragments and omissions in these descriptions; it's like he doubts his ability to create a totalizing description of the place"). Drawing parallels between Hemingway's sparse, fragmented style and the discontinuities and lack of totalizing explanations characteristic of modernity, students discover the multiple ways, in both content and style, the novel engages with the modern metropolis, helping them get beyond mere plot summary or reportage.

For our third class, things come full circle as we discuss the fiesta scene and Bill's anti-Semitism in light of the "Human Zoos" exhibit and our time at the Museum of Jewish Art and History. While some find painful parallels between Cohn's treatment by the expatriates and the propaganda of the anti-Semitic newspapers, others express relief that in light of the era's virulent anti-Semitism, Cohn's treatment was not worse. Still others wonder if Hemingway represents these anti-Semitic attitudes as a way to critique them. Turning next to the Fiesta scenes, we note the symbols of colonialism hanging over the parade ("cigar-store Indians, thirty feet high, Moors, a King and a Queen, whirling and waltzing solemnly to the riau-riau" [*SAR* 159]) and discuss the characters' different ways of conceptualizing otherness—from Cohn's naturalized privilege ("'Where are the foreigners?'" [158]), to Brett's erotic admiration ("'And those green trousers'" [169]), to Jake's primitivist ideals ("'He knew everything when he started. The others can't ever learn what he was born with'" [172]). After our time at the Anthropology Museum, these responses to otherness take on greater significance, and students come to see the fiesta scenes as more than just an enviable party but as part of the novel's ongoing negotiation of contact, spectacle, and strangeness.

When I teach the class next, I imagine adding another assignment, in which we visit the newly reopened Musée Galliera (Paris Fashion Museum) as a prelude to a journal assignment about gender.

> Journal 5: "How were the fashions of Coco Chanel (and other designers of the 1920s) different from the fashions that had come before? In what ways did they challenge and/or adhere to traditional notions of femininity? Now, look back at the novel's descriptions of Brett's clothing (e.g., "She wore a slipcover jersey" [*SAR* 29–30], "She had no stockings on" [84], "Brett wore a black sleeveless evening dress" [150], "a woman with bare shoulders, at a table full of drunks" [180], or "He wanted me to grow my hair out" [246]). In what ways does the novel use the language of fashion to reveal Brett's character?

To explore the limits and possibilities of Brett's independence, the ensuing conversation might trace the different ways characters react to her fashion, from Jake's sexualized gaze ("She was built with curves like the hull of a racing yacht, and you missed none of it with that wool jersey" [30]), to Robert's homosocial pride ("It must have been pleasant for him to see her looking so lovely, and know he had been away with her and that every one knew it" [150]), to Montoya's loathing ("He did not even nod" [181]), and Romero's retro makeover ("He wanted me to grow my hair out. Me, with long hair" [246]).

Such assignments help alert students to how the novel engages with the historical world of Paris in the 1920s. For classes not taught in Paris, the assignments can be adapted with the use of classroom technology: the Dreyfus Affair archive at the Jewish Museum can be accessed online; the exhibition book to the "Human Zoos" exhibit can be purchased from Amazon and its images scanned and presented as a PowerPoint; and inexpensive posters of Cézanne's paintings can be hung around the classroom for student viewing. Yet, of course, reading the novel in Paris has particular advantages. Holding class in the café where the novel takes place creates a thrill of recognition that can be had only in Paris, and Paris's world-class museums bring early twentieth-century culture alive in ways that xeroxed handouts and PowerPoints simply cannot. Still, what I value most about teaching this class in Paris are the opportunities the experience affords students to connect their lives to their reading. Too often, students view literature as something they do for class, unrelated to their real lives. But reading *The Sun Also Rises* while exploring Paris breaks down this divide. In the context of our discussions about Williams and *The Sun Also Rises*, students' complaints about non-QWERTY computer keyboards can become conversations about the arbitrariness of language and modern experiments in form; in the context of our discussions about tourism in *The Sun Also Rises*, their disappointment about renovations to expatriate cafés can become conversations about the role of authenticity in modern society. Studying expatriate literature while living in Paris allows students to see their own questions about the "stimulating strangeness" of the city refracted back to them by the novel, and as they gain from literature new ways of thinking about their own encounters with difference in the modern metropolis, they experience literature as equipment for living, finding in *The Sun Also Rises* a tour guide by which to extend their own global understanding.

Notes

1. The Alfred Dreyfus collection has been digitized and is also accessible through the website of the Musée d'art et d'histoire du Judaïsme. See Musée d'art et d'histoire du Judaïsme, The Dreyfus Collection, www.mahj.org/en/2_collections/fondsDreyfus.php?niv=3&ssniv=0.

2. Although this temporary exhibition closed on 3 June 2012, Lilian Thurman's excellent exhibition book, *Human Zoos: The Invention of the Savage* (Paris: Musée du quai Branly, 2011) is available from Amazon and can be scanned and projected in class to recreate this experience.

3. All citations to *The Sun Also Rises* are to the following edition: Ernest Hemingway, *The Sun Also Rises* (New York: Scribner, 1926).

4. See Robert Forest Wilson, *Paris on Parade* (Indianapolis: Bobbs-Merril, 1924); John Chancellor, *How to Be Happy in Paris Without Being Ruined* (New York: Henry Holt, 1926); and Bruce Reynolds, *Paris with the Lid Lifted* (New York: George Sully, 1927).

5. This statement is based on Kenneth G. Johnston's "Hemingway and Cézanne: Doing the Country," *American Literature* 56.1 (1984): 2–37. For color reproductions of "L'Estaque" (V. 428) and "The Poplars" (V. 335), see Basil Taylor, *Cézanne* (London: Paul Hamlyn, 1961), plates 19 and 15. A color reproduction of "Farmyard at Auvers-sur-Oise" is not readily available, but a black and white copy can be found in Lionello Venturi's *Cézanne* (New York: Rizolli, 1978), 36.

Teaching the Avant-Garde Hemingway

Early Modernism in Paris

Adam R. McKee

When Ernest Hemingway arrived in Paris by way of Chicago in December 1921, he was a fresh young writer exploring an especially vibrant and experimental artistic climate. It was in Paris that Hemingway's artistic sense and writing style would enter its most important developmental phase. Most students of modernism are well aware of the later Hemingway, a key artistic figure of the Parisian Left Bank and a founding member of the "lost generation," but perhaps more important to any understanding of Hemingway's modernism are his early encounters with the Parisian art scene and avant-garde movements. This period must be described and understood adequately for any potential reader of Hemingway because, as Ben Stoltzfus notes, "Paris was an incubator for Hemingway's prodigious talent, and the people he met and the books he read gave him the college education he never had" (136). When focusing on these early interactions in Paris, readers will find the writing Hemingway began and/or completed around this time particularly rich. When teaching this Hemingway, the most pertinent texts for students to read are his "Paris 1922" sketches, the collection *In Our Time,* and two short pieces cut from that collection before publication: "Up in Michigan" and "On Writing." Here, I will examine potential strategies for teaching these texts in the context of the influences on Hemingway's early, experimental modernism. (See Appendix F: Discussion Questions for a list of discussion questions I use in this process.)

As a graduate teaching assistant at Florida State University I was assigned to teach a sophomore-level survey course on the short story as a genre. I initially chose to teach a course directed toward understanding the short story cycle as employed by modernist writers. The primary texts for this course were Virginia Woolf's *Monday or Tuesday,* Jean Toomer's *Cane,* James Joyce's *Dubliners,* and Hemingway's *In Our Time.* My pedagogical focus here comes from my efforts, in teaching this course, to draw connections among the modernist texts in question and to place them in context for students in terms of the historical period and the writers' experiences. Most of the students had little or no previous experience with Hemingway's writings or with literary studies in general. As I planned the course, and during my first semester teaching it, I gradually emphasized Hemingway's early work in concert with other texts, both literary and cultural.

One major obstacle that all instructors must overcome in teaching Hemingway's early work and in encouraging students to engage in scholarship on Hemingway is the use of outside literary criticism. In my course and other lower-level courses at Florida State University, many of my students are unfamiliar with and/or reluctant to properly engage literary criticism in exploring the course materials. Seeking not only to teach students literature but also to teach them appropriate critical research skills, I require them to engage critical pieces in a scholarship explication project. At the beginning of the semester, I inform students that one of their core semester assignments will be to find, read, and summarize the arguments of several scholarly pieces (mentioned throughout this essay) by Milton A. Cohen, Theodore L. Gaillard Jr., Robert E. Gajdusek, J. Gerald Kennedy, and Ben Stoltzfus. Instructors may chose to provide these pieces for their students, but I find that requiring them to find the essays themselves, either through library databases or by physically going to the library, helps students to more accurately understand and experience the research process. Students are asked to read all of the selections and then choose one to focus on in writing a short (2–3 page) critique and summary throughout the semester. This assignment allows an instructor to bring outside scholarship into the classroom while also teaching students the proper way to conduct research and read criticism.

After introducing the course and assignments, I have found it important for students to begin studying early Hemingway writings through the "Paris 1922" sketches. These six sentences, which never appeared in any of Hemingway's major works, are reprinted in J. Gerald Kennedy's *Imagining Paris* (1993) and represent perhaps the most experimental prose writing of Hemingway's career. They are important for students to read at the beginning for several reasons. First, their short length allows a teacher to have students read them in class (either aloud as a class or individually) and thus more effectively walk them through the pieces. Second, these sentences allow students to see two things about a modernist Hemingway at this point in his career: his multilayered experimentalism and his famous use of descriptive and direct prose. A teacher can emphasize these characteristics by discussing the critical conversation surrounding the sketches by several prominent Hemingway scholars. Milton A. Cohen, for example, has explained how the sentences link Hemingway to modernist experimentation by showing the internalized influences of Ezra Pound and T. S. Eliot on Hemingway's early work. Similarly, in *Imagining Paris*, J. Gerald Kennedy notes that these sentences mark "an effort to achieve a more experimental form, perhaps reflecting the immediate influence of [Gertrude] Stein" (88), before describing the sentences as a "collage of images [which] projects a frenzied, cosmopolitan city of violent contrasts and illustrates the degree to which Hemingway had internalized the spectacle of Paris" (90). Lastly—and this is perhaps a crucial point of departure for instructors teaching Hemingway's early modernism—Kennedy explains that these "'true sentences'" (87) influenced the later composition of *In Our Time*'s vignettes. Scholars such as Cohen and Kennedy not only show how these sentences demonstrate Hemingway's early experimentation but also provide a solid introduction to *In Our Time*.

Once students have read the "Paris 1922" sketches and familiarized themselves with Hemingway's early experimentation, reading *In Our Time* allows them to apply this information to Hemingway's first major composition. Hemingway may have extended the experimentation of "Paris 1922" into *In Our Time*'s vignettes, but his composition of the longer pieces in the collection also displays the influence of Paris on his early writing. It is two pieces that were cut from *In Our Time* before publication, however—"Up in Michigan" and "On Writing"—that perhaps most clearly illustrate these influences. Teaching these two omitted pieces is important, because they introduce students to the influences of Gertrude Stein, James Joyce, and Paul Cézanne on Hemingway's early writing, enriching their exploration of *In Our Time*. Teaching "Up in Michigan" before the collection and "On Writing" after the collection works nicely to frame the content of *In Our Time*, but an approach that teaches both of them before examining *In Our Time* would also allow students to spot the influences explicitly mentioned in "On Writing."

"Up in Michigan" strongly demonstrates the direct influence of Gertrude Stein on Hemingway's compositions; it is equally strong as a pedagogical tool. Much has been made of the almost mythical status of Hemingway's and Stein's life on the Left Bank, and studies of Hemingway often mention Stein's early quasi mentorship of the young writer. "Up in Michigan" is in a unique position to demonstrate these influences. For this reason, I have students read very brief excerpts from Stein's "Composition as Explanation" (1925) before reading "Up in Michigan." Once again, scholarship allows instructors to make this connection in class by introducing Milton A. Cohen's assertion that by the time Hemingway paid Stein his first visit in March 1922, he probably had already read her work in *Three Lives* and *Tender Buttons* (10). Cohen also notes that Hemingway had begun composing "Up in Michigan" while in Chicago, and he argues that the work exhibits how "Stein was increasingly aware that the narrative conventions of nineteenth-century literature were inadequate for capturing a contemporary experience of time and space as increasingly fragmented and disjointed" (10-11). Cohen continues: "Progressive narration, moving from beginning to middle to end, must now yield to a time sense in which each moment becomes self-contained and freed of a linear hierarchy, as important as any other moment" (11). This new approach finds expression in the concepts of "beginning again and again" and "the continuous present" described in "Composition as Explanation" (1925), but it also can be found in Hemingway's "Up in Michigan." While I have students read selections from "Composition as Explanation" on their own, it often helps to walk students through the essay by reading selections aloud in class.

"Up in Michigan," which Hemingway originally intended as the opening piece of *In Our Time*, richly demonstrates Stein's influence on Hemingway, and by exploring it before beginning the published text of the collection, in the position originally envisioned by Hemingway, students can trace Stein's influence in other parts of the collection. The most explicit example of Stein's influence in the short story comes in the third paragraph, where a reader can see the internalization of Stein's "beginning again and again." This concept was evident in her early writing in *Three Lives* (1909) and "Composition as Explanation." The paragraph reads,

> Liz *liked* Jim very much. She *liked* it the way he walked over from the shop and often went to the kitchen door to watch for him to start down the road. She *liked* it about his mustache. She *liked* it about how white his teeth were when he smiled. She *liked* it very much that he didn't look like a blacksmith. She *liked* it how much D. J. Smith and Mrs. Smith *liked* Jim. One day she found that she *liked* it the way the hair was black on his arms and how white they were above the tanned line when he washed up in the washbasin outside the house. *Liking* that made her feel funny. (*CSS* 59; emphasis added)[1]

We read this paragraph aloud in class, and students are asked what this repeated usage accomplishes for Hemingway and how the story's opening is both similar and dissimilar from openings to other stories in *In Our Time* and other stories students have read. It is easy to see Hemingway's use of "the continuous present" in this paragraph, but it also can be found in other moments described elsewhere in *In Our Time*.

In addition to illustrating this connection between Stein and Hemingway, Cohen explains that Stein was instrumental to Hemingway's early writings because her "most radically fragmented writing may have inspired Hemingway to cut explanatory contexts from his own brief sketches in *in our time* and to begin many of his narratives in the middle" (15–16). It is easy to show students how the vignettes, in their brief, sketchlike composition, drop a reader abruptly into the scene, but this influence can also be seen in the composition of many of the longer pieces win the collection. I make students aware of this at the beginning of our reading of *In Our Time* by directing their attention to specific openings that place the reader immediately within the story, openings such as "At the lake shore there was another rowboat drawn up" ("Indian Camp"), "The rain stopped as Nick turned into the road that went up through the orchard" ("The Three-Day Blow"), and "Nick stood up" ("The Battler"). We then examine these openings closely through class discussion.

While Hemingway's relationship with Stein has been much discussed and could be the basis for a semester-long course, James Joyce, a different type of expatriate writer, also greatly influenced Hemingway's early work in Paris. Many students know of Joyce but have read almost none of his work. I usually attempt to introduce students to Joyce's experimentalism in *Ulysses,* often by showing a section of "Wandering Rocks" on the overhead for in-class discussion, and I briefly discuss scholarship on Joyce's magnum opus. Students can be led in a number of directions, but I discuss with them Catherine Flynn's assertions, in her online article "Joyce and Benjamin in Paris," that *Ulysses* uses "an aesthetic of constant disruption and new, open forms that are crowded with fragments of fact, of the irrational and of the subliterary and that place new demands upon the reader to find his or her way" and that "the stream of consciousness is only one of the disorienting and fragmentary forms through which *Ulysses* responds to the modern city." I demonstrate to students that the composition of *In Our Time* is firmly located within Paris and that the collection reflects the influences of the city through influences on Hemingway, in much the same way it influenced Joyce.

To examine these implications more closely, I have the students read *Dubliners* in connection with *In Our Time*. Once again, turning students to scholarship on the matter helps them to see the correlation more clearly and allows them to enter into the academic discourse for their papers at the end of the semester. The article "Dubliners in Michigan: Joyce's Presence in Hemingway's *In Our Time*," by Robert E. Gajdusek, explains in detail Joyce's influence on Hemingway. "There is good evidence," Gajdusek notes, "that Hemingway almost uniquely among his contemporaries recognized Joyce's techniques and early put them to use" (48). If students read *Dubliners* first, it is a valuable exercise to have them read *In Our Time* with an eye toward examining these influences, but the order could certainly be altered with similar success. As Gajdusek notes of *In Our Time*, "The organization and movement is very much that of the stories in Joyce's *Dubliners*, and it is not difficult to see that Hemingway almost concomitant with his association with Joyce began to use similar structure and strategy" (51). A close examination of the stories from both *In Our Time* and *Dubliners* shows several thematic continuities.

Both collections begin with youthful encounters with death ("Indian Camp" for Hemingway and "The Sisters" for Joyce) and end in conflicted accounts of adulthood ("Big Two-Hearted River" for Hemingway and "The Dead" for Joyce), and among many other similarities both also show female characters struggling with their lives and relationships ("Cat in the Rain" for Hemingway and "Eveline" for Joyce). Most important for students to observe, as Gajdusek notes, "The larger vision that Joyce and Hemingway ultimately share in *Dubliners* and *In Our Time* is a vision of the necessity for the reconciliations that take place in 'The Dead' and 'Big Two-Hearted River'" (59). In addition to these similarities, several of the revelatory endings in Hemingway's *In Our Time* warrant discussion and certainly appear to be influenced in part by his admiration of Joyce's writing.

After helping the students to explore the influence of Stein's work on the style of Hemingway's writing of *In Our Time* and the possible influence of Joyce's work on its content, it is useful to direct their attention to another early Parisian influence on Hemingway's form: the painter Paul Cézanne. While Cézanne was not Hemingway's contemporary in the way that Stein and Joyce were, Hemingway experienced Cézanne's work firsthand when he arrived in Paris. As Kennedy illustrates, "at the geographical and symbolic center of Hemingway's Paris lay the Luxembourg Gardens" (83). Ben Stoltzfus adds that the gardens were most important for Hemingway because he would visit them "to study the Cézanne's at the Musée du Luxembourg and the Louvre—landscapes and bathers, card players, the courtyard at Anvers, and the house of the hanged man" (3). Cézanne's position as a bridge figure between the impressionism of Monet and the cubism of Picasso and Braque influenced Hemingway's early work in many ways, such as fostering his interest in perspective(s) and the visual composition of landscapes.

Once again, scholarship helps to reliably demonstrate this; as Stoltzfus explains, "the impact of cubism on Hemingway is enormous and painting and painters [have been] an ongoing presence in his work. His collection of short stories *in our time*, inserts a brief paragraph in italics between each fiction. . . . This procedure adds a layered and disruptive quality to the conventional short story technique and allies it with cubism" (19). Carlos Baker confirms Hemingway's connection to the visual art scene in Paris by noting that "his chief interest centered in short, impressionistic pieces, where every word must count both for itself and for its effect on all the others" (85). However, Hemingway's "On Writing," originally meant to be a coda to "Big Two-Hearted River," provides students with a very thought-provoking examination of Cézanne's influence on Hemingway.

Finally published as "On Writing" in *The Nick Adams Stories* (1972), the coda to "Big Two-Hearted River" links Nick Adams to Hemingway's own experiences in Paris. One particular element of this text that is valuable to discuss with students is the fact that it reveals Nick Adams himself to be the author of several of the stories in *In Our Time*. Hemingway writes, "The only writing that was any good was what you made up, what you imagined. That made everything come true. Like when he wrote 'My Old Man' he'd never seen a jockey killed and the next week Georges Parfrement was killed at that very jump and that was the way it looked" (*NAS* 237). The coda also implies that Nick is the author of "Indian Camp": "Nick in the stories was never himself. He made him up. Of course he'd never seen an Indian woman having a baby. That was what made it good. Nobody knew that. He'd seen a woman have a baby on the road to Karagatch and tried to help her" (238). These moments of authorial revelation in "On Writing" are interesting to students in a course for several reasons. The first concerns the value attributed to invention within the stories. Students often have a difficult time separating Hemingway from the characters within the text, and these sections provide an opportunity for instructors to move students toward an understanding of Hemingway as a creative fiction writer rather than a writer modifying autobiographical facts. Second—and this would be valuable in any course examining Hemingway in the context of modernism—the selections cut from *In Our Time* illustrate early Hemingway working through of metafictional techniques in a way not attempted by many of his contemporaries. Without teaching "On Writing" in conjunction with *In Our Time,* this element of Hemingway's experimentation is not apparent.

Having students read "On Writing" at the conclusion of *In Our Time* allows for reflection and probing questions about their understanding of the collection's stories and the influence of his contemporaries. Kennedy notes of "On Writing" that Hemingway's "allusions to Pound, Joyce, Stein, Cummings, and Robert McAlmon connect Nick to the scene of Hemingway's apprenticeship" (93). As with other material cut from Hemingway's published writing, such as introductory passages cut from "Indian Camp," "On Writing" provides direct insight into Hemingway's influences. However, the decision to cut such passages also yields insights into Hemingway's writing process, reinforcing Hemingway's famous iceberg theory, stated in *Death in the Afternoon,* in which he asserts that omitting certain things a writer knows adds substance to the writing, just as an iceberg's "dignity of movement . . . is due to only one-eighth of it being above water" (*DIA* 192).[2]

Interestingly, scholars have noted the connection between this iceberg theory and the influence of Cézanne. "In several of his later paintings," notes Theodore L. Gaillard Jr., "Cézanne would intentionally leave small areas of canvas blank in the midst of a sea of roofs or on the side of a hill, causing viewers to fill spaces with preconscious constructs of complementary line and color, subtly moving towards the substitution of impression and feeling from cognition" (67). The influence of Cézanne's technique of omission on Hemingway is overtly stated in "On Writing," as Hemingway writes, "[Nick] wanted to write like Cezanne painted. Cezanne started with all the tricks. Then he broke the whole thing down and built the real thing" (*NAS* 239); moreover, "he could see the Cezannes. The portrait at Gertrude Stein's. She'd know it if he ever got things right. The two good ones at the Luxembourg, the ones he'd seen every day at the loan exhibit at Bernheim's. The soldiers undressing to swim, the house through the trees, one of the trees with a house beyond, not the lake one, the other lake one. The portrait of the boy. Cezanne could do people, too" (239-40). While it is nearly impossible to infer which of Cézanne's paintings Nick is thinking about at this point in the piece, many of Cézanne's works fit the general pattern, as he painted dozens of landscapes, portraits, and bathers throughout his career. Nick's wish "to write like Cezanne painted" is a statement that provokes lively conversation when explored with students in the classroom.

When approaching Cézanne's influence on Hemingway, I shift modes from purely literary conversation in the classroom, explaining to students that the influence comes more from Cézanne's position within modernist Paris than through any direct interaction between the two figures. Additionally, after completing a reading of the assigned Hemingway works, I show students images of several of Cézanne's paintings, focusing on his technique, to demonstrate what writing "like Cezanne painted" could mean. Cézanne's paintings offer numerous interpretive possibilities, since, as stated earlier, his works include many landscapes, portraits, and bathers. I generally show my students five paintings—"The House of the Hanged Man Auvers Sur Oise" (1873), "The Turn in the Road at Auvers" (1873), "The Banks of the Marne" (1888), "Bathers. Mont Sainte-Victoire in the Background" (1902), and "Riverbanks" (1905)—which represent several elements useful in comparison to Hemingway's work. "The House of the Hanged Man," "The Banks of the Marne," and "Bathers" all appear to represent images described in "On Writing," for example, while both "The Turn in the Road" and "Riverbanks" provide excellent examples of compositions in which Cézanne left blank spaces and/or gaps within his paintings. Since many of my sophomore students are even less familiar with Cézanne than they are with Hemingway, I ask them directly what Hemingway meant when he wrote that Nick "wanted to write like Cezanne painted." Responses vary but often provide a lively and creative discussion, with students most often wishing to discuss the "blank spaces" in Hemingway's stories and his desire to alter the formal aspects of his writing in a way similar to Cézanne's challenging of formal realism in his painting.

Any pedagogical approach to Hemingway's early writing in *In Our Time* must situate the Hemingway of that period in the context of his environment: the artistic climate and scene of 1920s Paris. In my own course, I have ordered the materials useful in accomplishing this goal so as to best serve my own pedagogical approaches; this order may, of course, be altered to fit any instructor's purposes. My own approach to the material follows Ben Stoltzfus's approach, in exploring Paris as an "incubator" for Hemingway's talent and striving to illustrate how his modernism was nourished, if not born, through his interactions with Parisian figures Gertrude Stein, James Joyce, and Paul Cézanne. The material can be challenging to teach, especially introducing Stein's writing to students unfamiliar with her work, but any understanding of Hemingway as a modernist must address his beginnings.

Notes

1. All citations to "Up in Michigan" refer to the following: Ernest Hemingway, *The Complete Short Stories of Ernest Hemingway: The Finca Vigía Edition* (New York: Scribner, 1998).

2. Hemingway's original versions of these pieces were cut from the final composition of *In Our Time*. By cutting opening passages from "Indian Camp," originally serving as a formal introduction to the piece, from the published version, Hemingway drops the reader into the middle of the story, a technique more typical of his short fiction; by cutting "On Writing" from the end of "Big Two-Hearted River," Hemingway avoids, according to J. Gerald Kennedy, "reductive sentimentalizing" of Nick Adams's story (95).

Teaching Hemingway Beyond "The Lost Generation"

European Politics and American Modernism

David Barnes

In the 2011 Woody Allen film *Midnight in Paris,* the American protagonist and would-be writer Gil Pender is on holiday in Paris, irresistibly drawn to an idealized vision of the city in the 1920s, when American writers like Ernest Hemingway, Gertrude Stein, and F. Scott Fitzgerald attended artistic salons on the Left Bank. As his fiancée Inez puts it, he is "in love with a fantasy." Yet at midnight each night the fantasy becomes reality, as he is transported in a vintage car into the past, meeting Hemingway, Fitzgerald, and others at parties, showing his book manuscript to Stein, and encountering Picasso. The problem with our received images of American writers in early twentieth-century Europe is that they are inherently "fantastical," which is to say that even being drawn to write about Hemingway in Paris or in Spain runs the risk of capitulating to the powerfully mythic ways such discourses are received, as a "lost" and glamorous past, divorced from a developed sense of socioeconomic and political context.

As a relative newcomer to the world of teaching Hemingway, I cannot offer the fruits of decades of pedagogical experience in this essay. Instead, I wish to explore some of the ways my own research questions have been shaped by my experience of teaching Hemingway's work in context, primarily in terms of modernism and secondarily in terms of a cultural-historical approach. What would happen if we read Hemingway as part of an early twentieth-century cultural matrix, one in which the work of other writers, newspaper reports, and visual culture contributed equally to the picture? In this essay, I want to explore how we might show students the richness of the cultures, both European and American, from which this novelist emerges. My experiences here are collected mainly from a lecture given at the University of Cambridge's Institute for Continuing Education and from tutorials given at Somerville College, Oxford, and Emmanuel College, Cambridge. I also draw on my wider experience of teaching modernism in its cultural and political contexts, at institutions including the University of Birmingham and Queen Mary, University of London.

My particular focus is on European politics, which I approach by comparing Hemingway with another key American modernist figure (and friend of Hemingway's), Ezra Pound. If Hemingway—with his machismo and at times decidedly awkward racial attitudes—has sometimes been problematized in terms of literary canonization, so has Pound to an even greater degree. The only advantage of teaching Pound in the British context is that fewer students have heard of him—an ignorance that often turns to baffled dismay when they encounter the dense, allusive modernism of *The Cantos*. However, a comparative study of the two writers presents a pedagogically useful way of approaching American literary modernism, not least because the contrasts between Hemingway and Pound can illuminate differences between the types of modernism that emerged in the 1920s. This focus also allows for a shift of critical gaze; examining the political positioning of both writers can help students to construct a more complex and nuanced set of contexts for what Daniel Katz has termed (using it as the title of his book) as "American modernism's expatriate scene."

To model this approach, I will now describe my lecture entitled "Americans in Europe: Ezra Pound and Ernest Hemingway." I begin the lecture by getting students to picture the scene of a boxing bout between Hemingway and Pound in Paris in 1922. I describe the small, chilly flat in the Rue Notre Dame des Champs and the physical contrast between the two writers, playing up the comic elements of the scene as Hemingway struggles to teach Pound the basics: "He habitually leads wit [sic] his chin and has the general grace of the crayfish or crawfish. He's willing but short winded. Going over there this afternoon for another session but there aint much job in it as I have to shadow box between rounds to get up a sweat" (Hemingway, *Letters 1* 331). The description introduces the idea of a kind of contest, or struggle, between two rival versions of modernism. It also, I suggest, grounds our responses to literary questions in temporal, spatial, and physical dimensions. The time: 1922; the place: Paris; the setting: the small flat; the event: a boxing lesson. One of the persistent problems with the idea of the "lost generation" in American culture is that this time and place can remain perpetually "lost," its very conceptualization bound up with its irretrievability. Looking at Hemingway and Pound through the mythic lens of their membership in a "lost generation" makes it increasingly difficult to recover the sociopolitical contexts that informed expatriate American writing in the 1920s and 1930s, and too easy to succumb to clichéd ideas about the nature of the American experience of Europe in those decades. I suggest to students that an engagement with interwar European politics shaped the writing of both these figures in radical ways. I also suggest to students that the writers' particular visions of Europe forged two distinctive, rival versions of modern writing, expressed in the finely tuned, popular prose of Hemingway and the dense, allusive, and complex poetry of Pound. The Paris boxing bout serves students as an enticing and informative introduction to American modernism in its European contexts. Europe is, if you like, a "stage" for the formation of an expatriate American avant-garde. Yet the ways in which that stage shapes the "performance" of American modernism need to be examined with an eye to the sociopolitical realities of early twentieth-century Europe. In concrete terms, I make sure a balance is struck between practical criticism (where I might stop the lecture to open up a discussion around a particular passage of Hemingway's) and wider cultural awareness (where visual materials or historical data might be provided). For example, I might provide students with a projected or photocopied image of a Paris café in the 1920s, or a painting by Picasso, or a photograph of the Italian front during the First World War. I then get students to respond to these images, describing how they see them, and what kind of mood they evoke. I find that the use of this kind of material data provides students with a deeper understanding of modernism, as expressed by Hemingway, Pound, and others. As a follow-up in seminars, I might ask students how an understanding of the Great War (producing the World War I image described above) could help us to understand the context of Paris in the 1920s (producing the café image). Such methods help students to appreciate the fragile and tense mood of Europe in the 1920s.

Many readers regard Hemingway's journalism as a training ground for his prose fiction, a view reinforced by the fragments of war reportage scattered throughout *In Our Time*. Yet the *content* of Hemingway's early journalism is just as important as its style. Introducing students to this work at the beginning of the lecture provides a useful way to destabilize the "myth" of Hemingway. In the lecture, I read extracts from Hemingway's Toronto *Daily Star* articles, analyzing them just as I would his fiction, with attention to vocabulary, style, and syntax. By this process, I seek to get students to discern the patterns and themes that recur in Hemingway's work, to note the style of his journalism, and to think about the context from which it emerges. Is there, I might ask students, a sense in which the Europe that Hemingway describes for Canadian newpaper readers comparable to the Europe he depicts in *The Sun Also Rises* or in the stories and vignettes of *In Our Time?* In other words, might we see Hemingway's "Europe" as emerging from a particular historical context or set of circumstances? Hemingway's earlier writings can then be seen *in context*, and a version of Hemingway embedded within the discourses of tourism and politics emerges. In particular, I want to show—via a comparison with Pound—how the discourses of tourism may lead American expatriate modernists toward a more political engagement with European culture.

For a useful perspective on this touristic discourse, I turn to the literary critic James Buzard, who has developed a theory of the "elite" tourist, who yearns to be "in the know" and despises "the beaten track" (4). I introduce Buzard in the lecture to encourage students to think through what being a tourist entails and how some of the attitudes the elite tourist characterizes might be applied to Hemingway's writing. As Jeffrey Herlihy-Mera has commented, such attitudes characterize Hemingway's early journalism, which often acts "as an outlet to criticize the expatriate community and to express his own apparent cultivation" (70). A deeper examination of this conflicted attitude to travel and tourism tends also, I suggest, to problematic monolithic notions of the "lost generation." This loose term—applied to Hemingway, Pound, Fitzgerald, and Stein among others—is not entirely helpful for several reasons. The history of the term is chronicled in Hemingway's posthumously published memoir, *A Moveable Feast*, where it first appears in French ("une génération perdue"), attributed to a garage owner who serviced Gertrude Stein's car. Stein then applied the phrase to a younger generation who had been shaped by the First World War; it was a phrase she never intended to apply to her own writing but to the generation including Hemingway, Fitzgerald, and others—"'all of you young people who served in the war'" (61). Furthermore, Stein's meaning was not primarily that this generation was "lost" (to the United States), in the sense of being on the wrong continent—Europe as opposed to America—but that its members had in some way (themselves) been abandoned or lost by a failed American society after the war. The image of Hemingway frequenting the cafés of Paris amongst a circle of "lost" Americans thus needs some revision. One way of addressing this image would be to spend some time in postlecture seminars "brainstorming" popular images of Hemingway, getting students to think of as many different things as possible that they associate with Hemingway's life and work, in order to better interrogate these images or myths with use of contextual data.

Hemingway was, for example, anxious to be distinguished from the Paris American herd. In one article published in the Toronto *Daily Star* on 25 March

1922, "American Bohemians in Paris," he pours scorn on the American visitors adorning the Café Rotonde:

> The scum of Greenwich Village, New York, has been skimmed off and deposited in large ladles in that section of Paris adjacent to the Café Rotonde. New scum, of course, has risen to take the place of the old, but the oldest scum and the scummiest scum has come across the ocean, somehow, and with its afternoon and evening levees has made the Rotonde the leading Latin Quarter showplace for tourists in search of atmosphere... A first look into the smoky, high-ceilinged, table-crammed interior of the Rotonde gives you the same feeling that hits you as you step into the bird-house at the zoo. There seems to be a tremendous, raucous, many-pitched squawking going on, broken up by many waiters who fly around through the smoke like so many black and white magpies. (*DLT* 114)

Hemingway's description is a response to the rise and ubiquity of the tourist. He is concerned, in visceral and unpleasant imagery ("ladles of scum"), to assert the superficiality of the Café Rotonde experience as simply a constant recycling of the society of New York, and further implies that this society then attracts more American tourists "in search of atmosphere," perpetuating the inauthenticity of the experience. The image of the birdhouse, with its "many-pitched squawking" and unguided movement, seems to represent a kind of sound and fury, a strutting and fretting signifying nothing, an empty, touristic "showplace." Hemingway, sitting apart from the birdhouse, represents by contrast an engagement with Paris that is the "real thing," an authentic experience he would describe as integral to his craft in *Death in the Afternoon* (1932), as opposed to one that is merely superficial, surface, or touristic. One way to bring home this distinction in a teaching context is to introduce students to contemporary tourist guides to Paris from the 1920s. In postlecture seminars, we might examine Baedeker guides to Paris from the period, alongside American travelogues such as Robert Forrest Wilson's *Paris on Parade* (1924). These could be read in conjunction with Hemingway's journalistic descriptions of the city, and small groups of students could be asked to list similarities and differences between them. Students might further be directed to study John Raeburn's *Fame Became of Him: Hemingway as Public Writer* (1984), which contains very useful material on the mythologizing of Hemingway's European residence.

Hemingway was not alone in his anxiety to distinguish himself from the crowds of tourists visiting Europe during this period. Pound's *Canto* III, set in Venice and drafted around the time Pound met Hemingway in Paris, pictures the poet sitting on the steps of Venice's Dogana (customs house) because, we are told, "the gondolas cost too much, that year" (*Cantos* 11). The poem places the poet materially in the city ("I sat on the Dogana's steps"), yet exiles him from the typical touristic experience exemplified by the gondolas that he can't afford. Thus, both versions of American engagement with Europe are concerned to distinguish the writer's experience from the touristic: "I'm in *my own* part of Venice—not the San-Marco-tedesco-turisto [German-tourist] side," Pound wrote from Venice in 1910 (*Tragic Friendship* 36). The Venice he claims, Pound implies, is a cultured Venice, not like the one belonging to those vulgar German tourists. There is a delicious kind of authority about being the "one in the know" and the antitourism of Hemingway, Pound, and others is, I suggest, another kind of tourism: the tourism of the local secret, the back alley, the in-club. Writing of the Café Rotonde in Paris again, Hemingway says: "You can find anything you are looking for at the Rotonde—*except serious artists*" (*DLT* 115; emphasis added). Hemingway's viewpoint is one of condescension: unlike these fakes and frauds, in Paris for purely economic reasons (it was "twelve francs for a dollar" he points out), Hemingway is by implication the "serious artist."

For students, this way of thinking about Hemingway is easily conceptualized: we make choices about how and why we travel, which cafés or bars we frequent, which neighborhood we claim, and what role these choices play in the construction of our persona or self-image. We also tend to underline our personas by pointing to other people who are less knowledgeable. In discussions around these issues in seminars and tutorials, I like to get students to think about how fashions work, and the ways in which the truly "fashionable" person always stands apart from the crowd. One way to accomplish this is to ask students to think about what fashion is, and to identify (perhaps in small groups) the qualities of an "in crowd." Students could consider their own experiences in high school or other contexts. Another approach might be to spend some time looking at and discussing the phenomenon of "insider" internet blogs on cities and detailing how these blogs attempt to distinguish themselves and their readers from mainstream travelers to those cities. Insider blogs on cities like London and New York, for example, tend to stress the beauty of street art in contrast to that found in mainstream museums and galleries. These discussions are a useful starting point for thinking about the way the modernist writer positions him- or herself. Hemingway's anxiety to be seen as the insider can then be related to our own experiences of social positioning and tribalism.

For example, in *A Moveable Feast*, Hemingway's memoir of his life in Paris, he compares his and Fitzgerald's reactions to France. Hemingway is always calm, an old hand at living in Europe, while Fitzgerald is depicted as a neurotic Yankee, incapable of understanding European culture and yearning for home comforts. In Hemingway's description, Fitzgerald drinks too much and takes to his bed, convinced that he has congestion of the lungs yet unwilling to go near French doctors: "I want . . . for us to get on an express train for Paris and to go to the American hospital at Neuilly," he demands. "At that time Scott hated the French," Hemingway explains, "and since almost the only French he met with regularly were waiters whom he did not understand, taxi-drivers, garage employees and landlords, he had many opportunities to insult and abuse them" (*MF* 168). Scott, Hemingway adds, "hated the Italians even more than the French and could not talk about them calmly even when he was sober. The English he often hated but he sometimes tolerated" (*MF* 169). Fitzgerald becomes here a figure of American stubbornness, unwilling to integrate into, or even appreciate, European society, an attitude signified by his inability to hold his liquor. Hemingway, implicitly a better traveler and a better man, scorns Fitzgerald's "unhealthy" attitude to drinking, explaining that "in Europe then we thought of wine as something as healthy and normal as food and also a great giver of happiness" (*MF* 166). Again, Hemingway is the insider—"we"—here, drinking wine and speaking French while Fitzgerald languishes drunk on the bed demanding the American hospital.

Another way that Americans in Europe could show they were in the know was by understanding European politics. Hemingway's dispatches to the *Toronto Star* demonstrate that he was keenly aware of the changing currents in European society in the 1920s. Exploring Hemingway's journalism contextually provides a way of viewing the writer as more deeply embedded in, and shaped by, the political contexts of the period. In teaching Hemingway, therefore, studying his journalism alongside political writings by other authors, such as Pound, George Orwell and D. H. Lawrence (whose comments on fascism are critical yet ambiguous), can engage students with historical interests, as well as providing a more nuanced picture of Hemingway's political identity.

Again, a comparison with Pound proves useful. The responses of the two men to the emergence of fascism are informative, pointing to future political positionings. Of Italy's burgeoning Fascist Party, Hemingway writes in 1922: "The Fascisti are a brood of dragon's teeth that were sown in 1920 when it looked as though Italy might go Bolshevik. . . . In short, they are counterrevolutionists, and in 1920 they crushed the Red uprising with bombs, machine guns, knives and the liberal use of kerosene cans to set the Red meeting places afire, and heavy iron-bound clubs to hammer the Reds over the head when they came out" (*DLT* 131). This refers to the period of conflict between Left and Right in Italy when paramilitary Fascist groups—the *squadristi*—were known to use intimidation and violence against Communists and other enemies. Hemingway gets to the crux of Fascist counterrevolution here, the sense of revolutionary violence married to bourgeois conservatism. Hemingway stresses the impact of the violence; the "dragon's teeth" refer to the teeth sown by Cadmus that would grow into warriors in Greek myth. Here also are "bombs, machine guns, knives, kerosene cans"—the terrible reality of fascism.

By contrast, Pound's description, in *Jefferson and/or Mussolini* (1935), of an earlier encounter with a group of Fascists at Florian's, a café in Venice, is relatively subdued:

> What I saw was the line of black shirts, and the tense faces of cavalieri della morte . . . Suddenly a little old buffer rushed up to a front table and began to sputter forty-eight to the dozen. . . . It was a different kind of excitement, a more acrimonious excitement than the noise of the midday pigeon-feeding. Then came the file of young chaps with drawn faces and everyone stood to attention and took their hats off about something, all except one stubborn foreigner, damned if he would stand up or show respect until he knew what they meant. Nobody hit me with a club and I didn't see any oil bottles. (50–51)

It is probable that this encounter took place in the early 1920s (the exact year is uncertain); it is described as one of the poet's first experiences of fascism. Unlike Hemingway and others who wrote about the violence of the *fascisti*, Pound stresses the nonviolence of the encounter ("Nobody hit me with a club and I didn't see any oil bottles") despite his own "stubbornness" as the only "foreigner" in the scene—one, moreover, who would not stand up or take off his hat. There *is* an intimation of violence in this episode, suggested in the "acrimonious excitement," the orderly "line of black shirts," the "tense faces," and the standing to attention, yet in contrast to Hemingway's report, this violence is in the background, an implied threat. Where Hemingway emphasizes violence, Pound emphasizes possibility, change, renewal. Hemingway's politics are familiar—he is well-known as a staunch anti-Fascist, prodemocracy campaigner, volunteer on the Republican side in the Spanish Civil War, and so on. Pound, in contrast, had moved to Italy in 1924, and Mussolini's Fascist regime became for him the nexus of civilization. The poet would notoriously end up in 1945 indicted for treason on the basis of his pro-Fascist (and pro-Nazi) radio broadcasts during World War II. In the lecture, I usually get students to work through a passage from Pound's later *Cantos,* reading it aloud and showing, line by line, how he uses his modernism and poetic experimentation to bolster a pro-Fascist politics. Laudatory references to the Fascist "Era" in *Canto* 76, for example, are interwoven with the finest lyrical and intertextual poetry. I might ask students what they think the effect of this is, or how knowing more about Pound's political views changes their perception of his poetry.

Yet it is worth pointing out to students that the binary opposition between these two writers' political visions may not be as binary, or as opposed, as they might seem. Despite his opposition to fascism, Hemingway was in some ways fixated on violence. Europe was a theatre of violence for him, right from the beginning when he was wounded in Italy in World War I at the age of eighteen. From a Milan hospital bed, he writes to his family that he has some:

> fine photographs of the Piave and many other interesting pictures. Also a wonderful lot of souvenirs. I was through all the big battle and have Austrian carbines and ammunition, German and Austrian medals, officers['] automatic pistols, . . . helmets, star shell pistols . . . and almost everything you can think of. The only limit to the amount of souvenirs I could have is what I could carry for there were so many dead Austrians and prisoners the ground was almost black with them. (*Letters 1* 118)

Tourism, spectacle, and suffering interact here in disturbing ways. In the manner of a boy writing to his parents about his collection of seashells, Hemingway accumulates medals, ammunition, pistols, and helmets—a bric-a-brac of war. These are taken off "dead Austrians" and prisoners so thick on the ground that the earth is "almost black." What I think is fascinating about Hemingway's letter is that Europe takes shape here as both site of trauma and *touristic* vista. Hemingway can write of the "fine photographs of the Piave" (a river in this part of northern Italy) and a "wonderful lot of souvenirs," but those souvenirs are grim trinkets of death, scavenged from the slaughtered Austrians.

Getting students to work with this passage—which they might do line by line in pairs or small groups—in a close-reading exercise will uncover important aspects of the way Hemingway's writing works (a sense of being drawn unflinchingly to death or the grotesque), alongside the more disturbing question of where Hemingway's narrative voice sits. For although the political Hemingway is keen to distance himself from expressions of Fascist violence (the "lead pipe government" of Mussolini [*SL* 150]), the writer Hemingway is consistently drawn to violence, as his interest in the culture of the bull-fight attests. Here a close reading of a relevant passage from *The Sun Also Rises* (1926) helps students understand how Hemingway works through these issues in the major novels. In this passage, Jake Barnes is describing his first view of the charging bull: "I saw a dark muzzle and the shadow of horns, and then, with a clattering on the wood in the hollow box, the bull charged and came out into the corral, skidding with his forefeet in the straw as he stopped, his head up, the great hump of muscle on his neck swollen tight, his body muscles quivering as he looked up at the crowd on the stone walls" (*SAR* 143). What we see developed here is a kind of impressionistic writing, where the elements of "bull" are broken down and deftly and quickly sketched: the "dark muzzle," the "shadow of horns," the "hump of muscle," the quivering body muscles. Hemingway adeptly conveys a sense of *movement*: charging, clattering, skidding, quivering. The passage embodies tension and physical violence—tense necks and quivering muscles—but is also framed as an aesthetic spectacle. "My God, isn't he beautiful?" exclaims the British aristocrat Lady Brett Ashley, who is watching the scene (*SAR* 143). The problem is that this spectacle of aesthetic violence was an image associated in Spain with the political Right; many of Hemingway's bullfighting friends were on the side of the Falangists. Indeed, Hemingway's attraction to the Spanish *corrida de toros* coincides with and parallels the cultural projects of the proto-Fascist Primo de Rivera dictatorship. De Rivera, from an Andalucian family, propagated "an eternal metaphysic of Spain" based around myth and symbolism. Thus Hemingway's personal myth or "fantasy" of male empowerment or aggression meets with and parallels (however uncomfortable this may be) the cultural projects of rightist authoritarian politics.

Indeed, to return to where I began this essay, the dimensions of "fantasy" make a fascinating subject of dissection in literature teaching. The film *Midnight in Paris* explores the scope and limits of fantasy. For Adriana, a character Gil meets in 1920s Paris, the present is also a disappointment. She yearns for the nineteenth-century Paris of the Belle Époque, for her a golden age of art. Gil has a moment of realization: our images of the past are often conditioned by our dissatisfactions with the present. By providing students with historicized, nuanced, and complex ways into reading the expatriate or "European" Hemingway, we can enable students to scrutinize our myths and fantasies. Both Hemingway and Pound engage with a Europe that became for them the site of textual *and* political practices. For both writers, travel and tourism started them on a road of increasingly complex engagement with the politics of twentieth-century Europe, and for both, their travel and their residence in Europe shaped their writing. For both, Europe was a site of trauma and violence that attracted and repelled them in different ways; in this turbulent era, Europe could exist both as touristic ideal and arena of violence.

Twentieth-Century Titans

Orwell and Hemingway's Convergence
through Place and Time

Jean Jespersen Bartholomew

In a hotel room in Paris, in late February 1945, an unlikely pairing reportedly occurred. George Orwell, part of a contingent of writers covering the end of the war, had noticed the hotel guest roster carried the name of a fellow author: Ernest Hemingway. No doubt curious, Orwell knocked gently on Hemingway's door, introducing himself by his real name, Eric Blair. Then, when a gruff greeting barreled its way through the doorway, later quoted as "Well, what the f—ing hell do you want?" the visitor clarified: "I'm George Orwell."[1] And the doors to the chamber rolled open. One can only wish for a recording of any conversation the two authors had. What might have been discussed? What on earth did the author of *Animal Farm* have in common with the author of *The Sun Also Rises*?

As it turns out, plenty. For those who teach Hemingway or Orwell, the convergence on so many levels of the spirits of these two authors is rich and teachable. They had similar multigenred approaches to developing their crafts and acquiring materials by means of immersed experience. Their stylistic aims overlapped as well, with Hemingway working to achieve a clean, bold, new style and Orwell wanting to strip away all adjectives (Orwell, "Politics" 156–71). Considered together, the two deserve a serious look not typically given them in juxtaposition within modernism. The bas-relief for eternity, were there to be one, of their spiritual and artistic, even political, inner selves would be curiously similar, making them ripe for a highly illuminating pairing in academics.

The two shared journalism and commentary as writing interests from the beginning: consider Orwell's diaries and *As I Please* commentaries and

Hemingway's dispatches (*By-Line*). Both also turned to memoir: *Homage to Catalonia* and the later semiautobiographical *Burmese Days* for Orwell, and *A Moveable Feast* and the semifictional *Islands in the Stream* (among others) for Hemingway. Both wrote about Paris, about Spain, about war, and about political intrigue—writings informed by experiences of major events occurring within miles of one another and at virtually the same points in time. Stripped, lean prose; simple beginnings outside academia; roguish independence, and a blazing drive to write anything from memoirs to diaries to journalism, from stories to novels to war writing—even participating in political intrigue—all were shared. Freedom. Code. Vision. This is what they had in common.

Looking at their lives and work in terms of place—Paris, Spain, the European theater of World War II, and islands (Jura and Cuba)—avenues of parallel emerge clearly. Any teacher or professor may create engaging Hemingway/Orwell courses that facilitate discussion of key topics: the function of literature, the source of the literary imaginative spark, and the impact of war and politics on an artist. A course encompassing these two figures might best begin with common biographical elements, especially organized by intersecting places (discourse provided here), or perhaps also using slides and lectures, since many photographs from their lives are startlingly similar. Then the course could move on to the writers' main works: their memoirs of Paris, work arising from the battlefields of the Spanish Civil War and World War II (novels, stories, journalism), and, lastly, their masterworks (see Appendix H: Master Course Syllabus). One of the implicit life codes shared by Hemingway and Orwell involves the immersion of self in essence, both positive and negative, to achieve the fullest measure of living and to become capable of deep, meaningful writing.

Paris was the two writers' first shared stop, and the responses of both included reporter-quality observational skills in examining distant locales. Hemingway had served an apprenticeship in Kansas City, Toronto, and Chicago learning his newspaper skills, but by his early twenties he was living in Europe, following an earlier tenure in Italy during the Great War. Orwell had explored Burma for five years as an imperial policeman, observing all the way and learning to value time for writing (Agathocleous 8-18). *Burmese Days*, Orwell's first significant work, was published in 1934 (compared to Hemingway's *The Sun Also Rises*, published in 1926). Orwell's volume criticized a corrupt system (the British Empire in Burma), while Hemingway's first major novel spotlighted the corruptive social whirl of the jazz age. This outer world–inner world variation on a theme between the two writers is a recurring paradigm students may wish to explore. Hemingway increasingly looked to the inner track for core meanings; Orwell gravitated to the social and political frame.

Service to country abroad (and to humanity) was important to both. Hemingway had signed up for the ambulance crew in Italy; Orwell repeatedly tried to sign up to fight for freedom but except in Spain, he was always turned down because of his health issues (primarily tuberculosis).[2] Always on the move, with the direction determined by where the perceived action was, both managed to work their way into and around major war zones. Additionally, Orwell soon developed what he called his "tramping" to a virtual art form, allowing him, in disguise, to see how the very poor lived in various places (especially Paris and London) and to absorb writing material whenever it suited. (Students might emulate this model in abbreviated fashion, modifying it for safety in today's world, and usually will enjoy doing so; for a special short afternoon assignment, see Appendix G: Teaching Idea: Writing about Immersion, Place, and Experience within a Setting of Action.) Orwell spent months living this way, eventually producing *Down and Out in Paris and London*. Hemingway, too, sought saturation and immersion, for his part never missing a good bullfight or a good war. He did not "tramp," but he did live relatively poorly in the early twenties, thereby gaining valuable perspectives.

One early geographic convergence of the two authors that will interest students occurred in 1920s' Paris (twenty years before the short Parisian hotel meeting at the end of World War II), when Hemingway and Orwell lived within blocks of one another on the Left Bank. Hemingway lived in Paris from 1921 to 1928 (M. Reynolds, *Homecoming* 167–69), and Orwell was there for about a year, between 1927 and 1928 (Agathocleous 25). Orwell lived at a cheap hotel, Hotel des Trois Moineaux, on rue du Pot de Fer, near the Rue Mouffetard in the Latin Quarter (Agathocleous 25).[3] In the early 1920s, before Orwell's arrival, Hemingway had been living on rue du Cardinal Lemoine, just a few streets over from the rue du Pot de Fer, and when Orwell showed up, Hemingway was living at 6 rue Ferou, 6e, less than half a mile from Orwell (Fitch 64).[4] Hemingway was already acquainted with fellow expatriate James Joyce by this time, and had mentoring access to Gertrude Stein; meanwhile, the lesser-known Orwell thought he "perhaps" had seen Joyce once at Les Deux Magots (Taylor 94). We will likely never know if our pair encountered each other more directly, but these environmental overlaps inevitably fascinate students and might be presented via slides or become the focus of a student map and poster project.

Hemingway wrote lovingly of his expatriate city, whereas Orwell's *Down and Out* seems on the surface less fond (although he later apologized to Parisians for any such implication) (Sheldon 145).[5] Hemingway's view of Place Contrescarpe in "The Snows of Kilimanjaro" simmers with life and color: "There never was another part of Paris that he loved like that, the sprawling trees, the old white plastered houses painted brown below, the long green of the autobus in that round square, the purple flower dye upon the paving, the sudden drop down the hill of the rue Cardinal Lemoine [Hemingway's own street] to the River, and the other way the narrow crowded world of the rue Mouffetard" (*CSS* 51). With rue Mouffetard immediately adjacent to Orwell's home street, Orwell must surely have shared this sensory feast.

Flash forward a decade to the Spanish Civil War. At this time, Hemingway based himself mostly in and around Madrid (Vernon 3–47),[6] while Orwell was mostly living in and around Barcelona (Bowker 201–27). (Spain provides the opportunity for much active involvement by students, who can plot out the authors' locations on maps.) Teaching about Spain, the Spanish Civil War, and Hemingway's and Orwell's impressions from that war is a richly rewarding endeavor but a complicated one in terms of teacher preparation. (See Appendix H: Master Course Syllabus.)

In the Spanish Civil War, Orwell came to fight, whereas the older Hemingway brought his journalistic skills and his participation in *The Spanish Earth*, a collaborative documentary, to the support of Spain. Orwell, often in army gear, spent considerable time in muddy Spanish trenches, sometimes sharing space with rats, which may have benefited his writing by serving as inspiration for the ending of *1984* (Bowker 207–8). Meanwhile, Hemingway scouted film locations wearing a casual black French beret and pressed trousers (see his brief cameo in *The Spanish Earth*, which students enjoy looking for). Still, Hemingway and Martha Gellhorn's hotel in Madrid (Hotel Florida, Rooms 112, 113) took some heavy bomb hits, and few streets in Madrid were completely safe. At times, his life, like Orwell's, was in danger (M. Reynolds, *1930s Through the Final Years* 260–62; Vernon 22–23, 33).[7] Orwell spent more than one hundred days fighting in Aragon (Shelden 315); Hemingway visited Aragon near the end of the war, but mostly followed the International Brigade south of Madrid (Vernon 33–34). Students inevitably find the "close call" of Hemingway and Orwell both having been in Aragon of interest. About this point, too, it is often provocative to share Picasso's *Guernica* painting, along with the fact that Hemingway visited the bombed-out village just a few hours after its near-total demise. Throughout the course, bringing in paintings and poetry of Spanish artists adds texture to one's teaching efforts, especially as students realize that some of these artists died or were exiled as a result of the war. This was not a lightweight war, if there is such a thing; sometimes students do not fully appreciate its full ugliness. One interesting topic for discussion may be the cheerful music accompanying *The Spanish Earth*. Why is so much of the music upbeat? I ask students.

Another less noticeable aspect, even if one were in Spain during the war, involved the complications of all the politics involved. As Orwell stated in *Homage to Catalonia:* "Various people were infected with spy mania and were creeping round whispering that everyone else was a spy of the Communists, or the Trotskyists, or the Anarchists, or what-not. The fat Russian agent was cornering all the foreign refugees in turn and explaining plausibly that this whole affair was an Anarchist plot" (Orwell, *Homage* 148).[8] A crucial goal while exploring *For Whom the Bell Tolls* or *Homage to Catalonia* is to first sort out the Spanish Civil War factions. It may be wise to have students identify the key participants. When looking at the two primary warring groups—the Republicans and the rightist fascist Nationalists—it may be prudent to clarify these groups for the students and have them identify the key participants. Most of the International volunteers, such as Hemingway and Orwell, supported the leftist Republicans, while the fascist Nationalists were, of course, headed by Francisco Franco. I often have students make note cards to organize key Spanish Civil War factions and names and then keep the cards in their books as they are reading. This helps them memorize the groups expeditiously.

The Spanish Civil War was an early prelude to World War II. While no other countries formally joined the war, many had some involvement, escalating tensions among them, with Germany and Italy as leaders among those providing material support for the Nationalists and the Soviet Union and Mexico doing the same for the Republicans. The international perception that Spain constituted a front between two antithetical political philosophies, socialism/communism and fascism, prompted volunteers from all over the world—many writers and artists included—to flock to Spain, mostly on the Republican side; nearly forty thousand volunteers from foreign nations participated (Agathocleous 40). Meanwhile, within Spain, factionalism was rife, with hatreds forming even within the Republican side. To aid students in understanding the complexity of the war, it is useful to show them a summary film documentary, such as *The Spanish Civil War* from the History of Warfare Series.

Russia's support for the Republicans included intensive recruitment for the International Brigades as a kind of first front against Hitler. These and other factors impacted Orwell and Hemingway. Of special significance, Orwell found himself assigned to fight with a Trotskyite unit; these units, with ties to Stalin's political foe, became increasingly unpopular with the dictator and soon were targets of a Stalinist purge campaign. Some of Orwell's fighting friends were jailed or died as a result of their units' association with Trotsky and Lenin. Orwell himself barely survived Spain, and his wife, Eileen Blair, who worked in Barcelona at the headquarters of a Spanish communist party know as POUM, had her hotel room searched at gunpoint (Shelden 323). Orwell never forgot these experiences, or their Stalinist origin, and later targeted the Russian deceit, propaganda, and manipulation that he first saw in Spain in both *Animal Farm* and *1984*.

Hemingway, lacking Orwell's direct experience of Stalinist-Trotskyist infighting, apparently came out of Spain with more positive, or at least neutral, feelings about Stalin, a typical attitude in the West at the time. Understanding these distinctions is crucial for students; having them research, write, and then discuss paragraphs outlining the two authors' perspectives on Stalin and communism clarifies the political context. Hemingway appears to have accepted the idea of Trotskyite spies within the POUM, as evidenced in his play *The Fifth Column*. The play's main character is a gruff, independent reporter-turned-spy (who even looks like Hemingway), who uses Madrid nightspots to trawl for traitors to the cause. Stalin's people had initiated rumors of this "Fifth Column"—a kind of hidden unit within the Republic supposedly intending to turn on Spain at the appropriate time for Franco and fascism. Hemingway's play suggests that he believed the secret column existed. Interestingly, one of the few places where *The Fifth Column* was actually staged was the Soviet Union, in 1963 (Blum 55); Hemingway, rather than Orwell, has always been popular there. Students might try staging the play informally in classroom, as it is short enough to read in one long or two short sessions and they react with great interest to the issues related to spying.

The impact of Spain on both writers was life-changing. Hemingway's double *dicho*, "'Man can be destroyed but not defeated,'" took on new meaning and began to dominate his novels as a spiritual underpinning, always present; when Hotchner inverted it to "'Man can be defeated but not destroyed,'" Hemingway responded, "'Yes, that's its inversion, but I've always preferred to believe that man is undefeated'" (qtd. in Hotchner 73). Orwell was so opposed to fascism after Spain that, in addition to writing his very fine novels warning against fascism, dictatorship, and totalitarianism, he worked seventeen-hour days writing copy against Hitler for the BBC. Because of Spain, Orwell would now use words to fight effectively, in a way his weak body and his poorly equipped Trotskyist unit had failed to do. In July 1937, Orwell and his wife, who at the end was falsely charged with treason against the Republic as members of the rumored "Fifth Column," snuck out of Spain under cover on a train, in some fear for their lives. Carefully posing as a tourist reading Wordsworth, Orwell, along with Eileen and another friend, fled the controlling forces in Spain, who were increasingly hostile to POUM Republicans who had fought so hard for the Republican cause (Shelden 330).

A course built even solely around Spain's civil war and these two authors would enhance any curriculum, but including some of the many other internationally acclaimed writers were also went to Spain (e.g., Auden and Dos Passos) could round out the study. Feminism constitutes another interesting conduit into the subject. Spain was one war that involved women, and both Orwell's wife Eileen Blair and Hemingway's later wife, Martha Gellhorn (although at the time he was still married to Pauline Pfeiffer) took part in the battle against fascism there. The role of women in Spain's war is one that many female students will be anxious to explore. As Martha Gellhorn once stated, "[we] will continue to love the land of Spain and the beautiful people, . . . among the noblest and unluckiest on earth" (Gellhorn 17).

Only a few years later, Orwell would be in London surviving the Blitzkrieg at a time when Hemingway also frequented London (even meeting fourth wife Mary Welsh there). Orwell wrote extensively in his journals as to what it was like being bombed by Germany ("War-Time Diary" 58–108).[9] He supported the British government's efforts in print and on the radio, writing copy for many long hours a day intended to keep the public informed and sometimes to shape public opinion or reshape news for the sake of morale, compensating for or softening bad news. Even though this work edged into "positive" propaganda, he seems to have recognized the need for it, at least in some cases, and performed it willingly (Agathocleous 65), perhaps conceding that in those cases the end justified the means. (This idea alone might provoke quality student writing and debate on "negative" propaganda versus supposedly more ethical propaganda.)

At this time, both Orwell and Hemingway developed a stronger interest in the world of spying. Orwell began to keep a "Cryptos" list of people in art and literature whom he suspected either of being Communists or of spying for Stalin. Orwell had witnessed dictators shaping the world with masks or words to create artificial, controlling realities, and those experiences were now readying him rapidly for the creation of *1984;* Stalin's spies represented artificial, unknown control. Meanwhile, Orwell kept on typing: columns, articles, radio broadcasts, diaries. And the bombs kept dropping on England. But strange forces lurked in London and in much of Europe (Rubin).[10]

Hemingway was not on Orwell's list, but he might have been. After Spain, early in World War II, Hemingway was reportedly approached by the NKVD, the early version of the KGB, to spy for the Soviet Union. Neither of the researchers who uncovered this material, Alexander Vassiliev, a defector from Russia, and Nicholas Reynolds, an American historian from the CIA Museum, have found evidence of any actual spying by Hemingway, but both confirm at least five meetings between Hemingway (code name ARGO) and the KGB between 1941 and approximately 1945 (Haynes 152-55; N. Reynolds 1-11).[11] Reynolds suggests that Hemingway's willingness to meet may have been motivated in part by his respect for Soviet assistance to the Republic in Spain during the civil war. In any case, Hemingway's later fear and stress over Hoover and the FBI, at the time viewed as paranoia, may have been grounded in reality, perhaps based on concern about his own past discussions with the KGB. Did these secret meetings contribute to Hemingway's writing, or was he hoping that they might? Perhaps. Students engage easily in speculation regarding the purpose of the KGB contacts, resulting in some of my most animated classroom discussions.

One example of a fictional treatment of spying by Hemingway, "Nobody Ever Dies," concerns a very brief, ill-fated love affair in the midst of political and spying intrigue. I have asked students compare that story to the short-lived love affair in *For Whom the Bell Tolls,* with positive results. One might combine these pieces with work by several authors to create a spy literature class. Possible selections could include Orwell's *1984* and *Homage to Catalonia;* Hemingway's *The Fifth Column,* "The Denunciation," and some of his dispatches and diaries; Arthur Koestler's *Darkness at Noon;* and John Le Carre's *The Spy Who Came In From the Cold.*[12]

Orwell, like Hemingway, was approached by reputed Communists for service, but in the early thirties. He writes of the experience in *Down and Out in Paris and London,* and, ironically, seems to have seen little problem with the possibility of writing propaganda for the Communists. Nothing came of it, however: Orwell, like Hemingway, did not produce (Orwell, *Homage* 287-91).[13] By World War II, Orwell had become staunchly anticommunist, probably much more so than Hemingway. Orwell was one of the few in the West to see Stalin's dark side so clearly; after all, he had witnessed the power and resultant terror of Stalin's propaganda purge machine, and so became totally dedicated to Cryptos and to literature that would warn of the perils of totalitarianism.

Perhaps the worst that can be said for Hemingway's efforts in World War II—the last war he attended—is that he tried to make a contribution, and at a time when he was well into middle age (he was 46 in 1945) and aging quickly.

General Charles T. "Buck" Lanham said of Hemingway that he had "performed heroically." Hemingway was also awarded the United States Bronze Star for journalistic efforts in covering the war; this honor, infrequently discussed, was documented in the television biography "Ernest Hemingway: Wrestling with Life," an episode of *A&E Biography*. When the war ended, both Hemingway and Orwell were done with their extreme immersion in the era's large-scale events. Full circle, both may even have left Paris (or at least their common hotel) on virtually the same day in early 1945, having talked and shared a small encounter to wrap up the war. Hemingway says he gave Orwell a gun to protect himself from Communists,[14] but perhaps this gun was also for Orwell's march into Nazi Germany with the Americans just days later. Hemingway may have "liberated" Paris; it is less well known that Orwell may be said to have liberated Cologne. He certainly marched into Nazi Germany with the Western forces, perhaps even carrying Hemingway's revolver.[15]

After Spain and France, the two writers soon headed off to separate islands, literally and figuratively, for most of the rest of their days. Both had experienced a fast five years of masterful writing: no one would forget Big Brother, and no one would forget *The Old Man and the Sea*. Now, suddenly, nothing was the same. After World War II, the parallels between Orwell and Hemingway persisted, but the two lived and wrote on different continents and shared fewer direct thematic relationships.

With the sudden death of Orwell's wife shortly after that brief Paris meeting with Hemingway, Orwell's world became more insular. His tuberculosis worsened; he became a fully devoted father; and he largely isolated himself with his writing. *Animal Farm* and *1984* made him justly famous and highly regarded by many, yet an enemy to a few. The publishing, distribution, and censorship/book burning horrors surrounding both Orwellian masterpieces make for interesting research by students; even the U.S. Army reportedly supplied a burnable quantity of *Animal Farm* to the Russians (Hitchens 233). Living for a time on the island of Jura, Orwell was productive until his tuberculosis overtook him (Shelden 523–26).

The end of World War II likewise left Hemingway easing away from a life of participation in major world events. He hunted a bit in Africa but mostly, like Orwell, settled into island living, in Cuba. He became a world-class fisherman, a boat master; and, in 1954, a Nobel Prize winner for his 1951 tale about an old man and his fish, written in the refined and simple, adjective-free style that Orwell, too, had sought to achieve. Unfinished or then-unpublished works, ranging from *The Garden of Eden* to *Islands in the Stream*, show that during this period Hemingway also began working in a richer, more sensory style, giving increasing attention to ties with nature and focusing on an internal code that needed no material world support.

Both achieved a crush of wonderful late writing in the midst of island living, followed by fewer interactions and fewer immersions in major events or life itself. Both had peaked shortly after World War II and then accommodated themselves to personal physical decline in different ways, Orwell writing more feverishly than ever and Hemingway drinking heavily. Both had tackled the world, not only on the home front but the world front, in the major wars and other significant events and places. Hemingway's reaction to winning the Nobel Prize in Literature may have summed it up best: "For a true writer each book should be a new beginning where he tries again for something that is beyond attainment. He should always try for something that has never been done or that others have tried and failed. Then sometimes, with great luck, he will succeed" (Nobel Prize Banquet Speech, print).[16] Hemingway and Orwell each achieved "something that [had] never been done."

Teaching a course combining these two titans, whether a grand semester course covering all aspects or a smaller course focused on one location, period, or genre, yields many rewards. In designing the former, the standard treatments of these authors' masterpieces—*For Whom the Bell Tolls, The Old Man and the Sea, Animal Farm,* and *1984*—will likely best fit into a plan of chronology and geography combined with additional cultural and sensory materials (music, art, perhaps even cuisine) based on place. (See Appendix H: Master Course Syllabus.) The basic master plan developed here encompasses Paris (readings of *A Moveable Feast* and *Down and Out in Paris and London*), Spain (*Homage to Catalonia, For Whom the Bell Tolls,* and war correspondence), and World War II (Orwell's London diaries and Hemingway's dispatches and short stories), followed by exploration of Orwell's sweeping warnings for totalitarianism in our futures: *Animal Farm* and *1984*. Lastly, *The Old Man and the Sea*, winner of the Pulitzer Prize, elucidates a sense of the final reward coming from the fighting itself: the internal reward, achieved regardless of any external victory, of knowing one has done what one could and that no one can take that away, even in loss. Man is defeated not destroyed, destroyed not defeated, again and again. Voiced silently in that eternal bas-relief I alluded to in the beginning is an unspoken Hemingway and Orwell combination double dicho: Freedom (Orwell) does not sustain itself without a clear internal code (Hemingway), but one's inner code cannot sustain itself without freedom. Place, motivation, and immersion in life—what a tidal wave that brought.

Notes

1. Paul Potts, the Canadian poet and a friend of Orwell's, stayed at Orwell's home and later delivered a eulogy for the author. Potts provides Orwell's version of his meeting with Hemingway (Potts 85). Hemingway's written account, found in two letters to friends, the first to Cyril Connolly in 1948 and the second to Harvey Breit in 1952, stated that Orwell, not looking well, indicated Communists were still after him, so could he perhaps borrow a gun? Hemingway says in the letters that he gave Orwell a pistol. This material, presented early in the course, seems to motivate students to become involved in original research.

2. Orwell's attempts to join fighting forces over time are repeatedly mentioned in both the Agathocleous and the Shelden volumes noted here.

3. Orwell's exact address was 6 Rue du Pot-de-Fer, which Agathocleous notes was disguised in *Down and Out in Paris and London* as "Rue du Coq d'Or," a detail students and travelers to Paris will find interesting should they wish to walk the correct street.

4. Hemingway's address at this time was 6 rue Ferou 6e, where he had moved with Pauline Pfeiffer in 1927. While not as close to Orwell as his first Parisian home, this address still put Hemingway within blocks of Orwell. It is effective to note this geographical proximity early on in one's course; mapping it all out, using either small handouts or a wall poster, seems to cement the sense of a geothematic link between the two writers.

5. Michael Shelden quotes Orwell directly: "I would be distressed if they [the French] thought I have the least animosity towards a city of which I have very happy memories" (Shelden 145). The French edition carrying Orwell's correction to perception is titled *La Vachee Enragee* (Gallimard, 1935).

6. Alex Vernon follows Hemingway's presence in Spain closely. If each student has access to the work, a worksheet of questions, based on Vernon's materials, covering sourcing for *For Whom the Bell Tolls* is very profitable for discussion and overall student knowledge.

7. Vernon's book contains more than any teacher or professor could hope for by way of informative material and solid background regarding *For Whom the Bell Tolls* and Hemingway's presence in Spain.

8. Orwell's *Down and Out in Paris and London* was originally published in 1933; *Homage to Catalonia* was originally published in 1952. The dual volume is a frugal choice for teaching, as it combines both works in full.

9. Orwell's diaries were first published in 1998 in Britain and in 2012 in the United States. The collection *Facing Unpleasant Facts* provides good teaching material. See also, however, George Orwell, *Diaries,* ed. Peter Davison (New York: Liveright Publishing, 2012). Orwell comments on the various forces affecting the press and reshaping its function at this time, from the paper shortage to the impact of advertising and politics. Tanya Agathocleous amplifies this point in her book, *George Orwell: Battling Big Brother,* arguing that Orwell's involvement with the BBC and other writing accomplished during this time "conflicted wildly with his belief in telling the truth at all times. Nevertheless Orwell was willing to do it" (Agathocleous 65).

10. Orwell's list was finally released by the British government in 2003, and represents his best take (as of 1949) on which persons in the literary and arts world were Communists and/or Stalinist sympathizers, even spies. The article includes partial photostats, names, and notes. Sharing this provocative piece with students provokes strong enthusiasm for further research and debate, even when compared and contrasted with Joseph McCarthy's black lists.

11. Colonel Nicholas Reynolds (USMCR, ret.) reports—on the strength of Russian files (first published by the Yale History of Communism Project in *Spies* by Haynes et al. and now directly available at the Library of Congress)—that Hemingway met with KGB operatives in the early 1940s, and that he agreed in general terms to serve as a KGB resource. Reynolds indicates that Hemingway was not so much pro-Soviet or pro-Communist as anti-fascist; that is, "ever since his experiences in Spain during the Spanish Civil War, Hemingway had been a dedicated antifascist" (2, 8–11). Colonel Reynolds expands on these thoughts in a forthcoming book about Hemingway as spy and the reasons. Reynolds, a respected American military historian, is continuing his research and plans to offer additional material soon.

In classroom discussions, students have suggested hopefully that the KGB meetings might relate to Hemingway's "search for spy-related material," since he had some interest in writing spy stories (see, for instance, "The Denunciation," "Nobody Ever Dies," and *The Fifth Column*). Lastly, the Hemingway Letters Project, of Pennsylvania State University and Cambridge University Press, may eventually turn up further information in this regard, although that is hopeful speculation on my part.

12. Hemingway was familiar with Koestler's writing, and Koestler and Orwell were friends who shared strongly anti-Stalinist convictions. See Arthur Koestler, *Darkness at Noon* (1940, rpt. New York: Scribner, 2006), and John LeCarre, *The Spy Who Came in from the Cold* (1963, rpt. New York: Penguin, 2012).

13. See also Shelden (156), who makes reference to Orwell's later handwritten marginal notations, which assert the truth of the story.

14. See note 1, above.

15. This is my own theory as based on timing of events; certainly students find the entire Hemingway gun matter worthy of at least some discussion. Few westerners would wish to enter Nazi Germany without a gun at this point in time (early 1945), let alone an unhealthy westerner like Orwell, and Orwell headed into Germany shortly after talking with Hemingway. I also think the odds are high that Orwell was testing Hemingway's political views in that hotel room, and yet also had need of a gun, so saying the gun was for protecting himself against Communists (Hemingway's version, in writing, see note 1) would have made for an easy political probe. Hemingway did not appear on Orwell's list of communist Russian sympathizers. Was Orwell right? Speculative though it is, this issue really grabs the students, along with the morality of keeping such a list, which of course ironically bears similarity to Joe McCarthy.

16. Both the written speech and an audio recording of Hemingway later reading the speech aloud are available at the website of the Nobel Prize. Since Hemingway wasn't present at the award ceremony, U.S. Ambassador John C. Cabot, read Hemingway's speech at the banquet in Stockholm on 10 December 1954; Hemingway later read the

speech aloud, however. Students seem to become invigorated on hearing the author's voice. Audio recordings of Hemingway are few; those available for use in the classroom include the later recording of him reading his Nobel speech; his narration of *The Spanish Earth;* and a curiously stilted Cuban acknowledgement for the Nobel Prize, spoken by Hemingway in Spanish and available on black and white film on YouTube.

The Developing Modernism of Toomer, Hemingway, and Faulkner

Margaret E. Wright-Cleveland

In the 1920s and 1930s, American authors began to explore the postwar European aesthetic later known as modernism. Shattered by the costs of modern warfare exhibited in World War I, Europeans and Americans began to question all established institutions: religion, marriage, nation, race, and gender. Jean Toomer, Ernest Hemingway, and William Faulkner became leaders in American modernism, shaping not only their generation but future generations as well. This essay proposes an upper-division course for majors, focused on the earliest works of each writer—a short story cycle for each—in an effort to understand the genesis of modernism in American letters. I teach no literature to students unless I can demonstrate its relevance in their world today. The development of modernism in America was pivotal to the development of twentieth-century culture, literature, and politics and continues to influence today's culture. Indeed, understanding the shift in worldview explored through early twentieth-century modernism enriches one's understanding of current culture, literature, and politics. So our examination of these texts and writers from the 1920s and 1930s should increase student understanding of culture today.

It is not unusual for Toomer, Hemingway, and Faulkner to be examined as the vanguard in the development of American modernism; however, they are usually considered independently. Because they published contemporaneously, an effective pedagogy examines their early works as part of one cultural moment. I do not propose an examination of literary influence, but an examination of cultural concerns that help constitute a national identity. What these texts share may, indeed, be a common understanding of American identity, its strengths and its weaknesses, as well as a common sense of purpose and direction for the burgeoning American modernism with which these writers experimented, and understanding of each text is augmented by better understanding of the others. To initiate students into a thinking process that can identify and analyze a cultural moment, I begin with focused immersion in their cultural present. First, I ask them to do some free-writing, followed by small-group discussion to identify cultural concerns for which they can find evidence in the music, television, film, fashion, politics, web browsing, and live entertainment in which they or others they know engage. We then use a whole-class discussion to articulate the process they used to reach these conclusions about their current world. The reading assignments and the work for the next two class periods involve immersing students in the late nineteenth- and early twentieth centuries. We look at, read, listen to, taste, and talk about as many things as possible that people of the time could have experienced between 1890 and 1930. During the immersion activities, students are to use the process we have just articulated as a class to start collecting evidence of common cultural concerns in this historical moment. We process these discoveries in small groups first and then the small groups share with the whole class the lists they have composed through consensus. We use a class period to agree on the important issues of cultural identity to look for in the work of Toomer, Hemingway, Faulkner, and their common mentor, Sherwood Anderson. Students are now practiced in methods for close reading and cultural analysis and can begin forming questions about the connections between the past and the present.

Besides the convergence of a historical moment, there are other reasons to examine Hemingway, Faulkner, Toomer, and American modernism together.

- Although each writer's craft is different, the work of all is highly avant-garde in its innovation in form, conceptual challenge to established views, and wider influence. Their language shares remarkable innovation and skill.
- The work of all three writers remains influential. Hemingway and Faulkner in particular are still commonly listed as influential for present-day writers. Toomer scholarship investigating the role of *Cane* abounds.
- All three writers were among the first in America to experiment with modernist ideals and form, effectively setting the standard for modernist avant-gardism.
- They represent the three literary events of the early twentieth century traditionally identified as significant: the Harlem Renaissance, the lost generation, and the Southern Literary Renaissance. When considered together,

they raise questions about the role of race, gender, and region in broadly shaping American modernism.
- These (very different) writers also shared the same mentor: Sherwood Anderson.

An exploration of the early modernism of Hemingway, Faulkner, and Toomer must begin by examining Anderson's *Winesburg, Ohio* as a model of historically influential writing immediately preceding literary experiments with modernism. Investigating Anderson's professional and personal relationship with each writer and then working through close readings of Toomer's *Cane*, Hemingway's *In Our Time*, and the Faulkner stories originally published as *These 13* demonstrates how these texts question, support, criticize, or ignore various social constructions.

Such teaching requires both training students and giving them ample opportunities to produce open-ended, exploratory thinking about traditional topics. Students must be conversant with traditional understandings of modernism. Classroom discussions, readings, and writing assignments should be crafted to get students to address the following:

- What is American about Toomer's, Hemingway's, and Faulkner's modernism?
- How do these works reflect a common American identity?
- What do these works suggest about definitions of race and gender in America?
- What do these works suggest about the balance between the individual and society?
- How do these works revise *and* critique American culture and identity?

I begin this course with an overview of the historical moment, using such materials as the introduction and timeline from *1865 to the Present* (volume 2 of the *Norton Anthology of American Literature*, fifth edition), and the article "American Cultural History: The Twentieth Century" from the Lone Star College-Kingwood Library website (<http://kclibrary.lonestar.edu/decades.html>). To better understand the impetus felt by writers to create something new instead of perfecting old forms, students will need a sense of the breadth and depth of change occurring at the turn of the twentieth century. I make sure they can articulate a broad definition of and an argument for the importance of the following concepts and events: the American Renaissance; Reconstruction; realism; naturalism; industrialism; urbanization; the Gilded Age; the transcontinental railroad; the closing of the American frontier; the Progressive Movement;

women's suffrage; the rise of magazines, journals, and newspapers; World War I; the New Woman; the Great Migration; the New Negro; and the Immigration Act of 1924. As today's students will not be discomfited or surprised that artists question the status quo, it is important that the historical overview exposes students to how disorienting vast change can be and helps them understand the nineteenth-century value system that Hemingway, Faulkner, and Toomer inherited. Students must be able to identify nineteenth-century values (inherent in the American Renaissance, the Gilded Age, the failure of Reconstruction, and the relative success of the Progressive Movement) in order to understand how American modernism was revolutionary.

After exposing students to the historical moment, I introduce ideas about American literary modernism. Two excellent sources for teachers needing to clearly articulate the complex ideas of American modernism are "Towards a Definition of American Modernism" by Daniel Joseph Singal (1987) and *Literary Modernism and Beyond: The Extended Vision and the Realms of the Text* by Richard Lehan (2012). The ideas of American literary modernism are abstract and difficult, in part because *modernism* does not have a simple, direct definition. Students at my institution seek "the right answers," a means to control life with as few mistakes as possible; modernism appreciates paradox, ambivalence, and fragmentation, none of which lead to control or any single, "right" answer. Conversely, today's college students have come of age in a world in which technology gives great access to and creates comfort with multiplicity, fragmentation, and the constant experience of disparate elements. This dichotomy is heightened when addressing cultural study. The students in my institution experience multiplicity and fragmentation very differently than the early modernists and their audiences did, and their constant access to vast cultural experience from across the globe hinders their ability to thoughtfully process it. This life experience of separating oneself out of society at will allows my college students to accept chaos as merely a noise to be ignored, rather than a tension to be wrestled with. Students have learned to be "tolerant" and to not challenge those "different" from themselves; likewise, they see little need to challenge the status quo, for many do not believe racism or sexism or classism or privilege exist. Against the modern mythos that we can be very separate—holding no identity in common with others in our gender, class, race, or nation—and still value others and ourselves, today's students struggle to understand the need for or benefit from breaking apart what they see as a benign structure. They feel no pervasive disillusionment like that experienced by the early American modernists at the same age; for today's students to understand modernism adequately, this gap in experience and worldview must be bridged. I face this challenge by asking students to select three different elements of modernism and compose a visual or aural image or model of each as they understand them to work today and as they understand the early modernists engaged them. These models are presented and explained during the last week of class, but they are worked on throughout the semester. I schedule appointments with each student to preview the models and push the thinking. By working outside of words to explain abstractions, my students are breaking down all kinds of barriers to their own thinking and learning to see ideas and experiences with new eyes. This skill facilitates our required dance back and forth across time as we look to understand historical modernism and perceive its vast influence today.

Recognizing that I must develop in my students both an intellectual understanding of historical modernism and an empathetic understanding of the human need for the goals of modernism, I present the following ideas of Daniel Joseph Singal as pillars of the developing American modernism we will read.

- Developing modernism included "a determination not only for expanding the range of consciousness but for fusing together disparate elements of experience into new and original 'wholes'" (*Making of a Modernist* 10).
- Modernism aimed to create "the interpenetration, the reconciliation, the coalescence, the fusion—of reason and unreason, intellect and emotion, subjective and objective" (10).
- Paradox and ambivalence are means of joining opposites and contradictory emotions, a means not of "disintegration" but of "super-integration" (10).
- Personal experience demands the constant refashioning of meaning in our world (11).
- Modernism does not seek a resolved coherence but displays patterns or "regions of coherence," and temporality is key (114).

As we return to these ideas with every text assigned in the course, we look for manifestations of them, of course, in the themes and content of the stories. But we also look for evidence of them in the techniques developed by our writers. In particular ways, Hemingway, Toomer, and Faulkner all experimented with the following techniques: ways to use the narrative voice to privilege "perspectivism: the belief that reality stemmed from the way it was perceived" (Lehan 4);

a way to make "time present and time past simultaneous" (Lehan 8) through nonlinear storytelling; and the combining of myth with realism and symbols with the literal (Lehan 10). Additionally, I emphasize the difference between American literary modernism and what preceded it in the nineteenth century: "In short, where the Victorians saw art as didactic in purpose—as a vehicle for communicating and illustrating preordained moral truths—to Modernists it has become the principal vehicle for exploring and fashioning meaning in a world where meaning must constantly be re-created" (Singal 12).

The first literature students experience in this course is Sherwood Anderson's *Winesburg, Ohio* (1919), a text that is a precursor to American modernism. Two sources valuable for teachers preparing to introduce *Winesburg, Ohio* are Marc C. Conner's "Fathers and Sons: *Winesburg, Ohio* and the Revision of Modernism" (2001) and Clarence Lindsay's "'I Belong in Little Towns:' Sherwood Anderson's Small Town Post-Modernism" (1999). Generally, my students have found Anderson very accessible and claim to "get" what he is doing, making these stories a good place to first search for modernist concepts and technique. I place Anderson as someone who laid the groundwork for modernism and spend ample time outlining his specific mentorship of Hemingway, Toomer, and Faulkner. I present the following as thematic concerns Anderson introduced and the modernists picked up, either to develop and affirm or to expose and dismiss: the power of the past over the present; socially constructed gender roles; socially constructed racial roles; the status of institutions; the state of the American dream; and defining an American identity. Since *Winesburg, Ohio* is the first text we discuss, I present these thematic concerns first through lecture and then through modeling close reading for my students. After my demonstration, the students are asked to write a similar exercise for homework that will be worked through in small groups during the following class meeting. Small groups are organized by modernist theme, so each group builds quite an argument on how Anderson approached each looming concern. The texts addressed in this course hold in common their structure as short-story cycles. After reading Anderson, the students are receptive to the modernist sense that the structure of a short-story cycle—multiple points of view and events connected by setting or circumstance—demonstrates the textual nature of our reality; we, as individuals and as a species, are our stories. Additionally, I identify Anderson's development of a nonjudgmental narrator as a shift from nineteenth-century literary protocols and guide students to find examples of Anderson's use of digression, irony, and restraint. As we embrace the other authors, we will look for ways these techniques lead into stream-of-consciousness and nonlinear storytelling; the challenge of the status quo through paradox, ambivalence, fragmentation, as well as irony; minimalism or Hemingway's iceberg theory; and perspectivism to complicate any search for Truth.

After *Winesburg, Ohio*, students tackle Toomer's *Cane* (1923). I introduce the text with information on Toomer, the creation and reception of the book, and his relationship with Anderson. Though debate persists on what form Toomer used in *Cane*, in this course I teach the work as a short-story cycle and demonstrate how the characters are united by location (the American South, Washington, D.C., and Chicago), historical setting (the 1910s to 1920s), and themes. Regardless of how the structure of *Cane* is classified, however, Toomer makes far greater technical experiments than Anderson and prepares us well for Hemingway. Toomer's shift in language and structure is so striking that it must begin our class discussion of the text, which I open by reading aloud sections of *Cane*. I follow my reading of "Karintha" by having a student read aloud a selection from Anderson. The difference is immediately apparent, and we begin to process it.

Cane adds to the list of American modernism techniques the blending of poetry, prose, and script in a single text; parable; new forms of poetry; and fragmentary sentences. More importantly, perhaps, the increased use of sensory detail in *Cane* demonstrates the burgeoning modernist interest in recreating the moment, in having the reader experience in some small way what the character experiences. As this interest will be developed through very different stylistic choices by Hemingway and Faulkner, we spend a good deal of time on it. I ask the students to consider how these more technical innovations reflect deeper structural changes. As we catalog the multiple character and technical voices in the text, I guide the students to see that Toomer does not write a totalizing historical narrative; instead, this history is full of complications that cannot be reconciled into a unified historical perspective. With every unifying perspective the students suggest—the compromised status of the African American in America; the need for gender equity; the belief that no individual act matters—I play devil's advocate and push them to address whatever in the text distorts or challenges that unifying perspective. Toomer's historical complication is developed through the juxtaposition of communal wisdom and individuality and the paradox of beauty and brutality, particularly in the American South. Once students see a few points of such juxtaposition, they are equipped to see them throughout, and I ask them to test the evidence they are finding to see what Toomer does with this complicated history.

Hemingway's *In Our Time* (1925) draws many parallels with Toomer's *Cane*, including the same publisher (Boni and Liveright). Both short-story cycles alternate stories with poems (Toomer) or vignette chapters (Hemingway). Both present three sections of stories: *Cane* opens with six stories set in rural Georgia, follows with seven set in urban Chicago or Washington, D.C., and finishes with a long narrative return to Georgia, while *In Our Time* begins with seven stories set in the United States[1] continues with six set in Europe, and concludes with a two-part narrative return to the United States. *In Our Time* complements the work begun in *Winesburg, Ohio* and *Cane* exploring the relationship between the individual and community and between the past and the present by portraying a white privilege that demonstrates both who is allowed to transcend the past and what costs are borne by society for that privilege.

As with *Cane*, the most immediate confrontation with modernism in *In Our Time* comes through form. Instead of poetry, Hemingway explores sentence fragments; vignettes; dialogue representing real speech with much omission and little tagging; action without interpretation; multiple narrators that each provide a personal, interior view without omniscience; and the applications of Hemingway's iceberg theory, in which most of the story occurs between the lines of the narrative or by implication. Because Hemingway writes such minimalist text, I begin our work on *In Our Time* by reading the first vignette aloud while projecting it on the screen. I then proceed to model how to do a close reading of such a minimal text. I actually move word by word and ask questions about the cultural moment, the context we can garner from the vignette, the part of speech and its relationship to meaning, and how other word choices could have altered the meaning. In chapter 1, for example, we consider what difference it would make had Hemingway used *general* or *corporal* instead of *lieutenant*. We examine *Champagne, soused, adjutant*, the use of *we*, and what "It was funny going along that road" could possibly mean. Thematically, Hemingway embraces and develops the challenge of the status quo, a critique of established institutions, and the representation of otherness. He also presents chaos without resolution and creates characters that remain ambivalent throughout their development. That experience and meaning are personal is the only pattern Hemingway establishes. He consistently fuses reason and unreason, intellect and emotion, the subjective and the objective, and the personal with the communal.

Hemingway's tight prose demands attention to every word choice. For example, in chapter 8, Boyle and Drevitts shoot two people they see backing their wagon out of an alley behind a cigar store at 2:00 in the morning. We are told the location of the store, the type of store, and the make of the police car Drevitts and Boyle are driving. With all that information, it is hard not to notice that the narrator twice identifies the soon-to-be-dead men as Hungarians. Boyle, however, justifies his killing of them by identifying them as "wops" and "crooks." The "wop" identification is emphasized through dialogue: when Drevitts quizzes him, Boyle brags, "I can tell wops a mile off" (*IOT* 117). The iceberg of this story, then, not only identifies racism, it presents as factually errant racism's tenet that white and not-white are the only racial categories. There is nothing that identifies these men as "wops" (Italians) other than the assumption that they are stealing and Boyle's belief that Italian immigrants steal. Also, the names *Boyle* and *Drevitts* identify our policemen as Irish, an immigrant group likewise maligned as inferior for decades, although by 1925, when *In Our Time* was written, the Irish had been assimilated as white while the Italians had not. In this vignette without people of color, Hemingway has referenced an entire system of socialized racism that lives under the umbrella of whiteness. The mistake of the police officers is not caught or rectified; Drevitts regrets Boyle's actions only because he fears they might be caught; the institution of law and order is challenged; the disparate elements of ethnicity are fused into a new understanding of the limits and power of whiteness. Our personal experience of this story demands that we refashion our own understanding of ethnicity and whiteness. It is dialogue, not a narrator's special knowledge, that holds the key to the story. There is much that demonstrates American modernism in these 139 words.

Though Faulkner's *These 13* is not a familiar title, it includes some of his most assigned and anthologized stories. Published in 1931, *These 13*, like *Cane* and *In Our Time*, is a short-story cycle organized around three distinct sections. Part I contains four World War I stories; Part II has six stories set in the American South after the war; and Part III presents three stories set in both Europe and America yet outside the bounds of typical society and experience. Also like *Cane* and *In Our Time*, *These 13* presents multiple narrators, embraces paradox, works to fragment and then fuse anew the past with the present, and offers its most daring modernist experiment in the last section. Though Faulkner was writing novels in the 1920s that contributed to the development of American literary modernism,[2] this course examines the later *These 13* because of its connection in form to *Cane* and *In Our Time*.

Like Toomer and Hemingway, Faulkner explores the concerns of the post–World War I generation and employs those concerns as foundational structures for the new modernism. According to Lisa Paddock, the first section of *These 13* shows the most destructive effect of war to be "its propensity for alienating the individual from his roots" (19). With multiple characters suggesting that World War I was not their war, Faulkner secures the idea that war estranges individuals from each other and from their national identity. Toomer developed this tension between the individual and society through the socially constructed roles of race and gender; Hemingway did so by critiquing war, marriage, and whiteness. My students and I have been making connections all term: connections between texts and modernism, between texts and today, between modernism and today, between the stories within texts. As we add Faulkner to the mix, I push students to look for connections among the three modernists. We address Faulkner's stories and revisit our understanding of Toomer's and Hemingway's stories by marking ways in which these three writers and these three books broke from a literary tradition that had worked to establish a national identity within which individuals could find an identity and birthed in its place a literary tradition suggesting that personal identity was impossible within a national identity, for it could only be defined autonomously and against the constraints of national and cultural identities and ideologies. I emphasize that this is a particularly salient shift within a democracy, and we expand our discussion to consider if this tenet still holds and, if so, what it might mean. This allows the class to consider very broadly the role of literature in personal and national identity, as well.

These 13 continues the development of modernist themes we explored in *Cane* and *In Our Time*: tension between the past and the present; tension between the individual and the community; the questioning of institutions; acceptance of paradox and ambivalence; the breaking up of systems to restructure or fuse the parts into new meanings; and the importance of the individual. I guide the class to "discover" these themes in Faulkner through deduction, just as they have done in Toomer and Hemingway. In our first class on *These 13*, we address modernist themes in Faulkner by free-writing for twenty minutes followed by small-group discussion. During the second day of discussion on Faulkner, we hear reports from the small groups and create a class list of themes to explore in Faulkner. If I think the students have missed certain important themes, I suggest them and offer some evidence of their presence, but I am usually quite impressed with the level of expertise my students have achieved at this point and with their ability to read modernism.

Technically, *These 13* experiments with narrative form, the presentation of time, and sentence structure. It does not include poetry, but certain of its stories are highly abstract, devoid of traditional experiences with time, and heavily dependent on the symbolic or on experiences of the supernatural.

"Crevasse," "Mistral," and "Carcassonne" use the supernatural as elements of plot, to explore identity, to complicate the relationship between humanity and nature, and to expose paradox. "Carcassonne" even has a narrator that speaks beyond death, fusing his references to ancient history with a future beyond life that is barely knowable. Faulkner's experiments with form expand those of Toomer and Hemingway into the surreal.

As my students move through each of these three short-story cycles, I continually present definitions of modernism broadly to both refine their thinking and get them to see what distinguishes American literary modernism from the high modernism of Europe. In classes and in writing assignments, I return repeatedly to the following questions to focus students on the task at hand, that of identifying elements of modernism in these three writers.

- What examples of paradox can you identify?
- What is being fragmented?
- What disparate elements are being fused together in a new way?
- How is the relationship between the past and the present portrayed?
- How is the relationship between the individual and the community portrayed?
- How do the characters find meaning?
- How is the natural world portrayed?
- How are institutions portrayed?

After leading students through close readings of these stories and focusing on identifying elements of and understanding the effect of American literary modernism, I require my students to apply what they have learned by writing their own close reading of a modernist short story. (See Appendix I: Model Assignments.) Though students must read others' ideas about the story chosen (three critical articles are required), the assignment emphasizes student interpretation of the story, not student interpretation of criticism. This assignment has merit, then, to students interested in literary analysis and to those who are interested in reading or writing fiction. It allows individual students to focus on either content or form and gives them control over what they will argue. It has proven to be an assignment well received and well accomplished by students.

Though not even one element of this course can be truly understood by the end of a sixteen-week course—much less the complicated relations between these three texts, writers, and modernism—students finish with increased ability to read the text that was written, to examine how that text reflected and challenged the world in which it was published, and to identify and understand those elements of modernism that persist in their world: paradox, ambivalence, fragmentation, fusion, and identity. Additionally, Hemingway, who for today's students potentially exists as a figure so iconic that he inhabits no particular time period, geography, or literary movement, is once again firmly connected to modernism.

Notes

1. "A Very Short Story" begins in Padua but ends in Chicago.
2. Before *These 13*, Faulkner had published *Soldiers' Pay* (1926), *Mosquitoes* (1927), *Sartoris* (1929), *The Sound and the Fury* (1929), *As I Lay Dying* (1930), and *Sanctuary* (1931). Based on this publication record, one could argue that Faulkner was the most established modernist among the three we are considering. However, according to records Faulkner kept concerning the submission and acceptance of his stories, he began writing the stories in *These 13* before the first submission date in 1927 (Hans Skei, *William Faulkner: The Short Story Career: An Outline of Faulkner's Short Story Writing from 1919 to 1962* [Oslo: University Forl, 1981]).

The Futurist Origins of Hemingway's Modernism

Bradley Bowers

The emergence of futurism and modernism in the same early twentieth-century moment led to a rivalry among writers and artists claiming originality. It also led to ongoing disrespect for Italian futurists, who sparked the movement following F. T. Marinetti's publication of *The Futurist Manifesto* on the front page of the Paris newspaper *Le Figaro* on 20 February 1909 (see Appendix J: The Futurist Manifesto, Excerpt). To this day, the shared aesthetic and philosophical roots of futurism and modernism have been largely ignored or denied, in part because of futurism's close association with the rising Fascist government of Benito Mussolini after World War I, a perception that to this day still may provoke occasional moral outrage at any appreciation of the futurists of this period, despite their significant artistic contributions.

The centennial of futurism's birth in 2009 revived interest in futurism, both in Italy and elsewhere, and initiated a new appreciation of futurism's role in the larger modernist movement. However, while this interest generated many exhibitions and events in Italy and Europe, only one major American museum, New York's Metropolitan Museum of Art, hosted a centennial futurist exhibition, presented in part because the Met is the country's largest holder of futurist art. In both European and American culture, great misunderstanding persists about the role of futurism in the development of modernism; "to this day," as Günter Berghaus asserts, "the prevailing view of the reception of Futurism after 1945 is that the anti-fascist consensus in Italian politics cast a political anathema on Marinetti's movement" (377). Walter Adamson likewise suggests that after World War II, "there was a deafening silence about futurism in Italy"

(71).[1] However, futurism and modernism grew from the same revolutionary origins and retained many of the same aesthetic and philosophical elements, and certainly the American expatriates living in Paris knew of futurism's role in inspiring the Parisian modern movement.

It was, of course, Ezra Pound who delivered the modernist edict "Make it new!" but it was Benito Mussolini who ordered his futurist artists to "Make it new, ultramodern, and audacious!" (qtd. in Alfieri and Freddi 8).[2] When Ernest Hemingway arrived in Europe in May 1918, on his way to Italy as a Red Cross ambulance driver, he went first to Paris, where he immersed himself in the mix of artists, writers, and intellectuals who were the nucleus of the emerging futurist/modernist aesthetic. In June, he traveled on to Italy, and his service there began and ended in Milan, home to futurism's second wave after the war. The shared heritage of its artists and writers reveals that Italian futurism was essential to the development of American modernism, which itself drew on Italy's first wave of futurism. The experimental aesthetic and attitudes Hemingway expressed in *In Our Time* (1925), the carefully nuanced philosophical stance of *The Sun Also Rises* (1926), and the ruthless yet romantic heroism of *A Farewell to Arms* (1929) especially illustrate the writer's place in the developing futurist movement.

Recent studies in the English language, such as Christine Poggi's *Inventing Futurism*, have acknowledged more similarities; Poggi argues that, like modernists, futurist artists and writers were far more ambivalent in their responses to the shocks of industrial modernity than they were perceived to be in the long-accepted but naïve characterization of futurism as a blind plunge forward (x-xi). Italian studies have likewise moved beyond the earlier discomfort with futurism's links to fascism to look at its concurrent development with modernism and the exchange of ideas between the leading proponents of both schools. *The History of Futurism: The Precursors, Protagonists, and Legacies* (2012) attempts to locate the movement within a larger modernist context; one chapter, "The Audacity of Hope" by Marjorie Perloff, takes its title from a recent political autobiography to emphasize the continuing presence of futurist ideology in American culture. Günter Berghaus has also compiled the first edition of the *International Yearbook of Futurism Studies* (2011).

In America, there is more ignorance of futurism than outright disrespect; elsewhere, however, the animosity and vitriol persist. A 2005 art exhibit at London's Estorick Collection of Modern Italian Art, for example, "Futurist Skies: Italian Aeropainting," provoked condemnation as "fascist crap"; "Claiming 'aeropainting' as a major twentieth-century art," complained *Guardian* reviewer

Jonathan Jones, "amounts to rehabilitating fascist kitsch." When the British Museum purchased Marinetti's Tin Book, *Parole in Libertá Futuriste Olfattive Tattili Termiche* (*Words in Futurist, Olfactory, Tactile, Thermal Freedom*), David Barrie, director of the Art Fund, was defensive, yet more appreciative of futurism's historical value: "This metal book is an extraordinary invention, testifying to the revolutionary spirit of a movement that genuinely believed in the power of art to change the world. It also gives us an insight into the fascinating and complex relationship between Italy's creative elite and the forces of Fascism" (qtd. in Brown).

That an American icon of modernism such as Hemingway also embodies much of the futurist philosophy and aesthetic illuminates their shared beginnings. Separating out futurism's origins and influences from later associations with politics and war allows an American audience to recognize that Hemingway's celebrated "grace under pressure" is essentially and precisely an expression of the Italian futurist embrace of modernity, especially the dehumanizing dominance of technology exemplified in its brutal and previously unseen wartime applications. Hemingway, who became the face of American modernism while he was in Europe, exhibits this principle, along with other concepts similar to the Italian futurist aesthetic and philosophy, in his works. Although Hemingway (and most other modernists, with a few notable exceptions, such as Ezra Pound and Wyndham Lewis) did not acknowledge any influence from—much less appreciation for—the futurist movement, he did demonstrate an intimate knowledge of the founders of futurism—openly praising and later mocking Gabriele D'Annunzio, for example—and respected their application of the Old World ethos of the poet-warrior to a new world war. The work of other modernist writers, such as Virginia Woolf and F. Scott Fitzgerald, also reveals a remarkable affinity with the futurist philosophy.

Hemingway lived in Paris, where futurism was born, and went to war in Italy, where futurism, and World War I, were flourishing. Futurists in Italy celebrated war as "the world's only hygiene" ("sola igiene del mondo") and joined the conflict as poet-warriors, invoking the Byronic model of the complete man absorbed in his culture, a man of words as well as a man of war. In Italy, Hemingway experienced the atrocities of modern combat firsthand, while at the same time seeking to live as an Old World poet-warrior despite being in a modern wasteland. In *A Farewell to Arms*, Frederic Henry's inherent romanticism encounters harsh and extreme realities, and, like the Italian futurist poet-warriors, he eventually embraces total immersion in the war experience and savors the intensity of those existential moments. Like D'Annunzio, whose war cry "Morire non basta" ("To die is not enough") Hemingway cites admiringly, Henry accepts the death of romanticism and celebrates the new poet-warrior as the only heroic choice left. Henry recognizes that the machine already largely dominates the man and will eventually replace him. He rationalizes the dominance of the machine and the diminution of the individual soldier, especially the soldier's inability to become a war hero, by recognizing the new emphasis on speed and technology in war. His description of his own wounds includes the futurist concept of the machine-extended man, part human, part metal (see the emblematic futurist sculpture by Umberto Boccioni "Unique Forms of Continuity in Space," which now adorns the Italian Euro quarter). His first realization comes early, well before combat, when he summarizes the "smooth functioning of the business" of war and wounded: "Evidently it did not matter whether I was there or not" (*FTA* 16). Henry tempers his latent romanticism with a futurist's embrace of the superiority of technology; later, he wants to trade his wounded knee for a "metal hook," while his doctors note ironically that he will receive a piece of silver metal (a medal) for his heroism (97). Like Fillippo Tomasso Marinetti, Henry admires the technological advances which have revolutionized warfare and, like Jake Barnes in *The Sun Also Rises,* looks forward to a postwar world cleansed of romantic illusions.

Many studies of American modernists separate Hemingway and other expatriates from the rest, contrasting them with the American who most embraced futurism and then fascism, Ezra Pound. Pound ended up as a fascist propagandist charged with treason by the United States, yet Hemingway and Pound had a close and lifelong friendship, a fact that can buttress a teacher's framing of Hemingway's work within this modernism–futurism dialectic. After visiting him in Rapallo, Italy, in 1927, Hemingway said that Pound was "a sort of saint . . . the man I liked and trusted the most as a critic" (*MF* 88, 102).[3] He wrote to Pound in 1925 that bulls and bullfighting were "such a goddam relief from all this horseshit about Art. To hell with delicate studies of the American scene. Fuck the American scene. Fuck moers [mores], manners, customs and all that horseshit. Let us have more and better fucking, fighting bulls"—a remarkably futuristic comment about traditional art (qtd. in Vincent).[4] That said, Hemingway liked condemning intellectualism while acknowledging that his "literary forebears" include many painters, including "Tintoretto, Hieronymus Bosch, Breughel, Patinier, Goya, Giotto, Cézanne, Van Gogh, Gauguin, San Juan de la Cruz, Góngora. . . . I put in painters, or started to, because I learn as much from painters about how to write as from writers" (qtd. in Plimpton 23). Of course, the first wave futurist painters Umberto Boccioni, Carlo Carrà,

Luigi Russolo, Giacomo Balla, and Gino Severini all emerge from the same Parisian modern movement as Hemingway and his circle of artists and writers.

In the classroom, one useful method of distinguishing Hemingway's style from those who came before is literally to compare the opening lines of his works with those of earlier well-known novelists, both British and American. The exercise can be done in the form of a game, with students trying to identify famous opening passages (see Appendix K: Opening Lines of Famous Novels before Ernest Hemingway). Contrasting the opening words of *In Our Time* with those of *Tom Jones, Pride and Prejudice, The Scarlet Letter, Great Expectations,* and *The Adventures of Huckleberry Finn* illustrates how radically Hemingway breaks with tradition. Comparing his openings with those of any number of earlier novels could demonstrate equally well not only the shift between them and Hemingway in narrative stance and authority but also his break with a commonly held set of beliefs. What is most notably missing from Hemingway's novels is any narrative reference to any system of beliefs, whether cultural, moral, or simply humane. Like the futurists, who blatantly dismiss the past as irrelevant, stifling, and dead, *In Our Time* makes no reference to and draws no obvious connections with any moral metanarrative. A useful sidebar to this lesson is an exploration of Twain's *The Adventures of Huckleberry Finn*, somewhat ironically cited by Hemingway as the first example of truly American literature.[5] Twain's narrator makes only mocking reference to traditional moral codes, much like the defiant Marinetti. Later in his career, in contrast, Hemingway writes in his introduction to the anthology *Men at War* (1942):

> When you go to war as a boy you have a great illusion of immortality. Other people get killed; not you.... Then when you are badly wounded the first time you lose that illusion and you know it can happen to you. After being severely wounded two weeks before my nineteenth birthday I had a bad time until I figured out that nothing could happen to me that had not happened to all men before me. Whatever I had to do men had always done. If they had done it then I could do it too and the best thing was not to worry about it. (7)

This amoral acceptance of war as inevitable and necessary is, of course, the theme of *The Futurist Manifesto*.

To further explore the radical nature of *In Our Time,* students should be introduced to a concept of war that the *Manifesto* embraces: "It is sweet and fitting to die for one's country." Both futurists and modernists invoke the Roman history of war and its ability to recreate the world into its own image, whether it is construed as "the world's only hygiene" or, as in one of the component stories of *In Our Time*, "On the Quai at Smyrna," as "a most pleasant business" (12).

Two writers whose work it is useful to explore in this context are the Roman poet Homer and the British poet Wilfred Owen (see Appendix L: Horace and Wilfred Owen). The sentiment of sacrifice to the greater good was most famously expressed by Horace, who lived in Rome during the time of Augustus; his ode to war embodies the Roman attitude toward war that for centuries supported Roman empire-building. British poet Wilfred Owen first used the phrase, in English rather than Latin, in a poem drafted in 1915, initially called "The Ballad of Peace and War." He never completed the poem. One version reads:

> O it is meet and it is sweet
> To live in peace with others.
> But sweeter still and far more meet
> To die in war for brothers. (2:504)

Before he could complete the poem, Owen went to battle in World War I. When he came home, he wrote a new version, using Horace's Latin phrase "Dulce et decorum est" as its title. This version ends with the lines:

> My friend, you would not tell with such high zest
> To children ardent for some desperate glory,
> The old Lie: Dulce et decorum est
> Pro patria mori. (1:140)

Hemingway knew both poets and their work. Later, in 1935, reflecting on his experiences in war, he points out the difference between earlier civilizations and those of the twentieth century: "They wrote in the old days that it is sweet and fitting to die for one's country. But in modern war, there is nothing sweet nor fitting in your dying. You will die like a dog for no good reason" ("Notes on the Next War" 304).

Then we get to the opening of *The Sun Also Rises*—not so much the first lines but the thematic element of absinthe. Oscar Wilde at the turn of the twentieth century described the effects of absinthe: "After the first glass of absinthe you see things as you wish they were. After the second you see them as they are not. Finally you see things as they really are, and that is the most horrible thing in the world." Wilde continues, "I mean disassociated. . . . That is the effect absinthe has, and that is why it drives men mad" (qtd. in "Effects of Absinthe").[6] Hemingway paraphrases Wilde's description early on: "Pernod is greenish imitation absinthe. When you add water it turns milky. It tastes like licorice and it has a good uplift, but it drops you just as far. We sat and drank it, and the girl looked sullen" (*SAR* 3).[7] His point is that "things as they really are" lack meaning, much like the "nada" commentary in "A Clean, Well-Lighted Place" (1933). Absinthe does not drive Jake Barnes mad, though; his salvation is that he is a reluctant futurist throughout the novel, dragged down only by the romantic fantasies fostered by Brett Ashley. As Jake says of the fiesta after at least four absinthes: "It did not mean anything" (*SAR* 228). He begins to acknowledge the effect during the fiesta: "We watched the beginning of the evening of the last night of the fiesta. The absinthe made everything seem better. I drank it without sugar in the dripping glass, and it was pleasantly bitter" (87). Later, Bill consoles him:

> "Have another absinthe. Here, waiter! Another absinthe for this señor."
> "I feel like hell," I said.
> "Drink that," said Bill. "Drink it slow."
> It was beginning to get dark. The fiesta was going on. I began to feel drunk but I did not feel any better.
> "How do you feel?"
> "I feel like hell."
> "Have another?"
> "It won't do any good."
> "Try it. You can't tell; maybe this is the one that gets it. Hey, waiter! Another absinthe for this señor!"
> I poured the water directly into it and stirred it instead of letting it drip. Bill put in a lump of ice. I stirred the ice around with a spoon in the brownish, cloudy mixture. (117)

The response questions will guide students to make their own connections between Hemingway's modernism and Jake's emergent futurist sensibilities as the novel progresses (see Appendix M: Response Questions). Instead of using the inadequate model of a "code hero" to elaborate this novel, have students discuss the ideas of heroism in *The Futurist Manifesto*, and they will recognize the many small and large elements of that embrace of "grace under pressure" by Jake Barnes.

Several websites allow students to search for keywords in *The Sun Also Rises* and *A Farewell to Arms*, and these can be useful tools for studying a writer so careful with diction.[8] For example, a search for the word *seem* in *The Sun Also Rises* finds the word fifty-one times, but its appearances cluster heavily around Jake, first after he gets knocked out by Robert and later when he and Bill have finished off the four absinthes (at least) mentioned earlier, stressing for students the importance of both close reading and contextualizing.

When *A Farewell to Arms* was published in 1929, it was literally "banned in Boston" because of its vulgar depiction of Frederic Henry's war experiences. However, a reassessment of the novel in 1990 concluded that it "was a revolutionary novel that has only now begun to be understood—sixty years after publication" (Phelan 53). The love story is illuminated by Valentine de Saint-Point's *The Futurist Manifesto of Lust*, which defines love as a romantic illusion created by "words," "rhetoric" and the kind of "literary nostalgia" that Frederic uses to justify his early interest in Catherine. Frederic's description of his first sexual encounter with Catherine Barkley fits de Saint-Point's description of lust as "the painful joy of wounded flesh."

The war story details Frederic's dedication to the war machine, literally, as he kills another soldier who will not help extricate their truck from the primordial mud (whether this image comes directly from Marinetti's Bugatti in the ditch is speculative). However, Frederic brags that his legs are "full of trench-mortar fragments, old screws and bedsprings and things" (*FTA* 85), and his experiences echo Hemingway's own, who had written home, "I can now hold up my hand and say I've been shelled by high explosive, shrapnel and gas" (qtd. in Villard and Nagel 176). As Marinetti writes in "War, the World's Only Hygiene" (1915), "There is nothing for us to admire today but the dreadful symphonies of the shrapnel." Frederic also elaborates on the sentiments expressed by Horace and elaborated by Owen's poems: "I was always embarrassed by the words sacred, glorious, and sacrifice and the expression in vain.... I had seen nothing sacred, and the things that were glorious had no glory and the sacrifices were like the stockyards at Chicago" (*FTA* 165).

Virginia Woolf expresses the same argument for amorality when she echoes Marinetti's lament, "Literature has up to now magnified pensive immobility, ecstasy, and slumber," in his "Manifesto of Futurism": she says; "there is, unfortunately, such a thing as life" ("Phases of Fiction" 55).[9] Woolf complains of contemporary novelists that "the conditions of storytelling are harsh; they demand that ... the same values shall prevail.... But what will happen if ... the novelist finds himself out of facts or flagging in his invention? Must he then go on? Yes, for the story has to be finished: the intrigue discovered, the guilty punished, the lovers married in the end" (101). She proposes in her political treatise *Three Guineas* that women should seek to destroy the traditional values that oppress them: "We are determined to do what we can to destroy the evil ... you by your methods, we by ours" (143). As she writes her own manifesto, "she has collected enough powder to blow up St. Paul's" (Woolf, *Diary* 77). The traditional reading of Septimus Smith in *Mrs. Dalloway* (1925) is that he is a shell-shocked war veteran filled with remorse over the loss of his friend Evans. Ask your students to read him as a futurist soldier and a different picture emerges, one of enthusiasm for war as the solution to a world of deadening Proportion and Conversion, one in which his ultimate gesture of suicide is affirmative. Echoing Marinetti's correlation of youth, violence, and ecstasy, he reflects on his experience: "The War had taught him. It was sublime. He had gone through the whole show, friendship, European War, death, had won promotion, was still under thirty and was bound to survive" (Woolf, *Mrs. Dalloway* 86). When faced with submission to traditional social norms, he confronts the fact that "conversion, fastidious Goddess, loves blood better than brick, and feasts most subtly on the human will" (100). Like the futurist's paradoxical embrace of violence and death, but also passion and joy, he "did not want to die. Life was good" (149). So when he plunges to his death rather than submit ("I'll give it you!"), it is with joy and passion. Clarissa Dalloway says, "But he had flung it away. They went on living" (184). He had, however, created "a thing there was that mattered; a thing, wreathed about with chatter, defaced, obscured in her own life, let drop every day in corruption, lies, chatter. This he had preserved" (184). The recurring quotation in *Mrs. Dalloway*—"'Fear no more the heat o' the sun,'" from Shakespeare's *The Tempest*—is realized by Septimus: "She felt glad that he had done it; thrown it away.... He made her feel the beauty; made her feel the fun" (186).

F. Scott Fitzgerald, like others more entrenched in the Paris environment, was inevitably aware of the futurist artists and writers of that time. The five major thematic elements present in Marinetti's *Futurist Manifesto* subsequently appear as identical figures and tropes in Fitzgerald's *The Great Gatsby*, summarized here (for specific passages, see Appendix N: Italian Futurism and *The Great Gatsby*).

1. *Romanticized industrial settings.* A persistent theme in much of futurist art, this idea is also the Manifesto's eleventh point about industrial beauty; *The Great Gatsby* is of course likewise famous for its "valley of ashes."

2. *The "machine in the garden" (or, an automobile crashing into a ditch or a person).* Leo Marx's *The Machine in the Garden* (1964) is an excellent supplement to this point, but the obvious parallel is the dominance of the machine over all that is human and natural. See also chapter 25 of Henry Adams's *The Education of Henry Adams* (1918), "The Virgin and the Dynamo," for a similar appreciation of how technology has replaced spirituality.
3. *The automobile as the new beautiful.* Marinetti's Bugatti and Gatsby's convertible coupe—a richly provocative link.
4. *Peaking at the age of thirty.* Both writers are precise that thirty is the end, an idea that persisted into 1960s counterculture as the warning, "Don't trust anyone over thirty."
5. *Wanton pursuit of the future.* A future without hope is nonetheless the only future to be found, and although the modernists may have slightly more reticence and less ambition, in the end they share a lot with the futurists.

Modernism shaped the intellectual discussion of the twentieth century, and modernist writers such as Hemingway continue to define what has been called the American century. His work has endured several decades of glowing appreciation, scathing reinterpretation, and subsequent reconsideration in a new historical manner, taking into account the time and place of the works' creation. By reenvisioning the Hemingway hero as an icon of the futurist philosophy and aesthetic, students can see that the futurist ethos is often embodied in Hemingway's works, most precisely in the famed attitude of those characters who maintain the famous "grace under pressure" without a trace of romance and with the enthusiastic fervor of a futurist.

Notes

1. Günter Berghaus himself cites this statement by Adamson to illustrate how the connection of futurism with fascism was widely perceived to have essentially ended the movement. While futurism was shunned throughout the world after Mussolini, it in fact persisted in parts of Europe and actually thrived in Italy. Berghaus's study reveals an astonishing number of publications, conferences, and exhibits (the vast majority in Italy, however) that celebrated the futurists' continuing influence.

2. See also Jeffrey T. Schnapp, "Epic Demonstrations: Fascist Modernity and the 1932 Exhibition of the Fascist Revolution," in *Fascism, Aesthetics, and Culture*, ed. Richard J. Golson (Hanover, NH: UP of New England, 1992), 1–37.

3. All citations to *A Moveable Feast* are to the following edition: Ernest Hemingway, *A Moveable Feast: The Restored Edition* (New York: Scribner, 2009).

4. The author wishes to thank the Ernest Hemingway Foundation and Society for permission to publish this excerpt.

5. While this tribute to Twain is often cited (including in Woody Allen's 2011 movie *Midnight in Paris*), it is not the compliment it seems to be. In *Green Hills of Africa* (1935), Hemingway begins with praise: "The good writers are Henry James, Stephen Crane, and Mark Twain. That's not the order they're good in. There is no order for good writers.... All modern American literature comes from one book by Mark Twain called 'Huckleberry Finn'" (23). Often overlooked is the next part of this passage, where he accuses Twain of the literary sin of "cheating": "If you read it you must stop where the Nigger Jim is stolen from the boys. That is the real end. The rest is just cheating" (23). However, he immediately reiterates his praise: "But it's the best book we've had. All American writing comes from that. There was nothing before. There has been nothing as good since" (23).

6. The quotation is of Wilde in conversation, and it exists in more than one form. The Virtual Absinthe Museum at the Oxygenee website provides another version as well: "The first stage is like ordinary drinking, the second when you begin to see monstrous and cruel things, but if you persevere you will enter in upon the third stage where you see things that you want to see, wonderful and curious things." The site explains "that this famous quote isn't sourced from any of Wilde's books, or from his letters, or from any contemporary interview. It originates in this form from a book of humorous reminiscences called "My Three Inns" written in 1949 by an eccentric hotelier called John Fothergill. . . . It's highly likely that this quote was substantially embellished by Fothergill (or perhaps based on the much simpler version published by Ada Leverson in 1930." See also Ada Leverson and Oscar Wilde, *Letters to the Sphinx from Oscar Wilde and Reminiscences of the Author* (London: Gerald Duckworth and Co., 1930).

7. All citations to *The Sun Also Rises* are to the following edition: Ernest Hemingway, *The Sun Also Rises* (1926; rpt. New York: Scribner, 2006).

8. For *The Sun Also Rises*, see <http://marimarister.files.wordpress.com/2013/02/ernest-hemingway-the-sun-also-rises.pdf>, while for *A Farewell to Arms,* the website <http://vccslitonline.vccs.edu/afta/study_guide.htm> offers abundant guidance, including word and thematic searches that also provide some context; a particularly useful search is for the word *they* at <http://vccslitonline.vccs.edu/afta/they.htm>.

9. See also Woolf, *The Essays of Virginia Woolf,* vol. 5: *1929–1932,* ed. Stuart Clarke (New York: Harcourt Brace Jovanovich, 1982), 101.

Hemingway, His Contemporaries, and the South Carolina Corps of Cadets

Exploring Veterans' Inner Worlds

Lauren Rule Maxwell

In a final paper entitled "Posttraumatic Stress in Hemingway's Short Fiction," one of the cadets in my most recent twentieth-century American fiction class analyzed the author's depictions of veterans' psychological states. To introduce this topic, he wrote: "As an ambulance driver in World War I, Ernest Hemingway witnessed a wide variety of serious wounds and injuries that his patients incurred in combat. Hemingway likely witnessed some very gruesome wounds, but he does not elaborate on many physical injuries in his stories. Instead, Hemingway is fascinated with the psychological experience of the wounded warrior."[1] This fascination with veterans' experiences—psychological and otherwise—became a major focus in my students' examination of Hemingway's work. Given the military nature of my home institution, the Citadel (the Military College of South Carolina), it is not surprising that the cadets were preoccupied with Hemingway's depictions of veterans. But what is surprising is how my students came to view other modernist texts through Hemingway's veterans.

Here, I focus on my students' readings of the complex psychological portraits of veterans in several works by Hemingway that I teach in the twentieth-century American fiction course; I then relate those readings to discourses of identity and otherness the cadets identified in F. Scott Fitzgerald's *The Great Gatsby*. The cadets' discussions of Hemingway's stories also influenced their readings of other modernist texts—particularly William Faulkner's *Light in August* and its depiction of Joe Christmas and Percy Grimm—but because of space constraints here I describe only connections the students drew between Hemingway's stories and *The Great Gatsby*. Their analyses of these connections, which were facilitated in part by my asking the students to consider how all of the works we read over the course of the semester serve as meditations on American history, help explain how the cadets used Hemingway's portrayals of veterans in his short stories to develop an understanding of ways World War I experiences informed identity in modernist works on a broader scale. Although, unlike Hemingway's stories, *The Great Gatsby* does not center on the depiction of characters as veterans, my students focused on the characters with military affiliations, particularly Jay Gatsby, because of the involved discussions we had been having of veterans in relation to Hemingway's stories. I encouraged the cadets to extend traditional readings of Gatsby in relation to class and race by asking them to consider and write about how these categories are further complicated by his military involvement. In a sense, my students were reading Fitzgerald through the lens of Hemingway. In the following exploration of what is at stake in doing so, I will address the larger questions it raises about modernist constructions of identity in relation to World War I.

In the spring of 2012, I was lucky enough to once again teach the twentieth-century American fiction course, which the Citadel offers only every few years. As I teach it, the course covers several of the century's most popular and talented writers, including Fitzgerald, Faulkner, Cormac McCarthy, and Toni Morrison, but the cadets seem particularly impressed with Hemingway's works. In fact, each time I have taught this course, cadets have independently charted intensive studies of Hemingway, reading a wider selection of his work than that assigned, devouring critical materials on his writings, exploring his biography, and engaging in various forms of author-worship. When asked about why they are so taken with Hemingway, the cadets seem to always have the same answers—they can "get into" his works more, they can relate to his texts better than those of some other authors studied, and they can place themselves in the worlds he creates.

For this course, students read a wide range of Hemingway stories. Although they enjoyed discussing all assigned texts—including "Hills Like White Elephants," "Cat in the Rain," and "Indian Camp"—five stories most captured their attention: "Soldier's Home," "Now I Lay Me," "A Way You'll Never Be," "In Another Country," and "Big Two-Hearted River." Before introducing any of the individual stories, I read the cadets excerpts of Anders Österling's Presentation Speech awarding the 1954 Nobel Prize in Literature to Hemingway. I focused particularly on the closing lines of the speech, which celebrate Hemingway as an author who, "honestly and undauntedly, reproduces genuine features in the hard countenance of the age."[2] After clarifying what *countenance* meant, I explained to the students that in their readings of the stories I wanted them to locate these features and, using those depictions, to draw conclusions about what image of the time period they projected. It was with this charge that the students began discussing Hemingway's veterans.

I began our discussion of "Soldier's Home" by asking the students talk about the title; in the discussion questions they posted to the online conference before class, some of them noted the title's irony. In class, they elaborated on the alienation and discomfort Krebs experiences despite being "home" and removed from the war front. One student suggested that the title itself was ambiguous—that it could represent either the soldier's actual home or the fact that the soldier is home. In considering both possibilities, I asked the cadets to identify places in the text that suggest that war affected Krebs's sense of or relation to home. They pointed to many things: his relationship with his family members, the need to lie to his mother, his fixation on patterns rather than individuals. Some of the cadets likened Krebs's experience to that of friends or family members who returned from war; his disconnect was relatable in rich, explorable ways. One student, who has an Army contract, answered the exam question "What realities of war do Hemingway's stories lay bare?" by elaborating on the story's ironies, noting that "the soldier doesn't find comfort in his house, or in his own skin" and explaining that his "mental alteration" manifests itself in "his inability to love." Hemingway "creates a bleak hole" in this character, she concluded.

This characterization of emptiness carried over to our discussion of "In Another Country." In our discussion, I asked the students to examine the various types of loss depicted in the story; they focused not only on the major's loss of his wife, but also on war itself and the feelings—innocence, security, identity, wholeness—that might be compromised by wartime experience. I directed them toward the opening paragraph of the story and explained that it was important for highlighting the patients' emotional states. The images of the animals' bodies hanging from the shop windows emphasized the disconnectedness between mind and body that some of the students attributed to being wounded—mentally or physically—while in battle. They said that they understood why the major sat looking out of the window, the emptiness and loneliness he felt. Similarly, it was clear to them why Nick had such trouble sleeping in "Now I Lay Me." After one of the cadets read aloud the opening paragraphs of the story, the class as a whole speculated about what actually had happened to Nick. Ultimately, they decided that knowing exactly what happened was not as important to the story as examining his coping mechanisms; he had "invisible wounds" that could be charted only in his "inner world." They identified Nick's practices for self-treatment, explaining that when others don't understand what is going on in your head, you come up with strategies to compensate, and contending that Nick's responses seemed perfectly rational to them. They applied the same explanation to Nick in "Big Two-Hearted River": fishing was a form of therapy for him, and he removed himself from everyday society to make things seem simpler.

To encourage students to consider how Hemingway's style contributes to his unique depictions of veterans, I asked them in an exam question to describe how Hemingway presented the realities of war to the reader. One student responded,

> Hemingway is not sentimental in his writing. Most of the effect of his writing is through implication, whereby the reader is able to intuit the meaning. For example, in "Big Two-Hearted River" he never even mentions Hop['s] going to war and dying. The effects on Nick are so subtle, such as his not wanting to go into the swamp. Yet the realities, though never spoken directly, are implicitly transferred to the reader. Nick is using fishing as a means of catharsis because the reality of war has impacted his everyday life.

In answering the exam question, students also explored implied realities for other veteran characters in the short stories, drawing conclusions about how their wartime experience affected their emotional states. For "A Way You'll Never Be," one student discussed Nick's figurative references to the war after being "certified as nutty": "In 'A Way You'll Never Be,' Nick's rant about the grasshoppers [CSS 310] is reminiscent of the abuse that soldiers endure. This metaphor displays the reality of war, that men are ripped apart like animals."

This response reflected our earlier class discussion, in which the cadets proved to be particularly interested in the connection Nick makes between the grasshoppers and the American uniform. The cadets paid more attention than other students might to the mention of uniforms because, at the Citadel, they must wear military-style uniforms. Thus they wanted to consider what Nick meant in the story when he said, "I am demonstrating the American uniform" (CSS 312). The cadets discussed Nick's wearing of the uniform in the context of the new role he has assumed since he has been singled out as damaged. It was clear to the cadets that he had experienced great trauma in his service, but it was less clear what role he would really play now that he was "supposed to move around and let [the Italian troops] see the uniform," the "one American uniform that is supposed to make them believe others are coming" (308). Although at end of the story Nick worries about losing his way, the cadets surmised that he might already be lost.

Given the military environment of the Citadel, it was not surprising that the cadets' engagement with Hemingway focused on his short stories about wartime experience. What did come as a surprise was their approach to the work of Hemingway's contemporaries: they examined other modernist characters through the same lens they had applied to Hemingway's veterans. Although we had read *The Great Gatsby* before Hemingway's stories, at the beginning of the semester, the students wanted to revisit *Gatsby* after we finished discussing the Hemingway stories to reassess Gatsby's character and behaviors in light of those of Hemingway's veterans. After first focusing the discussion on the role of the uniform in Gatsby's story, I initated a deeper examination of his character in relation to his military experience by asking the students to recall the importance of the military uniform for Gatsby's meeting with Daisy.

During our original discussion of *The Great Gatsby*, I had drawn attention to the uniform as part of a larger examination of Fitzgerald's use of clothing in presentations of both individual and national identity. While facilitating these discussions, I tried to emphasize the importance of the symbolism of clothing to Fitzgerald's oeuvre by highlighting the importance of clothing in his lesser-known works. To relate his depictions of clothing to national identity, for instance, I pointed to his retrospective "Echoes of the Jazz Age" (1931), in which Fitzgerald claims that this period represents a turning point in U.S. history because it marks the passage of "the style of man" to America. I explained that America's new supremacy in setting of "the style of man," while seemingly "subtle" and superficial, signifies a much more meaningful transfer of global power from Great Britain to the United States: gentlemen's clothes represented "the power that man must hold that passes from race to race" (Fitzgerald, *Crack-Up* 15). I went on to share Fitzgerald's assertions that after the Great War he was part of "the most powerful nation" and that we Americans now had the prerogative to decide "what was fashionable and what was fun" (15). Noting Fitzgerald's irony, we discussed how his fellow Americans sought clothing produced by Bond Street tailors and pondered why they continued to fashion themselves—in terms not only of garments but also, more broadly, of identity—after British models. Although Fitzgerald's satire operates on multiple levels, I suggested to the students that his focus rests at least in part on American postures of class and authority that rely on materialism at the expense of substance. Critiques of this type, I explained, appear throughout Fitzgerald's work and are often symbolized by gentlemen's clothing.

In addition to discussing how clothing represented national identity in the novel, we explored how Fitzgerald staged individual characters' attempts at upward mobility in the novel through costuming—through both uniformity and ostentatious dress. This discussion prefigured nicely our examination of Nick's uniform and his ambivalent feeling about it in Hemingway's "A Way You'll Never Be." When introducing students to the characters' costuming, I explained that literary critics have traditionally focused on Gatsby's colorful shirts and pink rag of a suit or on Myrtle's various costumes as clothing worn in hopes of projecting social advancement. However, cadets at the Citadel were fascinated that it is "the invisible cloak of his uniform" that allows Gatsby, "a penniless young man without a past," access to Daisy's house when he is on leave from Camp Taylor (Fitzgerald, *Gatsby* 116). In class I posed the topic of the "invisible cloak" for discussion, asking the students why it mattered that Gatsby was "invisible"—a point we addressed from the perspective of race later in the semester in the context of Faulkner's *Light in August* and Ellison's *Invisible Man*. In considering Gatsby's invisibility, the cadets raised a valid point—that he was not really invisible, that he couldn't be invisible because he was clearly identified as an army officer. As the students clarified in class discussion, the uniform veiled his class status. This point led the students to related issues—what Gatsby's status was, what the uniform hid, and what Gatsby gained by wearing the uniform.

After covering the Hemingway stories, the students wanted to reconsider the uniform in *The Great Gatsby* and what it meant to James Gatz's self-created identity. When prompted to discuss the importance of clothing and self-fashioning, one of the students wrote that Gatsby "believes that successful gestures, combined with fashionable clothing, will assist in changing his character. As a result he orders colorful shirts direct from England in order to impress Daisy. However the narrator, Nick, and the audience understand that this status symbol is . . . a clear sign of the excess that typically characterizes new members of the upper class." The same student goes on to discuss the uniform in particular: "Just out of the War, Jay employs the aid of disguise by way of the military uniform, which allows him to appear both successful and as a member of the elite." What I found most interesting about this student's response was his suggestion that although Gatsby is no longer actually wearing the uniform, he is relying on his veteran status as a "disguise" that will win him entrée into social circles from which he would otherwise have been excluded.

To further explore how the uniform obscured class status, I directed my students to the work of Keith Gandal, who has addressed similar issues in the World War One fiction of Fitzgerald, Hemingway, and Faulkner. Students discussed the ideas in his essay "*The Great Gatsby* as Mobilization Fiction: Rethinking Modernist Prose," in which Gandal claims that Fitzgerald himself was "intensely interested" in the selection of U.S. Army officers during war. What was so interesting about this selection, Gandal explains, is that war created an opportunity for a wider range of Americans—including "ethnic Americans"—to move "from obscurity to wealth on a wartime rise 'through the ranks' in military training camps and on the front" (133). According to Gandal, readers can sense Fitzgerald's preoccupation with this new meritocracy for U.S. Army officer recruits because Nick focuses on Gatsby's military record and "pieces together the truth over the course of the novel—sometimes in minute detail" (134). Like Nick, my cadets were invested in sorting through Gatsby's military record; our discussions of military service in the Hemingway stories piqued their interest in noting where Gatsby served and what accolades he received for his service. Although only one-third of Citadel cadets go on to serve in the U.S. military, all students at the Citadel are required to take military science, military history, and leadership classes that give them a deeper knowledge than most college students acquire of the interworkings of the armed forces. Consequently, the cadets focused on passages that related to Gatsby's service record.

In one such passage that was of great interest to my students, Gatsby describes his wartime experience while attempting to convince Nick of his privileged life. I read it aloud in class:

> Then came the war, old sport. It was a great relief and I tried very hard to die but I seemed to bear an enchanted life. I accepted a commission as a first lieutenant when it began. In the Argonne Forest I took two machine-gun detachments so far forward that there was a half mile gap on either side of us where the infantry couldn't advance. We stayed there two days and two nights, a hundred and thirty men with sixteen Lewis guns, and when the infantry came up at last they found the insignia of three German divisions among the piles of dead. I was promoted to be a major, and every Allied government gave me a decoration—even Montenegro, little Montenegro down on the Adriatic Sea! (Fitzgerald, *Gatsby* 53)

The students found a lot to discuss in this passage. For starters, why was Gatsby trying so hard to die on the front if he was living such an "enchanted life"? Why does he describe this enchantment as a burden by claiming that he "seemed to bear" it? Was he really as brave as he says he was? Did he really receive medals? Gatsby does have the medal inscribed "*Major Jay Gatsby . . . For Valour Extraordinary*" (53), but does that validate and verify his story? Although the students tended to admire some of Gatsby's qualities, they found much in this passage to undermine his credibility, as does Gandal, who notes that, according to Nick, Gatsby was not promoted to major because of his bravery in battle, but was in fact a Captain before ever reaching the front (Gandal 134). The cadets wondered if Gatsby's souvenirs—for example, the medal and the photograph—functioned, as one student wrote, as "place holders" that helped him not only fashion his identity but also fill an emotional void. Readers have traditionally assumed that this void resulted from the absence of Daisy in Gatsby's life, but my students began to question if the war—because of what he did or did not do—had scarred him psychologically. Might Nick have misread Gatsby's "romantic readiness"? (Fitzgerald, *Gatsby* 16). What little we actually know about Gatsby's inner world forms what one student called "open puzzle pieces" that we must consider when interpreting his character.

Gatsby's reason for bending the truth, for showing Nick his souvenirs, is that he does not want Nick to think he "was just some nobody" (54). In looking back over the entire novel, the cadets concluded that it was not his suspect business with Meyer Wolfsheim or Dan Cody that allowed Gatsby to become someone important but instead his military service. It was through the military, after all, that he had been able to escape the small town in North Dakota where he had lived his former life as James Gatz—a life he desperately hoped to improve with his Ben Franklin-like schedule and his list of General Resolves (135). It was the Army that took him from North Dakota to Camp Taylor, mere miles away from Louisville and the house of Daisy Fay (116). His army career distinguished him from those whom Jordan harshly describes as the "flat-footed, short-sighted young men . . . who couldn't get into the army at all" (60). And it was his status as an officer that granted Gatsby access to Daisy's beautiful house. As the students pointed out, one of Gatsby's great tragedies is that he failed to realize that his uniform was not an invisible cloak but a signifier of his commitment to serve his country. It was this commitment to service that granted him character, that made him, as Wolfsheim ironically states, "the kind of man you'd like to take home and introduce to your mother and sister" (57). By making these claims about Gatsby's military service, the cadets wanted to comment on Gatsby's ultimate tragedy. They, like many critics, related his downfall to an absurd pursuit of things, but they also emphasized that his view of his service was equally tragic: he began to see his service—and the opportunities it opened up for him—as a means of winning Daisy rather than as a way to serve others while bettering himself. Gatsby strayed too far, they insisted, from his childhood resolve to be the best he could be.

Based on our class discussions, I would say that one reason the students were drawn to revisiting *The Great Gatsby* was that the passage about the uniform raised questions about Gatsby's character and, more broadly, about the way in which we view those who have served in the military. As Citadel cadets well know, a military uniform not only denotes uniformity but also represents rank within the organization and indicates whether the serviceperson is an enlisted soldier or an officer. The Army has its own hierarchy and status, but one that is based on seniority and meritocracy rather than on birth, wealth, or other markers important to social class. By comparing the status significance of the army officer's uniform to that of other items of dress in the novel, my students have enriched my own reading of the novel, showing me even more nuance and meaning in the novel's symbolism of the uniform.

Looking back on the semester, it is clear to me that Hemingway's stories influenced the ways my students ultimately read *The Great Gatsby;* they were well aware that both Hemingway and Fitzgerald had some military affiliation, a frustrated desire to serve in the war (which they respected), and the impetus to convey war experiences in their writing. In addition to rereading *The Great Gatsby* with greater attention to uniforms and military connections related to the war, the students were more invested in exploring the Gatsby's inner world and considering how he negotiated his identity before and after the war than they might otherwise have been: Might Gatsby's attachment to objects, for example, bear some relation to Krebs's attachment to patterns? They speculated about how the realities of World War I translated to the narratives we read, acknowledging the importance of gaps in the narration and the degree to which Gatsby and the other characters defy easy classification. Thus they developed their own understandings of the ways ambiguity, fragmentation, irony, and dehumanization shaped modernist identities, in part because of the connections they drew between Hemingway's veterans and other characters. As a primer for other modernist works, Hemingway's stories inspired my students to become more attuned to characters' inner worlds while complicating their readings of outer markers of difference, giving them a better understanding of the modernisms of the time.

Notes

1. I have taken all student quotations from the work of participants of my twentieth-century American fiction courses at the Citadel, Charleston, South Carolina.
2. For the full text of this speech, see the Nobel Prize website: Anders Österling, "Award Ceremony Speech," 10 Dec. 1954, Nobelprize.org, web, 25 Apr. 2013, <http://nobelprize.org/nobel_prizes/literature/laureates/1954/press.html>.

Teaching Hemingway's Modernism in Cultural Context

Helping Students Connect His Time to Ours

Sharon Hamilton

When I design my classroom activities, I keep in mind that Hemingway began to publish his fiction almost a hundred years ago. I know from experience that my students tend to look at me blankly when I mention, for instance, the Berlin Wall; since even relatively recent history is a mystery to them, I am aware that I must begin with the assumption that they will need help to understand, and step into, the world of the Jazz Age. For them, this is a foreign country. I approach my teaching, therefore, with the conviction that if they better understand Hemingway's cultural contexts they will also better understand the innovations in technique and subject matter of his modernist art. I believe students will more profoundly connect with a literary work if its contents become—literally—tangible for them. In practice, this has produced a classroom session during which two students (with the help of YouTube) taught the class how to dance the Charleston; another in which a trio of students (including an excellent saxophonist) performed live jazz; and a third encompassing a virtual escape to France for a student-led walking tour (thanks to Google Street Views) of Hemingway's Paris.

Recent criticism has stressed a pedagogical approach known as "transformative learning," a theory that emphasizes moments of personal connection between the student and the material, resulting in "aha" moments. When students actively, even physically, connect with the literary material they are studying, they are likely to experience such moments; I know, because I ask them (see Appendix Q: Self-Guided Field Trips and Reading Self-Assessment).

The transformative learning exercises for teaching Hemingway that appear in this chapter make use of the short-story collection *In Our Time*. I suggest using short stories because they provide the maximum flexibility for teachers designing courses for a variety of different curricular requirements. I discuss here strategies both for teaching Hemingway's modernism using *In Our Time* as a whole *and* for achieving the same pedagogical goals, with less time to spend on Hemingway, by using selected stories. I provide examples of how Hemingway's modernism can be taught in cultural context in ways that are transformative for students because they are concrete, accessible, and memorable.

When I teach any modernist fiction, I always begin by finding a way to help my students connect to the cultural context of the Jazz Age, and I have found that the best way to do so is through student–delivered cultural reports. In a small class, cultural reports can be delivered by individual students; in a larger class, by groups of two to four. I have had good results with both formats. Cultural reports are designed to take no more than ten minutes of class time; they can be combined with other classroom activities throughout the term, or you can have a cultural reports blitz, in which all the cultural reports are presented during a single week. As illustrated in the sample cultural report assignment in the appendixes, I require students to research for presentation something from either World War I or the 1920s (see Appendix O: Cultural Report Assignment).

Typically, sports, gangsters, and fashion are popular topics. One good technique for minimizing overlap is to ask students to report to you via e-mail once they have chosen their subjects. I then encourage any students whose topics overlap to communicate with one another and to present different aspects of the same topic. Students wishing to present sports, for example could concentrate on boxing or baseball; those interested in fashion could pick such subtopics as flappers in film, trends in fashion advertising (including the makeup industry—e.g., Max Factor), or the biographies of major designers, like Coco Chanel. The main point of the exercise is that students should pick subjects that engage them, so they feel a strong connection with the historical material.

After the reports are given, to help students connect the 1920s to today, I ask them what things about the Jazz Age particularly interested them. What has changed since that era? What things seem similar today? They will make excellent connections. Students who have lived through the mortgage crisis will have no problem seeing its similarities with the Wall Street crash of 1929; discussions about Prohibition will inevitably lead to current debates about the war on drugs; and organized crime is still very much with us.

Once your students have been exposed to topics from World War I and the 1920s in this way, they are ready to discuss the era's fiction—and to connect it to their own time. If I have a week or two to devote to Hemingway, I teach all of *In Our Time*. Once students have seen the cultural reports, they are better attuned to Hemingway's modernist themes and are likely to point out, for example, in a discussion of "Soldier's Home," that Krebs's sister plays indoor baseball, that his father owns a car (at a time when car ownership was becoming much more common), and that the women in his home town now seem more complicated. They will also be aware that something seems wrong with Krebs and may raise the idea of possible war-related trauma. The cultural reports also provide students with a way to start thinking about what they would like to investigate for their research papers. (See Appendix P: Make It Swing! Interdisciplinary Research Paper, for a sample research assignment that asks students to analyze period fiction, including Hemingway's, in cultural context.)

To help students better connect with Hemingway's place and time, I also try to incorporate field trips into my classes, both actual and virtual. At the beginning of the semester, I give my students an assignment that requires them to each conduct two self-guided field trips. (See Appendix Q: Self-Guided Field Trips and Reading Self-Assessment.) In addition, I use videos and online resources in the classroom to take students on virtual field trips to the places that influenced Hemingway's modernist writings. I might inspire students to take a virtual walking tour of Hemingway's Paris, for example, by directing them to Riana Lagarde's "Hemingway's Steps Through Paris," an online resource giving directions for an actual walking tour that draws on addresses from *A Moveable Feast*.[1] Ask your students to use those addresses to virtually re-create a walking tour of Hemingway's Paris (using Google Maps and Google Street Views). Alternately, *Ernest Hemingway: A Life in Michigan*, a DVD,[2] provides a virtual field trip to the Michigan Hemingway recalls so vividly in such stories from *In Our Time* as "The End of Something," "The Three-Day Blow," and "Indian Camp," and in his descriptions of writing these stories in *A Moveable Feast*.[3] Cultural reports and field trips broadly familiarize students with the cultural context for Hemingway's modernism.[4] In what follows, I suggest ways for students to explore in greater depth two major themes of Hemingway's modernism: the sexual revolution of the 1920s and the aftermath of World War I.

With respect to the women's suffrage movement, which came so dramatically to a head with the ratification of the nineteenth amendment to the Constitution in 1920, a good primer for students is Ken Burns's *Not For Ourselves Alone: The*

Story of Elizabeth Cady Stanton and Susan B. Anthony.[5] This documentary provides students with information on the history of female suffrage in America. Watching it will help students better appreciate the shift in gender roles in the 1920s, personified by all those independent, bob-haired women in Hemingway's fiction. This background helps students discuss, with more historical awareness, details in stories like "Cat in the Rain," in which at least some of the relationship tensions clearly relate to new cultural options and expectations for men and women. In teaching students about the first American sexual revolution, I have also found it effective to compare Hemingway's modern female characters with those of his contemporaries, such as the heroines in F. Scott Fitzgerald's "Benediction" (1920) and Willa Cather's "Coming, Aphrodite!" (1920). Fitzgerald's short story concerns a young woman having an affair with a married man; the story uses the phrase "birth control," which is remarkable for the time. When I teach this story, I ask my students what the story means by "birth control"; they rarely know, and I have to explain that this meant condoms. That detail alone engenders interesting discussion. Cather's equally bold story concerns a young career woman and her sexual relationship with an artist.

Teaching the Fitzgerald and Cather stories together with Hemingway's "Up in Michigan" (1923) leads to rich discussions of censorship and period boundaries concerning depictions of sex. Hemingway had problems finding an American publisher for "Up in Michigan," while Fitzgerald had to turn to *The Smart Set*, a low-paying but permissive mass-market magazine, for publication of "Benediction."[6] As originally written, Cather's "Coming, Aphrodite!" contains a voyeurism scene in which the heroine dances in the nude while her neighbor watches her through a knothole; some critics have read masturbation into this scene.[7] Although, like Fitzgerald's "Benediction," it also initially appeared in the *Smart Set* (as "Coming, Edith Bower!"), the magazine censored it for publication, clothing the protagonist and making other changes; it appeared later in the year, as originally written, in a collection of Cather's stories. Thanks to the Willa Cather Archive, it is possible for students to compare the censored and uncensored versions of this story.[8] For students studying these stories within the cultural context of American censorship law, I recommend selected readings from Edward De Grazia's *Girls Lean Back Everywhere* and Nicola Kay Beisel's *Imperiled Innocents*. With specific consideration of "Up in Michigan," Nancy R. Comley and Robert Scholes's "Reading 'Up in Michigan'" is an excellent teaching tool, particularly as it opens up classroom debate by allowing students to examine the story's original manuscript ending (in which Hemingway's depiction of events the next morning suggests the date sex of the night before was consensual), making interpretations of the story's sexual relationships much more ambiguous.

In response to such gender-centric themes, many Hemingway critics have noted how attentively and sympathetically Hemingway describes women in labor throughout his fiction. Students are interested in speculating why so many women in labor appear in the stories. Of course, it makes sense either to raise, or to let your students discover through their own research, that Hemingway's father was an obstetrician. Such background information can inform general discussions about how Hemingway portrays women in labor and why this was such a common thematic choice for him. When reading all of *In Our Time*, students can link these discussions to the work's general depictions of trauma and suffering. A specific exercise that can be used to explore Hemingway's artistic choices in his depictions of women in labor involves comparing different versions of chapter 2 from *In Our Time*. Students can compare the story as published in 1925 with Hemingway's original news report of the incident, "A Silent, Ghastly Procession" (46), and with Milton Cohen's article "'There Was a Woman Having a Kid,'" in which he reveals that in the original manuscript Hemingway adopted the woman's point of view (105-8).[9] All three readings are short enough that students can perform these comparative readings and discuss them in groups during class time. Another exercise that can be illuminating is asking students to pick a news story about which to write their own one-page fictionalization. Afterward, the class can discuss the perspective each student chose and why, and what details each decided to include and omit.

Moving from Hemingway's depictions of modern women to his interest in the theme of modern warfare, I begin by having students compare fictional accounts of American soldiers coming home from World War I. I introduce Hemingway's "Soldier's Home" and "Big Two-Hearted River" together with Fitzgerald's "May Day" (1922).[10] Fitzgerald's story is based on a real event: the 1919 May Day riots in New York, in which socialists attacked returning soldiers. Have the students try to find this news item using the *New York Times* webpage; I give them the key word *soldiers* and the date of the event (1 May 1919), and let them figure out for themselves that any reporting on the riots would not have appeared until the next day, one way of getting them to do primary research.[11] In reading the short stories, I ask them to look at each for evidence of trauma and to note the stylistic choices Hemingway and Fitzgerald make to artistically represent the sense of dislocation experienced by soldiers returning home—in Fitzgerald's case through the experimental nature of the story's narrative form (students like comparing the multistrand narrative to the contemporary movie

Crash [dir. Paul Haggis, 2004]), and in Hemingway's, through his strategic uses of omission and repetition to indicate psychological stress.

Hemingway's exploration of the theme of modern warfare (including the incredible toll it takes on civilians) can also be explored in cultural context through having students read and discuss "On the Quai at Smyrna" from *In Our Time* as compared with accounts of the actual events (uncovered by searching online or in a historical newspaper database for "Smyrna" and "1922"). Students can also read Hemingway's dispatches for the *Toronto Star* on the massacre in *By-Line Ernest Hemingway,* and I recommend assigning Matthew Stewart's superb "It Was All a Pleasant Business: The Historical Context of 'On the Quai at Smyrna'" for critical context. Some questions I pose are:

- Is it appropriate to write fiction about this kind of real historical event?
- In writing about such events, what sorts of things can fiction accomplish that nonfiction cannot?
- What are the advantages and disadvantages of each genre in trying to help people connect to the reality of an exceptional human tragedy?

Discussion also can explore students' reactions to the story as compared with their reactions to events currently in the news: for example, refugees fleeing from Syria. An important note for instructors who are teaching all of *In Our Time* is that Hemingway wrote "On the Quai at Smyrna" as an author's introduction to the 1930 edition. If you are using an edition that includes this story, it is a good exercise to ask students whether they think it is an appropriate introduction and why.

With respect to Hemingway's depictions of modern war, another activity I have found effective is to explore the different possible meanings of the phrase "in our time." Why this title? In what ways can we interpret it? I have students give their theories on the significance of this title, and why it matters, before moving to the next part of the exercise, in which they discover where it came from. I give them a photocopy of a page from "The Order for Evening Prayer" liturgy of the Anglican *Book of Common Prayer* (1662). After the Lord's Prayer comes a twelve-line communal prayer, beginning with the line, "O Lord, shew thy mercy upon us" and ending with "And take not thy Holy Spirit from us." I read aloud the part of the priest and ask the students to answer together where the text says "answer." They are usually surprised to hear me saying, "Give peace in our time, O Lord."[12] If your students are studying all of *In Our Time*, you can ask them how this knowledge—that the title comes from a prayer for peace—changes their understanding of Hemingway's thematic connections between the stories. How does Hemingway show us the opposites of peace? In what ways does his interest in the nature of peace and war (which is not always war between nations) make a book about his time more relevant to our time? Such thematic explorations of Hemingway's depictions of modern warfare can be augmented by field trips to a local war museum, a local American Legion hall, or a historical society with photographs from World War I on display; or by an arranged talk by a visiting veteran. Virtual field trips can also be illuminating; a good option is to take a virtual tour at the website of Vienna's Museum of Military History, allowing students to see the car in which Archduke Franz Ferdinand was assassinated and the Austrian weapons Hemingway saw used.[13]

Just as it is possible to apply the interactive principles of transformative learning to teach Hemingway's modernist themes in cultural context, similar approaches can be used to help students better understand his key modernist literary techniques: especially his experimental uses of repetition, omission, and composition. To explore the modernist techniques that Hemingway used to push the boundaries between prose and poetry, I ask students to compare selected passages from Gertrude Stein's poetry or prose (either one works) and Hemingway's writing, noting echoes in uses of rhythm and repetition. For this exercise, I especially like to use the passage in "Soldier's Home" beginning, "when he was in town their appeal to him was not very strong" and ending "it wasn't worth it" (*IOT* 92). Another good passage for teaching Hemingway's Steinian uses of rhythm and repetition is the passage on eating oysters in chapter 1 of *A Moveable* Feast that begins, "As I ate the oysters with their strong taste of the sea" and ends "to make plans" (6). When examining these repetition-filled passages, I ask students to consider:

- Which specific words repeat, and how many times?
- What sound patterns repeat?
- Why do you think Hemingway repeats those sounds?
- What emotional effects does this passage create when read aloud, and why?

For a fun way to connect Hemingway's and Stein's modernist uses of repetition to present-day artistic expression (in this case a cult TV show), have your students read Erin McNellis's blog "Mostly Everyone Loves Some One's Repeating: Gertrude Stein and *Lost*."[14]

To place Hemingway's genre-bending experiments with language within the cultural context of the history of ideas, I recommend assigning one or more of the following: Martha Harris's 1895 *PMLA* essay, "A Study of the Nature of Rhythm"; Fred Newton Scott's 1904 *PMLA* essay, "The Most Fundamental Differentia of Poetry and Prose"; or Scott's 1905 *PMLA* essay, "The Scansion of Prose Rhythm."[15] These papers were typical of the period academic work on the intersections between science and literature that were resulting, by the turn of the century, in radical new conclusions about the essential flexibility of literary forms. Harris argued, for example, that there is no essential difference between poetry and prose, since "impassioned prose," like poetry, relies on rhythm (xxiv). Reading such articles emphasizes for students that Hemingway lived and wrote in an exciting intellectual environment, in which four-hundred-year-old boundaries between poetry and prose were being widely challenged, and shows that such experimental blurrings between genres were being taught to writers of Hemingway's generation, both in American academies and by other writers, such as Stein.

Exploring the work of influential literary critic H. L. Mencken can be useful in providing a cultural context when teaching Hemingway's modernist technique of radical omission; students can read contemporary reviews by Mencken about new techniques for achieving psychological realism in prose, especially his reviews of Joseph Conrad and Sherwood Anderson—both, as we know, strong influences on Hemingway's experiments with representing human psychology by saying less, rather than more.[16] In the context of Mencken's reviews of Conrad and Anderson (which Hemingway read), students can also compare Hemingway's prose directly to that of Conrad and Anderson. The *In Our Time* story easiest to compare with Anderson's work (because it is so obviously imitative) is "My Old Man," but any Anderson story works for discussion; I am particularly fond of "I Want to Know Why." Conrad's preface to *The Nigger of the "Narcissus"* is another useful reading in discussing models for Hemingway's technical innovations, and it can also be effective to assign Hemingway's beautiful tribute to Conrad on his death. Owing to its underlying theme of trauma and its extensive use of omission, the best Hemingway story in his *In Our Time* collection to compare with Conrad's *Heart of Darkness* is "Big Two-Hearted River." Even though the writing styles of the two authors are very different, students will note that in each case we are left to figure out from hints in the text what things may have happened in the past to cause the psychological traumas of the present.

Another way students can explore the cultural context in which Hemingway learned radical new prose techniques is to pay a virtual visit to a Chicago magazine stand of the 1920s (through babel.hathitrust.org), where they can read the copies of the *Smart Set*, in which H. L. Mencken's criticism appeared. Hemingway read this magazine's new issues and, I believe also, Anderson's back issues on Conrad when he was in Chicago in 1920–21.[17] Students can flip the pages of this magazine—the era's equivalent to the *New Yorker*—to explore what Hemingway learned to do, and what *not* to do, by reading contemporary writers in such magazines. An issue of particular interest is that of July 1921, which contained Anderson's story "Unlighted Lamps,"[18] at a time when Hemingway knew Anderson personally. Students can also look through these magazines for interesting covers and advertisements. The cover for the March 1922 issue, for example, shows the head and shoulders of a heavily made-up flapper, who may or may not be wearing any clothing and who is smoking (followed, on the next page, by an advertisement for the radical little magazine *The Dial*);[19] and the issue for December 1922, contains an advertisement for "Woman and the New Race" by the birth control rights activist Margaret Sanger.[20] Just by looking through such magazines, your students will acquire a much better idea of the cultural context out of which Hemingway's modernism emerged—both its subjects and its forms.

Finally, in terms of teaching Hemingway's modernist techniques, the best exercise I have found for helping students appreciate how carefully Hemingway structured his stories (with a cubist's attention to composition)[21] is a variation I developed based on an activity in McRae and Vethamani's *Now Read On* (14). For this exercise, get an electronic copy of the interchapter to chapter 5 of *In Our Time* ("They shot the six cabinet ministers") and enlarge it. Separate the vignette into individual sentences, and place a random number, between 1 and 11, by each of the sentences; make enough copies of the story for your class to analyze in small groups of two to four, and cut each story up into individual sentences. I give a complete cut-up story in an envelope to each group and ask the students to reconstruct it without consulting the text. (This exercise works even if they have previously read the story.) Ask each group to list, by number, the order in which they think the sentences originally appeared. Only after each group has given their guess should you tell them the correct order. Then you can ask them, why does Hemingway order his sentences as he does? If there is time, also ask them to identify sentence parts: the adjectives, nouns, and verbs. What does Hemingway rely on most? What least? Why? What emotional effect does he create by highlighting so few adjectives? What are they? This method of close analysis works precisely because the story is, basically, a prose poem. It is also an excellent story for underscoring the modernist technique of omission: What do we know? What do we have to guess?

• • •

When I was teaching at Georgetown University in Washington, D.C., I had the privilege of taking my students to see a painting Hemingway had owned: Joan Miró's 1922 painting "The Farm" (it can be visited virtually as well).[22] While looking at it, we talked about Miró's declaration that it took him "nine months of painting every day and wiping it out and making studies and destroying them all" (Miró 1). He spent, he said, "hours and hours making the ant come alive" (Miró 1). The exercises I have proposed here to help students explore Hemingway's modernist fiction within its cultural context—both his modernist themes (including the realities of modern warfare and shifting sexual relations) and his modernist forms (including his experimental uses of rhythm, omission, and composition)—work, precisely because when students see something concrete in front of them, they become more open to transformative educational experiences. Suddenly, somewhat abstract concepts (such as modernist artistic techniques) become as real, and as accessible, as Miró's tiny ant.

Notes

1. See Riana Lagarde, "Hemingway's Steps Through Paris," Slow Travel France. Web. 18 Jan. 2013. <http://www.slowtrav.com/france/paris/rl_hemingway.htm>.

2. The Clarke Historical Library has a number of suggestions for how to use this DVD in the classroom. See "Teachers Guides," Clarke Historical Library, Central Michigan University, web, 18 Jan. 2013, <http://clarke.cmich.edu/hemingway_tab/teachers_guides/teachers_guides_index.html>.

3. See, especially, Hemingway's description of the composition of "Big Two-Hearted River" in *A Moveable Feast* (1964; rpt., New York: Scribner, 2003), 76.

4. For more ideas on how to design virtual field trips of Hemingway's America, the National Archives offers a fabulous collection of primary source teaching materials and suggestions for classroom exercises on their website, "The Emergence of Modern America (1890-1930)" (National Archives, web, 18 Jan. 2013, <http://www.archives.gov/education/lessons/modern-america.html>).

5. Since this documentary is relatively long, I suggest showing just the first hour, which provides enough coverage of key events and issues, including the women's rights convention of 1848 at Seneca Falls. PBS also offers lesson plan ideas. See "Resources [*Not for Ourselves Alone*]," PBS WETA, web, 19 Jan. 2013, <http://www.pbs.org/stantonanthony/resources/index.html>.

6. For Fitzgerald's publishing relationship with *The Smart Set* and its willingness to publish fiction that pushed the boundaries of American censorship law, see Sharon Hamilton, "Mencken and Nathan's *Smart Set* and the Story behind Fitzgerald's Early Success," *The F. Scott Fitzgerald Review* 4 (2005): 20-48.

7. See, for example, Mary R. Ryder, "'Looking for Love in All the Wrong Places': Voyeurism in Cather's 1920s Fiction," *Willa Cather Newsletter and Review* 49 (2005): 4.

8. The Willa Cather Archive is a website designed as an online resource for Cather scholars, created through a collaboration among four groups at the University of Nebraska-Lincoln. See Willa Cather, "Coming, Eden Bower!" *The Smart Set,* August 1920, 3–25, and Cather, "Coming, Aphrodite!" in *Youth and the Bright Medusa* (New York: Alfred A. Knopf, 1920), 11–78, both in The Willa Cather Archive, web, 19 Jan. 2013, <http://cather.unl.edu/index.wcse.html>.

9. For other assigned reading options, see especially Lawrence R. Broer and Gloria Holland, eds., *Hemingway and Women: Female Critics and the Female Voice* (Tuscaloosa: U of Alabama P, 2004).

10. If you are teaching this material from a publishing history perspective, see Sharon Hamilton, "Mencken and Nathan's *Smart Set* and the Story behind Fitzgerald's Early Success," *The F. Scott Fitzgerald Review* 4 (2005): 20–48, for information on the original magazine publication of "May Day" in *The Smart Set.*

11. See "Soldiers and Sailors Break Up Meetings," *New York Times* 2 May 1919, NYTimes.com, web, 19 Jan. 2013, <http://query.nytimes.com/mem/archive-free/pdf?res=9E03E1DB1E3BEE3ABC4A53DFB3668382609EDE>.

12. See "The Order for Evening Prayer," in *The Book of Common Prayer* (1662; Oxford: Oxford UP, n.d.), 61; the text is available online at The Church of England website, <http://www.churchofengland.org/prayer-worship/worship/book-of-common-prayer/the-order-for-evening-prayer.aspx>. In case your students wonder, Hemingway was raised in a Congregationalist church which would not have used *The Book of Common Prayer;* he probably heard these readings at home from his Anglican grandfather.

13. See the website of the Heeresgeschichtliches Museum [Museum of Military History], <http://www.hgm.at/de/museum/360-virtuelle-tour.html>. The default language of the website's homepage is German; click on the pointer labeled "EN"at the top of the page to get the English version. There are two rooms that are particularly relevant to teachers of Hemingway: "Franz Joseph, Sarajewo" [Sarajevo] and "Weltkreig" [World War I]. In the virtual tour, the rooms are labeled in German only. Before the students virtually tour these rooms, it is useful to have them read the explanatory text for each room, which is the same text they would be reading were they to actually visit the museum. Find these by going to the museum home page, hovering over the tab "Exhibitions," and then clicking the link "Exhibition Sheets." Select "Exhibition Sheets English" and then click on the links for "Franz Joseph" and "First World War," which give the text for the Exhibitions "Franz Joseph Hall," "Sarajevo," and "World War I."

14. See Erin McNellis, "Mostly Everyone Loves Some One's Repeating: Gertrude Stein and *Lost,*" 25 May 2010, Uncomplicatedly (blog), 19 Jan. 2013, <http://uncomplicatedly.wordpress.com/2010/05/25/>. For other methods for teaching Hemingway's modernist uses of rhythm, see Katie Owens-Murphy's essay on Hemingway and Stein, "'Miss Stein Instructs': Revisiting the Paris Apprenticeship of 1922," in this volume.

15. For more information on the late nineteenth- and early twentieth-century teaching in American classrooms of challenges to traditional genre demarcations, see

Sharon Hamilton, "The *PMLA* and the Backstory to Making Poetry New," *Journal of Modern Periodical Studies* 2 (2011): 54–85.

16. See H. L. Mencken, "Joseph Conrad" and "Sherwood Anderson," both in his, *H. L. Mencken's Smart Set Criticism,* ed. William H. Nolte (Washington, DC: Regnery Gateway, 1987): 224–39 and 272–76, respectively.

17. In the original manuscript for *The Sun Also Rises,* Hemingway's characters specifically discuss reading Mencken's "serious criticism," including one of his long pieces "about Conrad" (*SAR: A Facsimile Edition* 151). My thanks to Hemingway scholar Robert Trogdon for bringing this reference to my attention.

18. See Sherwood Anderson, "Unlighted Lamps," *The Smart Set* 65 (July 1921): 45–55. This story, as reprinted in the collection *The Triumph of the Egg* (New York: B. W. Heubsch, 1921), 64-92, is available online at The Hathi Trust Digital Library, web, 19 Jan. 2013, <http://babel.hathitrust.org/cgi/pt?id=uiug.30112002000591;view=1up;seq=1>.

19. See Albert Barbelle, cover image of smoking flapper, *The Smart Set* 67 (March 1922), available online at The Hathi Trust Digital Library, web, 19 Jan. 2013, <http://babel.hathitrust.org/cgi/pt?id=uc1.b3874450;view=1up;seq=7>.

20. See "A radiant bride at twenty—at twenty-five—what?" advertisement for Margaret Sanger, "Woman and the New Race," *The Smart Set* 69 (Dec. 1922): 157, available online at The Hathi Trust Digital Library, web, 19 Jan. 2013, <http://babel.hathitrust.org/cgi/pt?id=uc1.b3874452;view=1up;seq=659>.

21. On this subject, see especially Jacqueline Vaught Brogan, "Hemingway's *In Our Time:* A Cubist Anatomy," *The Hemingway Review* 17.2 (1998), 31–46.

22. Hemingway's widor, Mary Hemingway, donated "The Farm" to the National Gallery. To view and learn about this painting, see The National Gallery of Art's guide, *An Eye for Art: Focusing on Great Artists and Their Work* (Chicago: Chicago Review Press, 2013); chapter 6, "Questioning Traditions," has a section on Miró entitled "Joan Miró," 137-40. This guide is available online at the National Gallery's website, <http://www.nga.gov/content/dam/ngaweb/Education/learning-resources/an-eye-for-art/AnEyeforArt-JoanMiro.pdf>.

On Teaching "Homage to Switzerland" as an Introduction to Postmodern Literature

Jeffrey Herlihy-Mera

I developed this approach to "Homage to Switzerland" for a course on Western culture and contemporary creation at the University of Puerto Rico. While considering how to integrate texts on Europe for a group of students who would travel there in the summer term, I refocused the introductory sessions on postmodernity around the straightforward, yet complex, protagonists in this Hemingway text. I found that the structures in the story are useful in making postmodern concepts—and their links to the physical sciences and psychology—accessible to students. The various iterations of "one" reality often become a lens through which our class conversations transition into discussions on multilingual and multicultural societies; these are of particular relevance to our class, which is usually conducted in several languages (Spanish, Spanglish, and English). The primary purpose of the session is to introduce postmodern thought and to characterize the modern and postmodern literary tendencies of the twentieth century.

Hemingway is usually regarded as most representative of American expatriate modernism, yet an important dimension of his work is vested in an array of postmodern devices. A distinguishing characteristic of his use of repetition, dialogue, wordplay, nonlinear narrative, pastiche, and polysemy is its playful tone: while modernists are often defined through their lament for (and attempts to control) the chaos of twentieth-century existence, postmoderns generally appreciate and sometimes participate in the chaos. Much of Hemingway's use of these devices demonstrates a nonconformist, alternative stance toward the construction of literature itself. "Homage to Switzerland" constitutes an excellent example of his use of postmodern mechanisms, and a close examination of its departure from standard literary tropes should reveal an ever-present and yet generally unstudied dimension of Hemingway's work.[1]

Several texts by other modern authors also could be perceived as postmodern tracts. *Yes, Mrs. Williams* by William Carlos Williams, for instance, is a semi-memoir constructed through an array of irregular, multilingual glances into the Caribbean life (displaced to New Jersey) of the Puerto Rican/Dominican-American author. Williams's mother was Puerto Rican, and his father was raised—from ages 5 to 29—mainly in the Dominican Republic; the memoir hinges on the interplay of Caribbean and U.S. cultural, linguistic, and societal norms, in which no one system permeates as a cultural standard. In what is arguably Williams's most experimental text, *Yes, Mrs. Williams* in some ways is a veiled autobiography—constructed through a memoir about his mother—that addresses many informing dimensions of his boyhood and of his perceptions of language as a communicative tool. Similarly, *The Autobiography of Alice B. Toklas* by Gertrude Stein is constructed through a veiled, third-person autobiographical format, which is nearly as revelatory about the author as the subject treated.

Before our class session, I assign as homework the text of Hemingway's story "Homage to Switzerland," two videos on YouTube, and an excellent short article on the story by Michael Reynolds, "'Homage to Switzerland': Einstein's Train Stops at Hemingway's Station."[2] The first video, "Simultaneity—Albert Einstein and the Theory of Relativity," uses a train station to discuss Einstein's theories on separate realities; the second video (from Yale's open-access courses) is an introduction to Freud's influence on the twentieth century (we view the first thirty minutes).[3] The first half of the class session is an introduction to postmodernism in general; we discuss its links to scientific and psychological progressions and how it relates to modernism. The second half of the ninety-minute period is an applied analysis of how postmodern tropes exist in "Homage to Switzerland."

Before the lecture, I write several key terms on the board (see below). We begin with a short review/summary of the readings and videos assigned as homework, and I pose a rhetorical question that guides us into the lecture: How would a new sense of time and space influence the way people perceive their surroundings?

Einstein (and Freud)
What is Postmodernism?
Reality into Realities
Existentialism

In the beginning of the twentieth century, some established concepts, such as knowledge and truth, were falling before great advances in the sciences, such as Einstein's theory of relativity in physics ("Simultaneity") and Freud's theories in psychology ("Foundations: Freud"). The power and depth of these new perspectives was altering how people understood the most basic components of life itself. Einstein's and Freud's work fractured concepts as fundamental as time and place, self and identity, and these new dynamics of the composition of reality became driving forces in Western creation. Postmodern thinkers were forging a new way of perceiving the world, and writers and painters made art out of this revolutionary philosophy. Indeed, the new ways that words and concepts were expressed began a literary revolution that was no less profound than the scientific revolution underlying it. Writers and artists were relocating concepts as momentous as value, beauty, and selfhood through new forms of narration and new techniques of using paint on canvas.

Postmodernism is difficult to define: it is not, as its prefix implies, an essentially after-modernist phenomenon. The movement could be defined perhaps as a reaction *against* modernism, which is generally optimistic about the potential of human reason and the constructs of objective knowledge and objective truth. The modern way of thinking maintains that we can exist on a neutral plane, observing reality; that there is a unity of knowledge; that human thought and technology and their "progressions" are generally positive phenomena; and that human reason will enable us to come to truth. Modernist approaches are troubled by the reshaping and distortions of "truth" that occurred in the midst of the technological "advancements" that were radically reshaping reality in the late nineteenth- and early twentieth centuries (for example, mechanized warfare, the consequences of industrialization, and other shifts in human existence occurring at that time). Much of modernist writing, perhaps for this reason, is pessimistic: it often treats the doubt regarding universal conceptual bases (that is, concepts such as "truth" and "God") as orientations.

In a sense, Western postmodern thought began with Copernicus, whose work demonstrated that we are not the center of the universe: we experience a space within a reality that is contingent upon many others realities. Before the conceptualization of these new senses of being, God (that is, humans with authority to disseminate ideas) put stories in motion about reality itself: time, place, community, identity, consciousness, morality, and so on, such that all of these stated concepts, like reality, are contingent upon a set of fixed and uniform circumstances. Postmodernists have rejected these sets of circumstance and the supposed "oneness" of experience and reality that dominates the modern mindset. The idea of many contemporaneous, coexistent realities is a useful platform to begin thinking from a postmodern perspective.

For postmodernists, truth is constructed from surroundings—it is the product of a place and time, a language, a background, a climate, a set of experiences, and so on. In this philosophical and sociohistoric approach, no single concept of truth—even that which is constructed through scientific means—has meaning once it is disentangled from the system that articulated its existence. We are culturally and socially situated, argues the postmodernist, and there are myriad correct and authoritative answers (precisely as described on Einstein's train in the video we watched for homework). No one (and no one's) "truth" has more currency than any other('s). From the postmodern perspective, claims to truth are impositions of power; we produce our own truth and our own knowledge, and, perhaps because of this, existentialism is paramount to postmodern orientations.

This is not to say that postmodern characters, artists, and thinkers, including Hemingway's protagonists, do not have systems of values or that they live in a world that lacks truth. Postmodern characters tend to orient themselves by rearticulating those concepts through other forms that do not have a systemic basis. Through their experiences and emotions, postmodernists establish patterns that resemble traditional systems. For this reason, existentialism and postmodernity are somewhat difficult to disentangle, as they are complementary and are often used to define one another. Existentialism maintains that we are the sum of our experiences, so people whose experiences are outside the common run are likely to be especially aware of the relative nature of truth. For this reason, exile and cultural disorientation are common literary devices in postmodern texts, such as Jack Kerouac's *On the Road*, Kurt Vonnegut's *Cat's Cradle*, and Julio Cortázar's *Hopscotch*. As basketball star Bill Russell put it, "the one certainty is that a man can never be certain of what he thinks. He can only strive and learn and fight against the frustrations of his life, and continue that struggle to the point that he develops a philosophy. A man who asks for a philosophy will never have one. My philosophy is only the result of what has happened in this life." Born in a segregated Louisiana and rising to fame in Boston, a city with a tepid atmosphere toward African-Americans, Russell could not rely on the frameworks of others for orientations. The postmodern element here is that he could not apply external systems of value to sort out his existence, his sense of self, and his identity. (Incidentally, Russell has defended Hemingway's approach to literature [Russell and McSweeny 9].) Russell's words—at once existentialist and postmodern—could have come from Santiago, Frederic Henry, Jake Barnes, or Francis Macomber.

In general, shifts from modern to postmodern have been applied to literary theory more broadly in Europe than in the United States. Indeed many of the poststructuralist and deconstructionist giants whose work informs postmodern approaches—such as Foucault, Barthes, Lacan, Derrida, Bourdieu, and Lyotard—are French academics. For those seeking to make the work of these scholars accessible for undergraduates, Mary Klages's text, *Literary Theory: A Guide for the Perplexed,* is a fine introductory examination that comprehensively and concisely surveys these topics. Klages's lively writing style is intended for undergraduates and her book offers a basic orientation that guides students toward more sophisticated argumentation.

The shifts in perceptions of reality from modernism to postmodernism were of great importance to the evolution of visual art, music, and film in the twentieth century. The sequence of aesthetic movements from postimpressionism (Cézanne and Van Gogh) to cubism (Picasso and Braque) to abstract expressionism (Pollock and Rothko) very closely parallels the philosophical shift from structuralism to poststructuralism—but in visual form. Trends in musical composition likewise echoed these philosophical shifts: in particular, we see postmodernism and postructuralism in the prevalence of the nonstructural "jam session" and the crucial role of improvisation in jazz, hip-hop, freestyle rap, and other genres that rose to prominence in twentieth-century music. Many films also employ what could be understood as postmodern devices, such as a nonlinear narrative and antihero protagonists, which are characteristic in such movies as *Citizen Kane, Pulp Fiction,* and *Twelve Monkeys.*

At this point, in order to help students connect these topics with Hemingway's "Homage to Switzerland," I ask another rhetorical question: Given the dimensions of postmodernity that we've looked at thus far, what would a postmodern text be like? Postmodern literatures themselves are often described and studied through a few common characteristics. In order to help students explore how postmodern aesthetics function in "Homage to Switzerland," we first examine some literary devices that are common in postmodern writing:

Form: Nonlinear, fragmented, repetitive, dialogue-based, exhibiting final irony

Theme: The archetypal postmodern character is in a state of cultural and social disorientation. His or her sense of value and aesthetics are constructed (perhaps determined) existentially, through his or her response to this situation. The postmodernist appreciates and sometimes participates in the disorder. (*Disorder* is a relative term here, of course.)

. . .

Hemingway wrote "Homage to Switzerland" in 1932; it is composed of three ostensibly contemporaneous episodes at three different train stations in Switzerland. At 9:30 P.M., an English-speaking American (or apparently American) man in each station flirts with a waitress and speaks with other men at the station (porters or other passengers) while waiting for the northbound Simplon-Orient Express, which has been delayed an hour. The haphazard, seemingly unconnected plot lines form a style that, as Susan Beegel observed, "challenges the assumptions of Western critics" (qtd. in M. Reynolds, "Homage" 255). The story is, moreover, an unswerving exploration of Einstein's new theories of time and space, employing a metaphor—the train—that Einstein himself used to illustrate the theory of relativity. Beegel has also noted that Hemingway's treatment of these approached a reality in which time and space "were not absolute values but relative to the speed of light" (255).

As the lecture part of class shifts to an open conversation on the postmodern concepts in the story, I mention that "Homage to Switzerland" is similar to much of Hemingway's other fiction in that it uses what are generally understood to be postmodern literary devices: a live-for-existence attitude toward daily affairs; a nonstandard attitude toward sexual and cultural behavior; a focus on individual, independent action; and cultural disorientation as a backdrop. In order to remedy this sense of disorientation—which is common to many of Hemingway's texts set abroad, such as *The Sun Also Rises*, *For Whom the Bell Tolls*, and *Across the River and into the Trees*—the characters often rely on an etiquette common to a group of people with whom the protagonist shares a perspective, experiences, or situation.

As a class, we begin a postmodern analysis of "Homage to Switzerland" first by outlining the events in each episode, using the categories "Character, Background, and Purpose at Station," "Language of Dialogue," and "Themes of Conversation" to guide the process.

Montreux
Character: Wheeler; American; going to Paris
Dialogue: In English, French, German
Themes: Language, sex, alcohol

Vevey
Character: Johnson; cultural origin unclear (ostensibly American); northbound
Dialogue: in English, Italian, German, French
Themes: Language, smoking, alcohol, sex, divorce, employment

Territet
Character: Harris; American; going to Paris, then the United States
Dialogue: in English
Themes: Language, smoking, suicide, National Geographic

After the above sections are filled in, I go on to note on the board student responses to the questions of how the text is nonlinear and fragmented and uses repetition and dialogue. As we discuss the nature of dialogue in "Homage to Switzerland," I take care to compare the story to two postmodern-style uses of dialogue that are often already familiar to the students: the television show *Seinfeld* and the film *Pulp Fiction*. The *Seinfeld* series is driven by dialogue that treats as everyday, commonplace topics themes that were considered obscene or inaccrochable themes in the 1990s: masturbation, homosexuality, deportation, the sudden death of a fiancée. *Pulp Fiction*, too, overlays seemingly ordinary dialogues with images of extreme violence to get a similar effect. While the themes of the dialogue in "Homage to Switzerland" today read as somewhat prosaic, in the 1930s they were as edgy as Seinfeld's and Tarantino's work was six decades later. I also take a moment to note that both *Seinfeld* and *Pulp Fiction* experimented with nonlinear storylines, absurdism, fragmentation, and repetition.

I often use these open discussions as a central part of class because the group brainstorm is often a lively forum for new ideas and student engagement. The students' reflections nearly always complement and enhance my own understanding of texts we study. I feel that this student-centered group approach encourages students to consider the historical and social contexts of the story in relation to their own lives. As Puerto Rico, like Switzerland, is multicultural and multilingual, the students' reflections on this text have significant critical currency—and I encourage them to develop and nourish these perspectives as they think about Hemingway's story and postmodern themes in general. If it does not arise from the students' responses, I make sure to mention the clear multicultural similarities between Switzerland and Puerto Rico. (I also express my interest in reading a term paper or a senior thesis exploring such a topic.) Given the cultural backdrop of our classroom, I invite the students to compare how the languages and cultural markers in the story function as purveyors of value. I also invite students to think about this in relation to the languages and cultures of our campus and our classroom. The students' reflections on such themes are particularly refreshing to me as a scholar, and many issues raised in class discussions have made their way, directly or indirectly, into my own scholarship on Hemingway. I also suggest that the students further develop these thoughts during small-group activities and in writing assignments. (See Appendix R: Small-Group Activities and Writing Assignments.)

By applying a postmodern approach to "Homage to Switzerland," students are engaging several disciplines (mainly physics and literature, although there is room for discussions of Freud) in their contemplations of literature. I feel that postmodern approaches in general allow students the latitude to embrace their own voices and opinions in a way that is not always possible in traditional academic structures. A reliance on the students' participation in the discussion is an empowering dimension of any pedagogical structure, and it is one that often creates a comprehensive learning environment for the students. Deemphasizing the teacher/student imbalance (that is, by making the teacher a student participating as an equal in the discussion) is a technique that is essentially postmodern in its inner parts, as the students' perspectives are as sanctioned as anyone else's in the room: and that concept is one that I hope students will take with them when they leave the *salón de clase* each day.

Hemingway is a useful figure for teaching both modernism and postmodernism, as his work and biography have close ties to the geopolitical events and philosophical movements of the twentieth century. As a war hero who endured a rather troubled homecoming, and then expatriation, Hemingway expressed perspectives on the "progressions" of humanity that were colored by the emptiness of the postwar landscape of America and Europe. His fictional characters likewise exhibit a loss of confidence in the stabilizing mores of civilization; these concepts are firmly modernist stations of experience and perspective. Hemingway's postmodern aesthetics, like the episodic playfulness of "Homage to Switzerland," occur comparatively seldom, and they tend to emerge only in his most radical and experimental texts. Nevertheless, these postmodern qualities are present in his work and remain a relatively unstudied dimension of Hemingway's body of literature.

Notes

1. Several of Hemingway's other texts—novels and short stories from the span of his career—are likewise open to modernist-postmodernist interpretation. Some early short stories, notably "Divine Gesture" (written before his arrival in Paris), "Up in Michigan," and the vignettes from *in our time* (and *In Our Time*), involve seemingly unconnected glimpses into what might be described as chaotic realities that are informed by nonstandard systems of value. *In Our Time* is a collection characterized by its episodic and pastiche nature, which plays with such opposing concepts as patriotism and independence, life and death, and home and abroad; Hemingway then unifies these concepts through a textual balance of traditional and radical aesthetics. In many ways a postmodern interplay of modern mores, *In Our Time* is colored by seemingly irrational thematic plays on some of life's most serious issues, like birth and unexpected death in "Indian Camp" and Krebs's traumatic incompatibly with his own mother in "Soldier's Home." The volume's diversity of voices (thieves, doctors, destitute kings, soldiers, and others) from around the globe (the Americas, Africa, Europe) enlighten a body of texts linked in their ostensible spontaneity and meaninglessness. Similarly, some of Hemingway's novels—like *The Garden of Eden, For Whom the Bell Tolls,* and *The Sun Also Rises*—are driven by comparable episodic, playful takes on the strains brought on by a reality that seems to lack a system of objective truth.

2. See Michael Reynolds, "'Homage to Switzerland': Einstein's Train Stops at Hemingway's Station," in *Hemingway's Neglected Short Fiction: New Perspectives,* ed. Susan Beegel (Tuscaloosa: U of Alabama P, 1992), 255–63. Modernist studies often note the work of Freud and Einstein; they also form part of the foundation of postmodern philosophy and literature because their work fractured previously stable ideas like identity, reality, time, and space. In a larger sense, one may argue that they set out to establish new grand narratives about humanity (Freud) and the universe (Einstein) and are thus more modern than postmodern scholars.

3. See "Simultaneity—Albert Einstein and the Theory of Relativity," last modified 5 May 2007, Our World—from EarBot.com, *YouTube,* web, <http://www.youtube.com/watch?v=wteiuxyqtoM>; and "Foundations: Freud," last modified 30 Sep. 2008, Yale Courses, *YouTube,* web, <http://www.youtube.com/watch?v=7emS3ye3cVU>.

Chasing New Horizons

Considerations for Teaching Hemingway and Modernism in a Digital Age

Andrew Fletcher

As part of his reception theory, Hans Robert Jauss describes a "horizon of expectations" (Jauss and Benzinger 14) to illustrate how different generations of readers understand and appreciate works of literature. I want to add that today's new generations of readers are not categorized strictly by age but more importantly by what else they have read, viewed, and listened to—all of which may contribute to their impression of a work. Increasingly, their reception of a given literary work is based more on relevant media input than their previous experience with genre, form, or language. As this horizon retreats, the "aesthetic distance" (Jauss and Benzinger 14) between the author's contemporary audience and the present-day reader increases. We should embrace classroom methods that give students glimpses of how contemporary audiences may have understood a literary work.

Whether we ask students to seek out supplementary materials or whether we provide these for them, the research they complete in trying to better understand the stories and novels we assign may be counterproductive, or even send them in the wrong direction. Teaching students that completing research is more than finding and analyzing information from the web is essential. We as instructors can direct them to relevant and credible websites and useful print resources, but relying on instruction without direct application in class fosters ineffective research habits. If our objective is to find the impression of a literary work on the author's contemporary audience, then we must incorporate research strategies and supplemental media—fictional and biographical, popular and scholarly, and primary and secondary, from both electronic and print sources—into our direct instruction that can contextualize the texts we teach, whether by Hemingway or others.

Using primary source material—such as an author's correspondence—can reveal a vivid context to literature that students may not otherwise find. When they can identify for themselves the pivotal historical moments and relevant biographical details available through other media, they can assign context to the fiction we are studying. If we use then use these supplementary materials to generate more questions, they can open avenues for further reading and subsequent bibliography. As I outline in more detail below, the books *Ernest Hemingway: Selected Letters 1917–1961* and *The Selected Letters of Thornton Wilder* can be used to emphasize how both authors saw themselves as part of a literary movement and to give us insight into the modernist characteristics of their art.

While valuable websites, like that for the Ernest Hemingway Collection of the John F. Kennedy Presidential Library and Museum, offer a range of useful materials—biographical and scholarly essays, scrapbooks, images, links to other credible sites containing further biographical material, and relevant articles from contemporary newspapers and magazines online—their offerings of digitized textual content of primary sources, such as original manuscripts, journals, and letters, are limited. I recommend the print anthologies and collections of letters that have compiled these same primary sources for easy access. Websites are helpful in gathering bibliographic information that can aid students in developing further research questions, but often they describe primary source records that may not be available online. To access most of the primary source materials in these collections, the student must actually visit to the museum, research centers, or library housing them.

Since we want students to find what interests them and take their own positions, our choices of teaching material should take into account what relevant media input students would seek without guidance. In addition to visiting blogs and wikis, for example, new generations of readers rely on more sophisticated search engines, online databases of periodicals and journals, and newspaper archives to present information relevant to their search. Remaining in a realm of generality, they can apply search strategies that produce predictable results and little divergence from clichéd notions about literary figures and texts.

One result of a Google search for Hemingway, for example, is the website of the Ernest Hemingway Home and Museum, based at the author's former Key West home. Given its affiliation with the author, this website may seem a likely source of information to a student. One tab, "The Legend," leads to a short account of the author's affiliation with Key West. The first sentence classifies him as a "member of the the 'Lost Generation' of expatriate artists and writers populating Paris during the 1920s."[1] While this idea may be true, it oversimplifies those artists and writers by classifying them under such a canned label.

Directly below this text is a link to a trailer of the 2012 HBO film *Hemingway & Gellhorn*, which illustrates that the rate at which students access information can also determine what they deem to be relevant media input. Students accessing this two-minute video will gain new impressions of the author, and, despite the fictional attributes of the film it advertises, are likely to regard it as an objective depiction of the author, convinced by its high production value and apparent historical accuracy with regard to its characters and the time period it depicts. They are likely to respond similarly to other films based on Hemingway's legend—even Woody Allen's 2011 fantasy film *Midnight in Paris*. Such impressions may influence their responses to Hemingway's writing.

We also should consider the rate at which students' access to academic media shapes their sense of what constitutes meaningful research. That students can scan thousands of texts, even searching through entire databases for keywords with a few keystrokes, may suggest thoroughness; however, keyword searching of mass amounts of information can also limit the chance for innovative research. As I demonstrate below, preliminary research gives students a base from which to expand on their own original searches. An intertextual approach to teaching modernism forces students who may overlook the artistic tendencies of other important modernist writers to broaden the scope of their search for relevant media input. Juxtaposing the work of an Ur-modernist like Hemingway with that of a less celebrated but equally prolific writer such as Thornton Wilder could allow students to discover the more nuanced tendencies, techniques, and style associated with modernism, rather than just the literary figures and times. When students get caught up in the appeal of the latter, they are frequently diverted from further relevant scholarship; although Wilder is an important modernist author, for example, his name does not typically surface in searches for modernism, Hemingway, or American expatriate writers.

My first introduction to modernism as it applies to American literature was in college, through a professor particularly interested in the American expatriates—notably Hemingway, Fitzgerald, and Pound—but having little regard for the lesser-known artists of the era. The professor's class was a survey course intended to cover a great deal of material besides these modernists, but his focus on and subsequent representation of these artists caused me to categorize their work as belonging to a particular historical era in a particular place (i.e., the 1920s in Paris). Although I still read these authors' works for common themes, ideals, and stylistic techniques specific to modernism, my initial introduction to them, particularly the biographical details that reinforced the "lost generation" construct, attached an underlying sentimentality to their works. The focus on biographical information taken at face value caused me to romanticize the movement (placing a certain lifestyle as prerequisite for inclusion) and, subsequently, the lives of the authors associated with it. Although I took the professor's word for it, I never actually saw evidence that these artists regarded themselves as part of something or that they recognized that something as a movement in art. Just as the films mentioned above seek to portray Hemingway as a charismatic, ultramasculine American legend, or to paint Paris in the twenties as a golden age in literature, so does much of the textual media students are sure to encounter on the web without our guidance, subsequently limiting their inventiveness with regard to scholarship. If students are to avoid the easy appeal of labels like "lost generation" and delve more deeply into the impetus toward modernism driving the writers of this period, they need to find the reasons for and details of the expatriate lifestyle adopted by Hemingway and some of his contemporaries, information that only primary sources can depict firsthand.

My professor's representation of these authors not only limited what I would read, watch, and listen to with regard to this literary topic but also how I would perceive this supplemental media. Since our first encounter with the idea of modernism in literature generally comes from a high school or college course through Hemingway, Fitzgerald, and others, we might miss the richness and nuance of modernism. To recognize the various forms of modernism, it is important to teach the tendencies of the movement while also delving more deeply into the authors' lives, exploring who they saw as important artists, even mentors. Instead I initially looked only for autobiographical evidence of their glamorous lives through their characters—characters like Fitzgerald's Gatsby, who embodied the mood of the twentieth-century Jazz Age New York, or Jake Barnes, whose tragic exploits in Spain evoked the horrors of war.

When my students pursue this same kind of autobiographical reading, I first provide them with evidence of the parallels between the authors' lives and their fiction from letters and memoir, but then complicate the picture by questioning the authors' own intent and subjectivity. In a November 1933 letter to his editor, Max Perkins, for example, Hemingway complains, "If I write about *anybody*—automatically they label that character as me . . . I write some stories absolutely as they happen . . . , others I invent completely" (*SL* 400). After reading such comments, I ask students to consider the context and situation of the letter by considering the audience, in this case his editor, and asking if the author's apparent defensiveness has influenced his comments.

I do not suggest abandoning research into the biographical components of modernism, since the artists under study were fascinating individuals whose lives are meaningful narratives in themselves. Rather, I suggest finding a relevant context between biography and text aside from obvious parallels. We should consider how students conduct their research in order to help them encounter new ideas and draw conclusions that they deem worthy of scholarship, especially when it leads them to read the fiction and biographical texts of other authors. To help them avoid overgeneralizing an entire literary–historical moment or casting an entire career into the realm of legend, we should choose media that will highlight the context that shaped the writing, such as its music, visual art, fiction, biography, interviews, literary reviews, and letters.

In order to illustrate my point, I present students with correspondence between Hemingway and Wilder, who published several works in the same years as one another, works often of the same genre and intended to achieve the same avant-garde goals. Using the biographical primary sources as a guide or segue into such parallel works as *The Sun Also Rises* and *The Cabala*, or *The Fifth Column* and *Our Town*, together with others I will discuss below, makes comparing the tendencies, techniques, and styles of those artists that much more interesting for students. Essentially, the students' preliminary research will determine what works of fiction they read.

I begin my introduction of primary source research to students by moving backward from the text of a letter into a footnote, to point out what the editor of the volume of letters has deduced from the content of the correspondence. Whether a specific note gives an explanation about an unnamed person or story, or a reference to a biography, memoir, or journal, using footnotes and endnotes can lead students to further reading that allows them to track a researcher's reasoning and to move backward from his conclusion to the texts he used to reach it. For example, I begin a class meeting with another letter by Hemingway to his editor from June 1930, in which Hemingway tells Perkins, "enclosed is the story ["Wine of Wyoming"]. I think you will like it. It is nearly 6000 words long. Don't let anyone tell you it's not a good story or has too much French in it" (*SL* 323).

The editor of the collection of letters, Hemingway biographer Carlos Baker, determined the title of the letter's unnamed story to be "Wine of Wyoming"; Baker bracketed this title to indicate that it was inserted and then followed the insertion with a footnote citing a page in his biography, *Ernest Hemingway: A*

Life Story (1969). Following the reference in the footnote, Baker explains that Maxwell Perkins had "asked for a new story for the August number of *Scribner's Magazine*. Ernest had already set down an account of the Moncini family of Sheridan under the title "Wine of Wyoming" (Baker 210). Here I prompt students to make deductive inquiries into how the biographer determined the title of the story that was mentioned in the letter. My goal is to demonstrate to students that as they search for evidence in other letters they will also find relevance, context, and direction for their own research. When students use indexes to find other letters to Perkins or letters that mention the story "Wine of Wyoming," the Moncini family of Sheridan, or *Scribner's Magazine*, they are ultimately broadening the scope of what they deem relevant media input.

If a student follows the reference to the Moncini family in the index of Hemingway's biography, she will find obvious parallels between the author's time in Wyoming in 1928 and "Wine of Wyoming." Baker tells us of the "French family that made and sold good wine" and how Ernest and Pauline "bagged nine prairie chickens on the Indian Reservation" (Baker 196). When we do read the story, students point back to these excerpts from the biography. To complicate easy assumptions, I produce another part of the same November 1933 letter to Perkins mentioned earlier, in which Hemingway writes, "That story—Wine of Wyoming is nothing but straight reporting of what [I] heard and saw when I was finishing A Farewell to Arms out in Sheridan and Big Horn" (*SL* 400). While this gives the story additional context with regard to the author's life, it doesn't foster oversimplified autobiographical readings.

This source-mining technique not only teaches students how to use indexes to find potential routes for research; it also facilitates a relevant segue into literary theory and criticism. For example, the title "Wine of Wyoming" appears again in Baker's biography when he tells of "a new outbreak of hostility among the New York reviewers." We learn that "Wine of Wyoming" was "generally admired" but that "the new collection" in which it was published, *Winner Take Nothing*, "was otherwise held to be the poorest and least interesting that [Hemingway] had yet placed on view." This allows me to return to my objective of finding the impression of a literary work on the author's contemporary audience. Baker continues, "Ernest chose to respond privately to Clifton Fadiman's review, which had appeared in the *New Yorker* as 'A Letter to Mr. Hemingway'" (Baker 246).

While students pursue the letter to Fadiman, using the index to the letters, they find only a mention of him in a letter Hemingway wrote to Perkins on 6 November 1933: "I can't write better stories than some I have already written—

what Mr. Fadiman asks for—because you can't write any better stories than those—and nobody else can" (*SL* 401). Having anticipated this, I produce the 1933 review, but before we read it I demonstrate the research methods I used to find this older article. I explain how I unsuccessfully searched through databases like JSTOR and Project Muse to find the full text. Since at this point I still didn't know which issue of the magazine contained the review, I checked the online archives of *The New Yorker*; this yielded the correct citation, but I didn't have further access. So, rather than subscribe, I found the full text in the microfiche in the basement of the library.

Fadiman's 1933 review, "A Letter to Mr. Hemingway," can help recreate the "horizon of expectations" of Hemingway's contemporary audience. Fadiman writes to Hemingway, "your school has been let out for a long recess," suggesting an end of modernism in the reviewer's eyes. Fadiman's review of the short stories in the collection consistently calls for the new. "They contain strong echoes of earlier work. They mark time whereas 'A Farewell to Arms' was a magnificent leap forward." He even suggests that Hemingway is allowing himself "to get stuck fast in yesterday" and that he is fixed "on things which smell of the early 1920's."

Fadiman then moves on to discuss Hemingway's brand of irony, his "brilliant trick of incongruous juxtaposition—placing two apparently unrelated aspects of life side by side so that each will unobtrusively bring out the horror of the other—it's a good device, beloved by young writers, but it should be only a vestibule leading to a deeper and more inclusive kind of irony" (Fadiman 58). Instead of deciphering this statement for students, I ask that they apply their own close reading. While Fadiman's call for the new is clear, there is much room to discuss the "incongruous juxtaposition" he mentions and to determine what he means by "a deeper and more inclusive kind of irony." Students create the meaning behind these descriptions by assigning them to the literature they read. While this practice may be applied to any of the stories in the collection, in class I ask students how Madame Fontan and her husband in "Wine of Wyoming" are juxtaposed to the narrator, as well as to the locals, both whites and Indians, that come to their small establishment (See Appendix S: Student Prompts for Using Contemporary Reviews, Close Readings, and Primary Sources, Part I.)

Having myriad print sources on hand, such as biographies, collections of letters, journals, and complete collections of authors' works, can allow students to search out answers to their research inquiries using the methods modeled in class. While many answers to research questions rest within the fiction itself, sometimes finding an answer requires strategies like reading other letters from that time frame, cross-referencing excerpts from a biography, or searching indexes for the title or other key words. If in the process of reading and creating bibliographies students find their own starting points for additional research, even better. After all, the idea is to lead them toward original scholarly writing and enhanced textual literacy.

Having led students to recognize the modernist qualities and tendencies in Hemingway's writing as described by himself, his correspondents, his biographer, and his reviewers, I share with them J. A. Cuddon's definition of modernism from his *Dictionary of Literary Terms and Literary Theory*. Cuddon describes a "breaking away from established rules, traditions and conventions, fresh ways of looking at man's position and function in the universe and many experiments . . . in form and style." To further expand the range of students' understanding of modernism, we discuss how this "comprehensive but vague term" (Cuddon 516) applies to another writer, Thornton Wilder.

To determine what of his work we will read, we start with letters written by Wilder around the same time as those written by Hemingway mentioned above. This will not necessarily point us in an obvious direction, although some letters can give us insight into the two writers' mindsets, purposes, and artistic goals. Rather than jumping straight in to the letters, I start with the introduction to part three of Wilder's letters, covering the same year "Wine of Wyoming" was written, which states, "After classes ended in June, Wilder spent a month at the McDowell Colony, working on six one-act plays" (Wilder 4258). When we take the next logical step, however, that of reading a letter by Wilder from this time, we discover an eighteen-month gap in the selected letters presented, so I ask the students where to look next. Since I have already spent time presenting the various resources available to them, students are equipped to seek more information in other collections of correspondence, journals, biographies, autobiographies, and other artistic works, in this case to find the title of the collection of one-act plays mentioned in the editor's introduction.

After referencing the "Collected Plays of Thornton Wilder," we find the collection, entitled *The Long Christmas Dinner and Other Short Plays*. Having anticipated this and read the six one-act plays, I either choose one well-suited for comparison with "Wine of Wyoming" or ask students to make that choice, based on the tendencies they notice in both pieces. Having read Fadiman's review and others contemporary reviews mentioned in Baker's biography, together with the author's own words about "Wine of Wyoming," I then use student observations and inquiries to bridge into traditional understandings of modernism. (See Appendix S: Student Prompts for Using Contemporary

Reviews, Close Readings, and Primary Sources, Part II.) The short write-up that follows may or may not be a starting point regarding what text a student chooses to complete an essay on, but it has allowed the students to apply research skills concretely and purposefully. (See Appendix S: Student Prompts for Using Contemporary Reviews, Close Readings, and Primary Sources, Part III.)

To begin another class, we continue reading Wilder's letters—again without any specific objective, although with the hope that students may draw conclusions about the relationship of the two authors and/or about whether they saw themselves as part of a literary movement. Wilder's letters to his family, for example, give us insight into his place in a new literary generation. He tells his mother of a meeting with Hemingway at Shakespeare & Company in Paris, describing him as "one of two other good artists of my generation," an opinion he develops in another letter to her, in which he comments, "He's wonderful. It is the first time I've met someone of my generation whom I respected as an artist" (Wilder 3629).

Having read Hemingway's letters and excerpts from his biography and memoir prior to reading Wilder's letters, students recognize that the two authors had many common friends, which leads me to begin another class by reading from letters both Hemingway and Wilder wrote to Scott Fitzgerald and other prominent literary figures, to determine the role these people may have played in their lives and crafts. The personal and professional relationship between Fitzgerald and Hemingway is abundantly portrayed in their correspondence and in scholarship on the authors. From their letters, it is apparent that they shared and discussed their work with one another, valuing and often acting on each other's artistic opinions. In an April 1926 letter to Fitzgerald, for example, Hemingway informs him of last-minute changes to *The Sun Also Rises*: "I've cut it to about 90,000 words . . . I'm hoping to hell you like it" (*SL* 199), After reading this in class, we follow by reading the unpublished opening of Hemingway's novel and Fitzgerald's letter suggesting he cut it. "I think part of *Sun Also* are careless + ineffectual . . . Ernest I can't tell you the sense of disappointment that beginning with its elephantine facetiousness gave me" (Fitzgerald, "Letter" 15–17). The volume of their correspondence manifests the authors' personal and professional ties.

Similar ties are also apparent when we read Wilder's letters. In a January1928 letter to Fitzgerald, Wilder responds to Fitzgerald's praise of *The Cabala* by writing, "As you see I am a provincial schoolmaster and have always worked alone. And yet nothing interests me more than thinking of our generation as a league and as a protest to the whole cardboard generation that precedes us from Wharton through Cabell and Anderson and Sinclair Lewis. I know Ernest Hemingway" (Wilder 4109). Not only is this evidence of Wilder's view of his place in a literary movement and that such a movement exists in his eyes, but this letter may also lead students to further intertextual analysis if they choose to research the other authors mentioned here.

Through their correspondence, we see that Wilder recognizes Hemingway's role in this literary movement. In a June 1928 letter, Wilder tells him, "I had a weekend with Scott and Zelda this spring. Scott read the opening chapter of his new book to us, perfectly fine. Your ghost crosses the stage every now and then, but so it does in all of our books willy-nilly, mostly willy." He goes further, telling Hemingway that he wishes "we could sit down for some more long talks. Honest. I'm more flexible than I was. And you modified me lots" (Wilder 4206).

Although we do not find any response to this letter in *Ernest Hemingway: Selected Letters 1917–1961,* when we search the index for Wilder we see another 1928 letter from Hemingway to Perkins, his editor, in which he praises Wilder's *The Bridge of San Luis Rey,* mentioning particular parts of the novel. "I thought Bridge S.L.R. [San Luis Rey] was a fine book of short stories—2 splendid ones—The Esteban and I think the other was about a girl who worked for Mother Superior" (*SL* 278). I use this opportunity to read chapters 2 and 3 of *The Bridge of San Luis Rey,* referred to by Hemingway, and even ask students why Hemingway refers to them as short stories. Again, I ask this kind of question not to shell out overused and constructed images of an era in American literature but to allow students to discover the modernism of the work for themselves through a kind of source mining.

So, whether it be to analyze the "incongruous juxtaposition" of characters or the level to which dialogue carries the plot of "Wine of Wyoming," to read Wilder's short play "The Long Christmas Dinner" for its portrayal of time, or to turn students on to longer works of both authors for intertextual analysis, the point is to introduce students to various forms of modernism. We could just visit several websites to find biographical information about the authors (with varying degrees of accuracy); however, the original documents reveal the authors' self-definitions and their views of the era's avant-gardism. Most importantly, though, such primary source materials give students direction that a simple web search cannot provide, direction that can illuminate a key age in American literature, giving relevance and purpose to research and yielding deeper understanding of the writers' work and its sources.

Note

1. See "The Legend," The Hemingway Home and Museum, web, 26 Mar. 2013, <http://www.hemingwayhome.com/legend/>.

Appendix A

Stylistic Consistencies Between Stein's *The Making of Americans* and Hemingway's *A Farewell to Arms*

From Stein's "Picasso":

> One whom some were certainly following was one who was completely charming. One whom some were certainly following was one who was charming. One whom some were following was one who was completely charming. One whom some were following was one who was certainly completely charming.... One whom some were certainly following and some were certainly following him, one whom some were certainly following was one certainly working. (104–5)

From Hemingway's "Soldier's Home":

> Nothing was changed in the town except that the young girls had grown up. But they lived in such a complicated world of already defined alliances and shifting feuds that Krebs did not feel the energy or the courage to break into it.... Most of them had their hair cut short.... They all wore sweaters and shirt waists with round Dutch collars. It was a pattern. He liked to look at them from the front porch as they walked on the other side of the street. He liked to watch them walking under the shade of the trees. He liked the round Dutch collars above their sweaters. He liked their silk stockings and flat shoes. He liked their bobbed hair and the way they walked.... He liked the girls that were walking along the other side of the street. He liked the look of them much better than the French girls or the German girls. But the world they were in was not the world he was in. He would like to have one of them. But it was not worth it. They were such a nice pattern. He liked the pattern. It was exciting. But he would not go through with all the talking. He did not want one badly enough. He liked to look at them all, though. It was not worth it. Not now when things were getting good again.

From Stein's *Three Lives:*

The good Anna had high ideals for canine chastity and discipline. The three regular dogs, the three that always lived with Anna, Peter and old Baby, and the fluffy little Rags, who was always jumping up into the air just to show that he was happy, together with the transients, the many stray ones that Anna always kept until she found them homes, were all under strict orders never to be bad with the other. . . . You see that Anna led an arduous and troubled life. (8)

From Hemingway's "Mr. and Mrs. Elliot":

Mr. and Mrs. Elliot tried very hard to have a baby. They tried as often as Mrs. Elliot could stand it. They tried in Boston after they were married and they tried coming over on the boat. They did not try very often on the boat because Mrs. Elliot was quite sick. She was sick and when she was sick she was sick as Southern women are sick. That is women from the Southern part of the United States. Like all Southern women Mrs. Elliot disintegrated very quickly under sea sickness, travelling at night, and getting up too early in the morning. (161)

From Stein's *The Making of Americans:*

Miss Charles was then one having general moral and special moral aspirations and general unmoral desires and ambitious and special unmoral ways of carrying them into realisation and there was never inside her any contradiction and this is very common in very many kinds of them of men and women and later in the living of Alfred Hersland there will be so very much discussion of this matter and now there will be a little explanation of the way it acts in the kind of men and women of which Miss Charles was one. (462)

From Hemingway's *A Farewell to Arms:*

I loved to take her hair down and she sat on the bed and kept very still, except suddenly she would dip down to kiss me while I was doing it, and I would take out the pins and lay them on the sheet and it would be loose and I would watch her while she kept very still and then take out the last two pins and it would all come down and she would drop her head and we would both be inside of it, and it was the feeling of inside a tent or behind a falls. (114)

Appendix B

Sample Assignments and In-Class Prompts

1. If Stevens and Hemingway alike are approaching meditative states of emptiness of thought, of unprejudiced reflection, how do they represent these states? What historical (extratextual) or dramatic (intratextual) compulsions are there for these empty, meditative states?
2. Can a meditative state be a heroic attitude? Does the meditative tone of "Big Two-Hearted River" help adjust the popular image of Hemingway as a connoisseur of physical force?
3. What is happening in Hemingway's descriptions of nature if the outlines and substance of the material object are not "mirrored"—that is, if his project is not *mimetic*? Students may consider how Hemingway's sentences come to be objects in their own right that suggest less the objects themselves than the sturdiness and quotidian reliability of his experience of objects; or they may discuss the reliability of objects (e.g., fish, rivers, coffeepots, meals of beans) themselves.
4. Students of American literature familiar with Emerson can compare his mandates in "The Poet" for a locally based literature unafraid to indulge the extraordinary to Stevens and Hemingway.
5. If students have had a world literature and/or a philosophy class, they might consider the meditative moments in Hemingway's fiction alongside accessible strains of ancient (e.g., Epicurean and stoical), modern (e.g., Santayana, Heidegger), and postmodern (e.g., Wittgenstein) philosophy that explore the relationship of perception to knowledge.

Appendix C

Hemingway and "the Code"

For many years it was argued, or assumed, that Hemingway's fiction was governed by a code of behavior that could be articulated as follows: Life in our time is subject to both predictable and random threats of violence, pain, and death. At any moment, an individual's pleasure, dignity, freedom, or life itself may be threatened by vast impersonal forces, over which he or she has no control whatsoever. In the face of this absurd condition, the following code of conduct is prescribed.

1. We should attempt to know things as they truly are, as a result of direct, immediate experience;
2. We should develop the specific understanding, skills, and habits of mind that will enable us to cope with these threats to our pleasure, dignity, freedom, and life;
3. We should cultivate vigorous physical talents, vital sensory responses, and authentic aesthetic tastes;
4. Our knowledge, skill, ability, and courage should be frequently tested in action;
5. "Don't talk about it." We should strive to be reticent, and to practice understatement, rather than to indulge in garrulousness and braggadocio, both of which should be avoided. This applies to both good things, which could be cheapened or tarnished, or could even disappear as a result of talking about them, and bad experiences, which cannot be changed or forgotten by dwelling on them.
6. "Don't think about it." We should not allow our minds to dwell on painful memories of the past or fearful anticipation of the future ("fishing the swamp"). If we think too much about these things, we run the risk of self-pity, despair, or paralysis. Similarly, if we yearn too nostalgically for lost pleasure or fantasize future happiness, we run other risks.

7. In any society, only a select few understand this code and live by it. They are in some sense, the initiates of a fraternity, and they recognize their kinship and their mutual bond almost instantly.

This presumed code remains one of the most familiar and pervasive myths of Hemingway studies. Although it is neither stated in a single work of fiction by Hemingway nor appears in this sort of detailed form in any single interpretation of Hemingway's works, scholars have inferred it from many readings of particular Hemingway texts. Its most important impetus comes from *Ernest Hemingway*, a 1952 book by Philip Young, and it was common currency among Hemingway's expositors and advocates for forty years or more. Over time, however, the close reading of Hemingway's texts also showed that no one of Hemingway's protagonists perfectly embodies every aspect of the code. While these characters may have sometimes judged themselves adversely according to these standards, they also show the limitations of the code itself. Eventually, the code came to be seen as arbitrary, limited, and reductive—an inadequate tool for interpreting the complex world of Hemingway's fiction.

Appendix D

Chronology and Lineage, *The Sound and the Fury*

Chronology

Saturday, 7 April 1928: "Benjy," 5-75
[Thursday], 2 June 1910: "Quentin," 76-129
Friday, 6 April 1928: "Jason," 180-264
Sunday, 8 April 1928 "Dilsey," 265-321

Narrative Scenes
1. 7 Apr. 1928: Luster and Benjy, 3:1-4:24: Looking for a golf ball; Benjy's birthday.
2. 23 Dec. 1908: Benjy and Caddy, 3:25-6:29: Uncle Maury's letter to Mrs. Patterson.
3. 1912 or 1913: Mrs. Compson, Benjy, T.P, 9:12-12:17: Trip to cemetery without Jason.
4. Spring or Summer 1908: Benjy, Mr. Patterson, 13:28-14:5: First letter to Mrs. Patterson.
5. 1900: Benjy, Quentin (I), Caddy, Jason, 17:18-9:13: Damuddy's death; Caddy's muddy drawers.
6. 25 Apr. 1910: Benjy, 20:25-22:23; Benjy, T.P., Quentin, Caddy, 20:25-22:23: Caddy's wedding.
7. 2 June 1910: Benjy, T.P., Dilsey, Roskus, 28:9-29:6; 29:11-30:5: Quentin's suicide.
8. 1912: Benjy, Roskus, Versh, Dilsey, 29:7-10; 30:6-32:19: Death of Mr. Compson.
9. 1915: Benjy, Dilsey, Luster, 33:9-12, 17-24: Roskus's death.
10. 1906: Benjy, Caddy, Dilsey 40:28-43:6 Caddy and Benjy give perfume to Dilsey.
11. 1908-1910 (?): Benjy, Caddy, Charlie, 46:16-25, 29-31; 47:1-48:18: Caddy and Charlie in swing.

12. Spring or Summer 1910: Benjy, girls, 51:19-53:10: Benjy at gate, "trying to say"; Attacks girl.
13. 1900: Benjy, Caddy, Dilsey, Mrs. Compson, 56:4-11: Benjy's name changed.
14. Nov. 1908 or 1909: Benjy, Caddy, Quentin, 66:20-29, & esp. 68:24-69:5: Caddy's loss of virginity.

Chronology of Scenes
1. Damuddy's death; Caddy's muddy drawers.
2. Benjy's name change.
3. Caddy and Benjy give perfume to Dilsey.
4. Benjy takes letter to Mrs. Patterson.
5. Benjy and Caddy take second letter to Mrs. Patterson.
6. Caddy and Charlie in the swing.
7. Caddy loses virginity.
8. Caddy's wedding.
9. Benjy misses Caddy, watches for her at the gate, attacks Burgess girl, is castrated.
10. Suicide of Quentin (I)
11. Father's death.
12. Mother and Benjy driven to cemetery by T.P.
13. Roskus; death.
14. Luster and Benjy look for a quarter; Benjy's birthday. They see Quentin (II) leave the window of the house and climb down the tree.

Lineage Chart

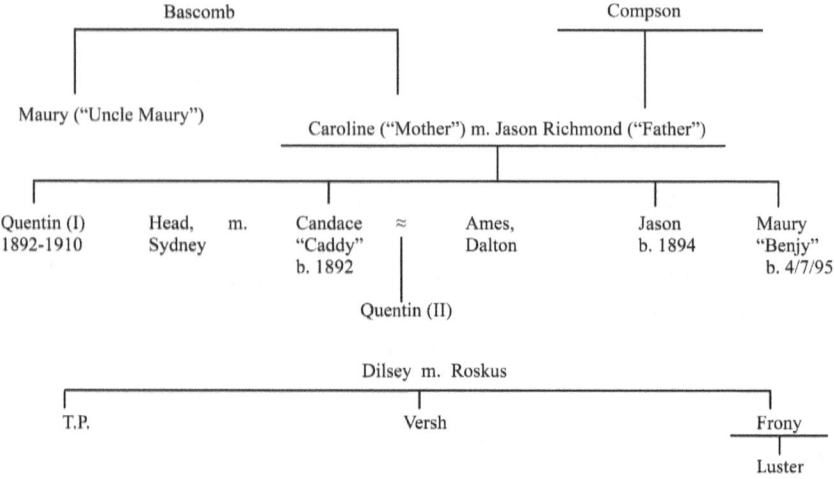

Page references are to Faulkner, *The Sound and the Fury: The Corrected Text*, ed. Noel Polk (New York: Random Vintage International, 1981)

This material was derived and adapted from Cleanth Brooks, *William Faulkner: The Yoknapatawpha Country* (New Haven: Yale UP, 1963); John T. Mathews, *The Sound and the Fury: Faulkner and the Lost Cause* (Boston: Twayne, 1991); and Stephen M. Ross and Noel Polk, *Reading Faulkner's* The Sound and the Fury: *Glossary and Commentary* (Jackson: U Mississippi P, 1996).

Appendix E

Discussion Questions and Writing Assignment

Discussion Questions

Note to educators: These questions are posted in my online American Literature II survey course. I divide the class of forty students into four groups. Each group is assigned its own questions, which all the students in that group must answer (in 250 words). One person in the group then summarizes the discussion and posts the summary for the whole class to read. Once all the summaries are posted, the class is required to engage in a discussion of any points on which students wish to comment.

1. Read T. S. Eliot's *The Waste Land*. Describe how *The Sun Also Rises* also depicts a waste land. What symbols or themes do the two works share? Are the post–World War I waste land inhabitants the same in the two works? Do the two works end with the same message?
2. Discuss the Jake-Brett-Robert triangle. Compare and contrast Jake's and Robert's characters. Why do Jake and Brett stay together? Ihab Hassan claims that Lady Brett is the "hollow center around which all the characters revolve." Do you agree that she is hollow? Why does she engage in gender confusion and act the way she does?
3. What makes Pedro a code hero? How does bullfighting contribute to his aura? Why would he be interested in someone like Brett? What danger does she hold for him and his bullfighting? Describe his bullfighting technique and its symbolism.
4. Discuss the ending of the novel and the ending of the pilgrimage. Have the characters transformed? Why does Jake say the last line in the novel? Has he moved beyond his affair with Brett? Has she?
5. What is the meaning of the title of the book? Does it shed light on Hemingway's worldview in the novel? Why does Hemingway turn to the Bible for his title?

6. View <http://www.youtube.com/watch?v=PANwrq_OuPM>. After watching the video, how would you describe Zora Neale Hurston's personality? Why do you feel we need to read and study her writing today?
7. Why do we need to recall the Old South as represented by Nanny in *Their Eyes Were Watching God*? Does Janie respect her advice? How do Janie's values differ from Nanny's? Do you think Janie is an embodiment of Hurston's personality and/or values?
8. View <http://www.youtube.com/watch?v=y_M-PfhgMsg>. What is the essence of Eatonville? How does the Eatonville setting affect Janie's life?
9. What are the gender issues in the novel, beginning with Nanny's position during the slavery and postslavery eras? How does Janie handle Eatonville's patriarchal society? Why does she put up with Tea Cake's beating of her and theft of her money? What do you think is Hurston's view of gender relations by the end of the novel?
10. Compare/contrast the physical effects of the storm in the novel with its emotional and spiritual effects. Explain the significance of the title in relation to the novel's themes.
11. What is Janie's state of mind at the end of the novel? Do you think she has transcended patriarchy? According to one critic, Houston Baker, she is transforming into a blues singer. Do you agree? Another critic instead claims that Janie has contracted rabies and is preparing to die. What do you think is her likely fate?

Writing Assignment

1. Write a 5-page (1250-word) essay on either Hemingway's *The Sun Also Rises* or Zora Neale Hurston's *Their Eyes Were Watching God*. Focus on the ending of the work you select and choose an aspect of the author's worldview that interests you (e.g., gender relations, self-empowerment, setting). These works are great modernist texts that culminate in a message that the author wishes to convey. As a reader, it is up to you to decipher that message. Be sure to construct your paper in the format of an argument and review my writing guidelines.
2. Create an electronic archive focusing on on either Hemingway's *The Sun Also Rises* or Zora Neale Hurston's *Their Eyes Were Watching God*. Be as creative as you wish, in order to familiarize your audience with your chosen author. The following authors have impressive electronic archives that pertain to

their works: Whitman, Hemingway, Cather, and Thoreau (walden.org). You can also view my Hurston archive at <http://pegasus.cc.ucf.edu/~zoraneal>. You should include the following materials in your project:

- A brief biography of the author (no more than 250 words).
- Photograph(s) of the author and/or the landscape about which he or she wrote.
- A brief overview of the historical, political, and/or social issues in the nation in which the author lived. Focus on the particular cultural aspects of the author's milieu that create meaning in his/her particular novel or play and enhance its key theme.
- Write an overview (1,000 words) of one key theme that embodies the overall meaning of the text and unlocks the meaning of the ending.
- Beyond these basics, add whatever material you find that illuminates the life and work of your author.

Appendix F

Discussion Questions

1. In "On Writing," what does Hemingway mean when he says that Nick "wanted to write like Cezanne painted"? Look at Cezanne's paintings in reference to Hemingway's writing and descriptions.
2. Gertrude Stein's influence on Hemingway's writing in "Up in Michigan" is undeniable. What other Hemingway stories from *In Our Time* perhaps illustrate Hemingway's internalization of Stein's influence?
3. By examining Hemingway's work and the influences he absorbed while in Paris, how might we be able to illustrate Hemingway as an urban writer in a collection, which offers very little discussion on the urban environment?
4. Robert E. Gajdusek notes similarities between James Joyce's "The Dead" and Ernest Hemingway's "Big Two-Hearted River." What similarities are apparent to you? How do Nick Adams and Gabriel Conroy resemble each other? How are they different?
5. Both "On Writing" and "Up in Michigan" were cut from the contents of *In Our Time*. How would their inclusion alter the collection? Give examples.

Appendix G

Teaching Idea: Writing about Immersion, Place, and Experience within a Setting of Action

Note to educators: Two possible ways for students to emulate Hemingway's and Orwell's techniques for acquiring writing material relate to strong immersion in experience. This may reflect the reporter present in both men, but it also relates to their common desire for passionate, intense experiences in living.

Orwell

Note to educators: I have found students studying Orwell enjoy becoming immersed in the author's favored activity of "tramping" (or in experiences similar to "tramping," with modest modifications). I also redefine "tramping" to ensure that students do not stumble into difficult situations.

Assignment: Experiment with versions of Orwell's "tramping." Operating in disguise, you are to go experience life wearing a totally new image for a few days, or even for just a few hours. *Tramping* in this sense might mean dressing like the upper crust and attending a fancy gallery opening, going to Tiffany's or other venues dressed to the nines, and/or the reverse—going out dressed and groomed poorly. It might mean wearing a fat suit and going to a few shops or restaurants to see how you are treated. If you are tramping as a homeless person, act accordingly, perhaps sitting on the bridge by Northwestern Station in Chicago, for example, with a cardboard sign and a pan for quarters and bills. How does it go? What observations can be made? How are you treated? What conversations do you have? Write it up! Refer to *Down and Out in Paris and London* as your model. You may write this as a journal or as fiction, but indicate your intended genre. Length: 3–5 pages.

Hemingway

Note to educators: For practice in Hemingway's methods, my approach is slightly different. Hemingway, like Orwell, favored immersion, but rather than employing

deliberate disguise or play-acting, he simply immersed himself in active living and loving life. It still can be argued, however, that Hemingway "played" the war hero, the sub-chaser, the fighter, the "spy"—even the troubled husband and father—mostly without artifice (but occasionally using some artifice, though). He typically chose very active, sensory-laden locales to visit.

Assignment: Visit a place of high activity related to current news or play a role you don't normally play that mimics Hemingway's huge immersion in life itself. You might, for instance, go trout fishing in a briskly rippling stream for an afternoon, then come back and write it. If there is a community rally going on about education cuts, go attend it and get involved and active: carry a sign and ask questions or lead some of the chants (think of Hemingway leading and motivating his small band of French fighters). There may not be a war to go to, but there will always be something happening out there. Remember that, for Hemingway, nature itself was always a "happening" event. Go for a nature hike or visit a large marsh or even a zoo and record your observations about a few of the animals you see, trying to describe them in the beautiful prose that Hemingway often saved for describing magnificent animals. Eyes wide open! Whatever you choose, please check in with me about your plan of attack before implementing the plan. Essay length: 3–5 pages.

Note to educators: After my students have produced writing related to one of these approaches, we share the writing and the experiences in class, sharing pictures or even, for those who were tramping, wearing the disguise used to class. This immersion produces strong and vivid writing and helps students see that writers don't always simply begin writing by writing; instead they often begin by deliberately seeking out life's experiences, experiences centered around place or events and amplified by their own passionate involvement.

Appendix H

Master Course Syllabus

Semester Course Description

In exploring the seemingly disparate pairing of Orwell and Hemingway, each author's contribution when viewed adjacent to the other's creates a surprisingly insightful paradigm. The two together create a dynamic of meaningful individual human experience within a world of political flux. One author (Orwell) was clearly political; one (Hemingway) playing on the fringes of socialism, yet was ultimately apolitical and much more focused on inner spirit; one was, ever after the Spanish Civil War, private (Orwell), yet driven by a world vision and churning with astute warnings about totalitarian states; one (Hemingway) was outgoing and worldly, traveled yet seeing a vision of clear inner core and code as key in this life. We will explore their interaction in the literary cosmos through geographic overlap in time and space as defined by key world events. This course will provide a study of shared writing genres, shared immersion in many of the same important twentieth-century events, and a shared search for a new stripped-down style reflecting modernism. Along the way, both used literature to promote inner individual or outward societal freedom.

Course Plan

This semester-designed course is organized with a chronological overlay beginning substantively in the late twenties, progressing to Spain and World War II, and then to coverage of later master works by both authors. Required student work will include a literary analysis (3–5 pages); a short comparative listing of the characteristics of the two authors' writing styles (2 pages); a reading journal with select quotations and commentary on each selection (12 entries); memoir/descriptive writing, including "tramping" or a "life study" immersion piece (3–5 pages); and one research paper (12+ pages). A few presentations will also be expected.

Unit One: Early Years (3 weeks)
Introduction: Reading journal explained
Immersion: Orwell's tramping (Paris and London); Hemingway's Paris years
Memoirs: Orwell's *Down and Out in Paris & London;* Hemingway's *A Moveable Feast (Note to educators: Courses emphasizing the twenties may include* Burmese Days *and* The Sun Also Rises *as a worthy comparative study, especially as related to fictionalized autobiography.)*
Setting: Begin mapping Hemingway's and Orwell's locations and locational settings for their works. We will prepare one large classroom map of Paris, Spain, and other intersecting locales, as well as individual 8 x 10-inch maps by each student.
Approaches to writing: compare and contrast Hemingway and Orwell approaches to memoir (discussion).
Student work: sharing of student reading journal entries throughout; tramping and/or immersion write-ups due in week 3; you will also present your experiences to the class.

Art and Music
Artists: Bonnard, Cezanne, Gris, Matisse, Modigliani, Picasso
Music (CDs): *Café de Paris* (accordion); *Souvenir de Paris: The Great French Stars, 1920–1933; Music in Paris in the 1920s*
Films (DVDs and VHS): *Paris, The Luminous Years: Toward the Making of the Modern; Ernest Hemingway: Rivers to the Sea; Ernest Hemingway: Wrestling with Life; George Orwell: A Concise Biography*

Websites for your Reference:
The Ernest Hemingway Foundation of Oak Park (near Hemingway's boyhood homes in Oak Park, Illinois: <http://www.ehfop.org/>
The Hemingway Society: <http://hemingwaysociety.org/>
The Michigan Hemingway Society: <http://www.michiganhemingwaysociety.org/>
George Orwell: <http://www.george-orwell.org/>

Unit Two: Spanish Civil War (5 weeks)
Background: history of the Spanish Civil War, including Russian influence, Axis involvement, and the International Brigade of Volunteers (lecture/

discussion/films—including Allegro's *The Spanish Civil War* and Hemingway's *The Spanish Earth*, the latter shown either at this point or near the end of this unit)

Works: for Hemingway, we will examine material from Seán Hemingway's *Hemingway on War*; Hemingway's *By-Line*; and the stories "The Butterfly and the Tank," "Night Before Battle," and "The Denunciation" from *CSTFV* (*Note to educators: It is possible to condense here and use only the Seán Hemingway volume for this portion*); and *For Whom the Bell Tolls*. For Orwell, we will examine *Homage to Catalonia* readings (factual material by Orwell about his Spanish Civil War experiences) and also Orwell's *Diaries*.

The Spy Motif in Spain: we will examine Hemingway's play, *The Fifth Column*, and relate it to Orwell's situation in a Trotsykite POUM unit (members accused falsely by Stalin as being part of the Fifth Column)

Closing discussions: we will compare and contrast Hemingway and Orwell and their attitudes toward Spain, Stalin, communism, fascism.

Setting: mapping project continues throughout Unit 2

Student work: short oral reports on more specific aspects of Hemingway's or Orwell's involvement in Spain, or on Spain's own civil war writers (your choice) will be due last week of this unit. Also due before the end of the unit will be a 2-page stylistic comp arison in bulleted list form, with quoted examples from Orwell and Hemingway

Art and Music

Spanish artists from the thirties and their art work: Miro's *Aidez l'Espagne* (Help Spain) and *The Giant Awakening*; Dali's *Espagne*; Picasso's *Femme en Pleurs* (Weeping Woman) and *Guernica*. See also Robert Trogdon's visual volume, *Ernest Hemingway: A Literary Reference* (note chapter 4 for Spanish Civil War propaganda posters); a Spanish poster art site called <http://libraries.ucsd.edu/speccoll/visfront/vizindex.html>; and the separate Spanish Civil War section on <http://posterart.com/>.

Spanish writers for individual short reports: Federico Garcia Lorca, Francisco Ayala, Ramon Sander, Alejandro Casona, Gamon Gomez de la Serna, Benjammin Jarnes, Carmen Lafore; as well as poets Germain Bleiberg, Miguel Hernandez, Leopoldo Panero, Luis Roslaes, and Luis Felipe Viranco

Music (CDs): *Music of the Spanish Civil War*; *Pasiones: Songs of the Spanish Civil War, 1936–1939*; *Songs of the Spanish Civil War*, vols. 1 and 2; and *Spain in My Heart: Songs of the Spanish Civil War*

Films (possible DVDs): Hemingway's *The Spanish Earth;* Terkel's *The Good Fight: The Abraham Lincoln Brigade in the Spanish Civil War;* Allegro's *The Spanish Civil War*

Websites for your Reference
The Abraham Lincoln Brigade Archives (ALBA): <www.alba-valb.org> (*Note to educators: this site also provides helpful classroom materials designed for teachers and professors.*)
La Guerra Civil Española, 1936-1939 (the largest Spanish Civil War site, presented in Spanish): <http://www.guerracivil.org/>
Spanish War page of the War Poets Association: <http://www.warpoets.org/conflicts/spanish-war/>

Other cultural activities
We also may share a Spanish Night Fiesta with music, food, and perhaps dance, in honor of what Gellhorn called "the most beautiful people on earth"

Unit Three: World War II (2–3 weeks)
Biography (lecture and readings); plus World War II historical overview (with emphasis on England, France, Russia)
Reading/Discussions: Orwell's *Diaries,* particularly on the London Blitzkrieg and so on, and his commentaries; lecture on Hemingway's arrival in Europe and various dispatches (augmented by a film about D-Day and a few of Martha Gellhorn's writings about D-Day)
Short Stories: we will look at several by Hemingway chosen from the following: "Black Ass at the Crossroads" and—from *Across the River and Into the Trees*—"The Taking of Paris," "The Valhalla Express," "The Pistol Slappers," "The Chain of Command," "The Ivy Leaf," and/or "The Dead." Other stories not directly about World War II but rather about war in general that may be covered include "A Way You'll Never Be" and "Under the Ridge."
Discussion: Hemingway and Orwell together at the war's end; back to Paris in 1945 (full circle)
Student work: Creative responses and creative writing may include writing creative dialogue or one-act plays about the writers' Paris meeting and, time permitting, writing fictional letters between the two writers, either discussing their writing or involving theoretical philosophical exchange of ideas or political views reflecting what is really known about their posi-

tions. A literary analysis or comparative journalism analysis of 5–6 pages (with a choice of works) is due during this unit. Term research projects (12+ pages) will be assigned at this point if not before and will be due at the end of the course.

Unit Four: Post–World War II Writing, The Masterworks (5 weeks)
Overview: Orwell to island of Jura; Hemingway to island of Cuba
Works: Orwell's *Animal Farm* and *1984*; Hemingway's *The Old Man and the Sea* and part 1 of *Islands in the Stream*
Short visual films and websites: *Accidental Eden* (on Cuba) and Rick Steves's *Ireland and Scotland* (with a portion on Jura). You may also wish to peruse the Isle of Jura website <http://isleofjura.scot/> for information about Orwell's island as we visualize the beautiful solitudes where these two writers were creating their masterworks in their respective towers/attics

Unit 5—Course Wind-Down, Best Days and Closings
Author Struggles and the Nobel Prize: See material on Hemingway on Nobel Prize website, <NobelPrize.org>
Student work: Creative writing idea: nominate George Orwell for the Nobel Prize and explain why he might have deserved it. Final research studies and presentations come due (last week of regular class)

Note to educators: A quarter-based system will require you to pick and choose quite selectively from this syllabus OR omit some portions entirely, focusing just on Spain, for instance. One could also recast this plan as two full courses, perhaps Hemingway and Orwell, parts 1 and 2. The syllabus as presented is heavily weighted, with many options from which any teacher may choose as materials are available, personal interest suits, or student needs dictate. The more you work with these two writers in juxtaposition, the more you will see intriguing ways to shape a meaningful learning experience around Hemingway and Orwell together.

Please see <http://jeanjespersenbartholomew.com> for additional course suggestions, syllabi, and amplifying materials. Syllabi variations available online include "Spy Literature," "A War for Authors: The Spanish Civil War," and "Freedom as Paradigm Shift—Hemingway and Orwell." Additional background books and additional media resources are also identified at this site.

Appendix I

Model Assignments

I. Understanding Modernism Model Assignment

Purpose
The tenets of modernism are both abstract and connected to a specific twentieth-century historical moment. Though still present in today's culture, these ideas are by their very nature fluid, unlimited by concrete definition, and structured by modes of thinking rather than finalized facts. These characteristics make these ideas both very valuable and very difficult. To increase your understanding of these ideas, I am asking you to think beyond traditional language and use more abstract means to them. Essentially, if you can't express the tenets of modernism in words, can you express them with a picture, a sculpture, a recording, an image, a demonstration?

Procedure
1. You are to develop a visual or aural model of your understanding of one tenet of modernism.
2. While you may define visual model or aural model as you like, be sure to get your idea approved by me. What you may not do is rely on the written word exclusively.
3. You will need to schedule one conference with me to discuss your model, what it means, how it portrays modernism for you, and how you plan to present it to your classmates.
4. You will present your model and explain it to the class. Time limit: 5 minutes.

Grading
1. You will be graded on content only. We will spend a great deal of class time developing your critical thinking skills. This assignment should demonstrate your best thinking. During your presentation to class, I will evaluate you on the following: How evident is it that you understand the tenet of

modernism you have chosen? How clear is your explanation in your class presentation? How well do you answer classmates' questions?
2. You will not be graded on the visual or oral quality of your model. This is not an art class. Since I am not teaching any techniques for model production, you will not be graded on art techniques.

II. Close Reading Essay Model Assignment

Each option listed should produce a 10-page paper presented in MLA format. The Works Cited should include two short stories and a minimum of three scholarly articles regarding the story not addressed in class.

Option 1: You may offer a historically contextualized close reading of a short story published in the 1920s or 1930s by an author other than Anderson, Toomer, Hemingway, or Faulkner. The purpose of the close reading is to demonstrate that the strains of early American modernism developed by Toomer, Hemingway, or Faulkner continue in others' work.

Option 2: You may write a historically contextualized close reading of two stories, one a story assigned for class and the other a story by another American author published in the 1920s or 1930s. You are to compare and contrast the elements of modernism you find in the two stories. The purpose of the comparison is to explore distinct developments of American modernism.

Option 3: You may present a historically contextualized close reading of a story published after 1936 by either Hemingway or Faulkner. The purpose of the close reading is to offer an analysis of the developments in stylistic and ideological modernism in the work of a specific writer.

Appendix J

The Futurist Manifesto (originally titled Manifesto of Futurism), excerpt

F. T. Marinetti, 1909

1. We want to sing the love of danger, the habit of energy and rashness.
2. The essential elements of our poetry will be courage, audacity and revolt.
3. Literature has up to now magnified pensive immobility, ecstasy and slumber. We want to exalt movements of aggression, feverish sleeplessness, the double march, the perilous leap, the slap and the blow with the fist.
4. We declare that the splendor of the world has been enriched by a new beauty: the beauty of speed. A racing automobile with its bonnet adorned with great tubes like serpents with explosive breath . . . a roaring motor car which seems to run on machine-gun fire, is more beautiful than the Victory of Samothrace.
5. We want to sing the man at the wheel, the ideal axis of which crosses the earth, itself hurled along its orbit.
6. The poet must spend himself with warmth, glamour and prodigality to increase the enthusiastic fervor of the primordial elements.
7. Beauty exists only in struggle. There is no masterpiece that has not an aggressive character. Poetry must be a violent assault on the forces of the unknown, to force them to bow before man.
8. We are on the extreme promontory of the centuries! What is the use of looking behind at the moment when we must open the mysterious shutters of the impossible? Time and Space died yesterday. We are already living in the absolute, since we have already created eternal, omnipresent speed.
9. We want to glorify war—the only cure for the world—militarism, patriotism, the destructive gesture of the anarchists, the beautiful ideas which kill, and contempt for woman.
10. We want to demolish museums and libraries, fight morality, feminism and all opportunist and utilitarian cowardice.

11. We will sing of the great crowds agitated by work, pleasure and revolt; the multi-colored and polyphonic surf of revolutions in modern capitals: the nocturnal vibration of the arsenals and the workshops beneath their violent electric moons: the gluttonous railway stations devouring smoking serpents; factories suspended from the clouds by the thread of their smoke; bridges with the leap of gymnasts flung across the diabolic cutlery of sunny rivers: adventurous steamers sniffing the horizon; great-breasted locomotives, puffing on the rails like enormous steel horses with long tubes for bridle, and the gliding flight of aeroplanes whose propeller sounds like the flapping of a flag and the applause of enthusiastic crowds.

Standing on the world's summit we launch once again our insolent challenge to the stars!

Note to educators: Often, students will react strongly to the manifesto, which, among other audacious statements, asserts a desire to "glorifying . . . contempt for women" and to "demolish feminism." First, it is best to place these comments into the radical context of the manifesto, which calls for disregarding almost all established traditions and institutions. Then, explore the surprising way that Marinetti later explains the first phrase. His argument is against romantic love— "nothing but an invention of the poets"—which limits the aspirations of both men and women to fully realize their (equal) potential as human beings unfettered by gender roles. His call to "fight feminism" aims at freeing women from traditional rules of femininity, calling those prescribed roles "intellectual and erotic slavery" (see "Contempt for Women," in Marinetti's Le Futurisme, Paris, 1911).

See <http://vserver1.cscs.lsa.umich.edu/~crshalizi/T4PM/futurist-manifesto.html>. Text of translation taken from James Joll, *Three Intellectuals in Politics,* New York: Pantheon, 1961).

Appendix K

Opening Lines of Famous Novels before Ernest Hemingway

1. The Introduction to the work, or bill of fare to the feast.

An author ought to consider himself, not as a gentleman who gives a private or eleemosynary treat, but rather as one who keeps a public ordinary, at which all persons are welcome for their money. In the former case, it is well known that the entertainer provides what fare he pleases; and though this should be very indifferent, and utterly disagreeable to the taste of his company, they must not find any fault; nay, on the contrary, good breeding forces them outwardly to approve and to commend whatever is set before them. Now the contrary of this happens to the master of an ordinary. Men who pay for what they eat will insist on gratifying their palates, however nice and whimsical these may prove; and if everything is not agreeable to their taste, will challenge a right to censure, to abuse, and to d__n their dinner without control.

2. It is a truth universally acknowledged, that a single man in possession of a good fortune must be in want of a wife.

However little known the feelings or views of such a man may be on his first entering a neighbourhood, this truth is so well fixed in the minds of the surrounding families, that he is considered as the rightful property of some one or other of their daughters.

3. A throng of bearded men, in sad-colored garments, and grey, steeple-crowned hats, intermixed with women, some wearing hoods and others bareheaded, was assembled in front of a wooden edifice, the door of which was heavily timbered with oak, and studded with iron spikes.

The founders of a new colony, whatever Utopia of human virtue and happiness they might originally project, have invariably recognized it among their earliest practical necessities to allot a portion of the virgin soil as a cemetery, and another portion as the site of a prison.

4. My father's family name being Pirrip, and my Christian name Philip, my infant tongue could make of both names nothing longer or more explicit than Pip. So, I called myself Pip, and came to be called Pip.

I give Pirrip as my father's family name, on the authority of his tombstone and my sister—Mrs. Joe Gargery, who married the blacksmith. As I never saw my father or my mother, and never saw any likeness of either of them (for their days were long before the days of photographs), my first fancies regarding what they were like, were unreasonably derived from their tombstones. The shape of the letters on my father's, gave me an odd idea that he was a square, stout, dark man, with curly black hair. From the character and turn of the inscription, "Also Georgiana Wife of the Above," I drew a childish conclusion that my mother was freckled and sickly. To five little stone lozenges, each about a foot and a half long, which were arranged in a neat row beside their grave, and were sacred to the memory of five little brothers of mine—who gave up trying to get a living, exceedingly early in that universal struggle—I am indebted for a belief I religiously entertained that they had all been born on their backs with their hands in their trousers-pockets, and had never taken them out in this state of existence.

5. You don't know about me without you have read a book by the name of "The Adventures of Tom Sawyer," but that ain't no matter. That book was made by Mr. Mark Twain, and he told the truth, mainly. There was things which he stretched, but mainly he told the truth. That is nothing. I never seen anybody but lied one time or another, without it was Aunt Polly, or the widow, or maybe Mary. Aunt Polly—Tom's Aunt Polly, she is—and Mary, and the Widow Douglas is all told about in that book, which is mostly a true book, with some stretchers, as I said before.

Answer key:
1. *Tom Jones,* Henry Fielding, 1749
2. *Pride and Prejudice,* Jane Austen, 1813
3. *The Scarlet Letter,* Nathaniel Hawthorne, 1850
4. *Great Expectations,* Charles Dickens, 1861
5. *The Adventures of Huckleberry Finn,* Mark Twain (Samuel Clemens), 1885

Appendix L

Horace and Wilfred Owen

Horace

The first recorded use of the sentiment "Dulce et decorum est pro patria mori" (It is sweet and glorious to die for one's country) was in an ode by Quintus Horatius Flaccus (BCE 8 December 65 to BCE 27 November 8), who is known as Horace in English and Orazio in Italian. Horace was the leading lyric poet in Rome during the reign of Rome's first emperor, Augustus. Horace worked under the patronage of Maecenas, a poetry-loving aristocrat who was close to Augustus. For centuries, the tradition of the citizen-soldier had underpinned Rome's military success and built an empire around the Mediterranean. For Roman society, the sacrifice of life for one's country was both common and admired.

> "Sweet and glorious it is to die for one's country."
> It is sweet and proper to die for one's country
> and death pursues even the man who flees
> nor spares the hamstrings or cowardly
> backs of battle-shy youths.

Or

> It's sweet and fitting to die for one's country.
> Yet death chases after the soldier who runs,
> and it won't spare the cowardly back
> or the limbs, of peace-loving young men.

Wilfred Owen

British poet Wilfred Owen first used the phrase, in English rather than Latin, in a poem drafted in 1915, initially called "The Ballad of Peace and War." He never completed the poem. One version reads:

O it is meet and it is sweet
To live in peace with others.
But sweeter still and far more meet
To die in war for brothers.

Owen's later poem, "Dulce et Decorum est," written in 1917, became one of the best-known poems of World War I.

DULCE ET DECORUM EST
Bent double, like old beggars under sacks,
Knock-kneed, coughing like hags, we cursed through sludge,
Till on the haunting flares we turned our backs,
And towards our distant rest began to trudge.
Men marched asleep. Many had lost their boots,
But limped on, blood-shod. All went lame, all blind;
Drunk with fatigue; deaf even to the hoots
Of gas-shells dropping softly behind.

Gas! GAS! Quick, boys!—An ecstasy of fumbling
Fitting the clumsy helmets just in time,
But someone still was yelling out and stumbling
And flound'ring like a man in fire or lime.—
Dim through the misty panes and thick green light,
As under a green sea, I saw him drowning.

In all my dreams before my helpless sight
He plunges at me, guttering, choking, drowning.

If in some smothering dreams, you too could pace
Behind the wagon that we flung him in,
And watch the white eyes writhing in his face,
His hanging face, like a devil's sick of sin,
If you could hear, at every jolt, the blood
Come gargling from the froth-corrupted lungs
Bitter as the cud
Of vile, incurable sores on innocent tongues,—
My friend, you would not tell with such high zest
To children ardent for some desperate glory,

The old Lie: *Dulce et decorum est*
Pro patria mori.

For the quotation from Horace's *Odes,* see ll. 13–16, Bk. III, 2, *The Complete Odes and Epodes,* trans. W. G. Shepherd (New York 1988), 131.

For the quotation from "The Ballad of Peace and War," see Wilfred Owen, *The Complete Poems and Fragments,* ed. Jon Stallworthy, 2 vols. (London: Chatto and Windus, 1983), 1:140; for that from "Dulce et Decorum est," see Wilfred Owen, *Poems* (London: Chatto and Windus, 1920, 15.

Appendix M

Response Questions

The Sun Also Rises:

- How do you interpret the epigraph from Ecclesiastes?
- Pound and Mussolini both said, "make it new." What's new?
- Can you find a microcosm of modernism?
- Can you find a microcosm of futurism?
- All literature involves a quest. What is it?
- Who or what is a code hero in this novel (in reference to the *Futurist Manifesto*)?
- How do you read the last line, with regard to both Jake and Brett, and also with regard to the futurist solution to the modernist dilemma?

A Farewell to Arms

- Is *A Farewell to Arms* a war story, a romance, an anti-war novel?
- Has futurism survived?
- Why does Catherine compare Frederic to "Othello with his occupation gone" (*FTA* 228)?
- Describe Hemingway the writer in a futurist context.

A highly useful website for researching *A Farewell to Arms* is a concordance to words and concepts found in the text at <http://vccslitonline.vccs.edu/afta>, hosted by the Virginia Community College System.

Appendix N

Italian Futurism and *The Great Gatsby*

The five major thematic elements present in Marinetti's *Futurist Manifesto* subsequently appear as identical figures and tropes in Fitzgerald's *The Great Gatsby*. The corresponding representations appear in the following passages:

1. Romanticized industrial settings

> We will sing of the great crowds agitated by work, pleasure and revolt; the multi-colored and polyphonic surf of revolutions in modern capitals: the nocturnal vibration of the arsenals and the workshops beneath their violent electric moons: the gluttonous railway stations devouring smoking serpents; factories suspended from the clouds by the thread of their smoke; bridges with the leap of gymnasts flung across the diabolic cutlery of sunny rivers; adventurous steamers sniffing the horizon; great-breasted locomotives, puffing on the rails like enormous steel horses with long tubes for bridle, and the gliding flight of aeroplanes whose propeller sounds like the flapping of a flag and the applause of enthusiastic crowds. (Marinetti, *Futurist Manifesto*)

> About half way between West Egg and New York the motor road hastily joins the railroad.... This is a valley of ashes—a fantastic farm where ashes grow like wheat into ridges and hills and grotesque gardens; where ashes take the forms of houses and chimneys and rising smoke and, finally, with a transcendent effort, of men who move dimly and already crumbling through the powdery air. Occasionally a line of gray cars crawls along an invisible track, gives out a ghastly creak, and comes to rest, and immediately the ash-gray men swarm up with leaden spades and stir up an impenetrable cloud, which screens their obscure operations from your sight. (Fitzgerald, *The Great Gatsby*, ch. 2)

2. The "machine in the garden" (or, an automobile crashing into a ditch)

> We drove on, crushing beneath our burning wheels, like shirt-collars under the

iron, the watch dogs on the steps of the houses. . . . I stopped short, and in disgust hurled myself—vlan!—head over heels in a ditch. Oh, maternal ditch, half full of muddy water! A factory gutter! I savored a mouthful of strengthening muck which recalled the black teat of my Sudanese nurse! (Marinetti, *Futurist Manifesto*)

In the ditch beside the road, right side up, but violently shorn of one wheel, rested a new coupe which had left Gatsby's drive not two minutes before. The sharp jut of a wall accounted for the detachment of the wheel, which was now getting considerable attention from half a dozen curious chauffeurs. (Fitzgerald, *The Great Gatsby*, ch. 3)

3. The automobile as the new beautiful

We declare that the splendor of the world has been enriched by a new beauty: the beauty of speed. A racing automobile with its bonnet adorned with great tubes like serpents with explosive breath . . . a roaring motor car which seems to run on machine-gun fire, is more beautiful than the Victory of Samothrace. (Marinetti, *Futurist Manifesto*)

At nine o'clock, one morning late in July, Gatsby's gorgeous car lurched up the rocky drive to my door and gave out a burst of melody from its three-noted horn. . . . He saw me looking with admiration at his car. "It's pretty, isn't it, old sport?" He jumped off to give me a better view. "Haven't you ever seen it before?" I'd seen it. Everybody had seen it. It was a rich cream color, bright with nickel, swollen here and there in its monstrous length with triumphant hat-boxes and supper-boxes and tool-boxes, and terraced with a labyrinth of wind-shields that mirrored a dozen suns. Sitting down behind many layers of glass in a sort of green leather conservatory, we started to town. (Fitzgerald, *The Great Gatsby*, ch. 4)

4. Peaking at the age of thirty

The oldest among us are not yet thirty years old: we have therefore at least ten years to accomplish our task. When we are forty let younger and stronger men than we throw us in the waste paper basket like useless manuscripts! They will come against us from afar, leaping on the light cadence of their first poems, clutching the air with their predatory fingers and sniffing at the gates of the academies the good scent of our decaying spirits. . . . The oldest among us are not yet thirty, and yet we have already wasted treasures, treasures of strength, love, courage and keen will, hastily, deliriously, without thinking, with all our might, till we are out of breath. (Marinetti, *Futurist Manifesto*)

I was thirty. Before me stretched the portentous, menacing road of a new decade.

It was seven o'clock when we got into the coupe with him and started for Long Island. Tom talked incessantly, exulting and laughing, but his voice was as remote from Jordan and me as the foreign clamor on the sidewalk or the tumult of the elevated overhead. Human sympathy has its limits, and we were content to let all their tragic arguments fade with the city lights behind. Thirty—the promise of a decade of loneliness, a thinning list of single men to know, a thinning brief-case of enthusiasm, thinning hair. But there was Jordan beside me, who, unlike Daisy, was too wise ever to carry well-forgotten dreams from age to age. As we passed over the dark bridge her wan face fell lazily against my coat's shoulder and the formidable stroke of thirty died away with the reassuring pressure of her hand.

So we drove on toward death through the cooling twilight. (Fitzgerald, *The Great Gatsby*, ch. 7)

5. Wanton pursuit of the future

"Come, my friends!" I said. "Let us go! At last Mythology and the mystic cult of the ideal have been left behind. We are going to be present at the birth of the centaur and we shall soon see the first angels fly! We must break down the gates of life to test the bolts and the padlocks! Let us go! Here is the very first sunrise on earth! Nothing equals the splendor of its red sword which strikes for the first time in our millennial darkness." (Marinetti, *Futurist Manifesto*)

Outside the wind was loud and there was a faint flow of thunder along the Sound. All the lights were going on in West Egg now; the electric trains, men-carrying, were plunging home through the rain from New York. It was the hour of a profound human change, and excitement was generating on the air. (Fitzgerald, *The Great Gatsby*, ch. 5)

Gatsby believed in the green light, the orgastic future that year by year recedes before us. It eluded us then, but that's no matter—to-morrow we will run faster, stretch out our arms farther.... And one fine morning——

So we beat on, boats against the current, borne back ceaselessly into the past. (Fitzgerald, *The Great Gatsby*, ch. 9)

Appendix O

Cultural Report Assignment

For this project, you will prepare a 10 minute oral presentation.

Research any aspect of World War I (e.g., a specific battle, medical care, shell shock, weaponry, women and war) or any aspect of American culture relating to the historical period immediately following the war (1919-1929), and prepare a ten-minute presentation through which you will teach the class about some aspect of Jazz Era culture.

You may research any aspect of this period that interests you: fashion; cars; the Red Scare; Prohibition; the changing role of women; the rise of talking pictures; the development of Hollywood, sporting events; art deco art and architecture; the stock market crash; the rise of organized crime; international flight; trans-Atlantic luxury liners; or advances in medicine, science, and technology.

Be creative: For example,

- Play jazz for the class and teach us how it works;
- Prepare a mock period sportscast with YouTube clips of actual sporting events. Teach us something about changes in sports during this period;
- Prepare slides of period clothing and help us to imagine Jazz Age fashion;
- Gather newspaper articles about an actual event (e.g., the stock market crash) and prepare a radio broadcast or PowerPoint presentation that recreates the events of a significant day or time;
- Teach us how to dance the Charleston or another period dance;
- Act out a short scene from a period play (e.g., one by Eugene O'Neill);
- Invite us onto an early flight, explain our destination and what we might expect to experience during the journey;
- Show us slides or film clips about World War I medical equipment; military uniforms; period weapons, and so on;
- Show us clips from period movies and explain changes in film. Read us period film reviews (*The New Yorker* magazine, for example, has film reviews dating back to 1925).

The use of audiovisual tools is highly encouraged; you may wish to show photos or period videos from YouTube, for example, or create a PowerPoint presentation on your subject. You have access to internet, audio, video, and/or DVD equipment in the classroom. If you use PowerPoint, remember to e-mail the presentation to yourself and make sure it will work in Microsoft.

Grading: This assignment will count as 10 percent of your class grade. You will be given one mark out of five for content (creativity, quality of information, interest, specific details, consistency, good overview, organization) and one mark out of five for presentation (professional delivery, volume, clarity, success in staying within the assigned time limits, good pace, eye contact).

Appendix P

Make it Swing! Interdisciplinary Research Paper

For this assignment, you will write a research paper of 10 to 12 pages. All papers should employ careful reading of the texts, attention to the cultural context of the art you are examining, and one other interdisciplinary critical focus (chosen from the list below).

1. Theology: Explore American traditions of spiritual seeking by comparing the religious-themed prose or poetry of an American writer from the Jazz Age or the Harlem Renaissance (e.g., James Weldon Johnson or Zora Neale Hurston) against the religious prose or poetry of an American writer today (e.g., Mary Oliver or Mary Karr). You could also consider the religious writing of a modern American rock or pop star (e.g., Bruce Springsteen's "I'll Work For Your Love," or Macy Gray's "I Can't Wait to Meetchu"). How do these writers seek and find God? In what ways are their eyes watching God?

2. Art: How does art influence the interpretation of a song or poem? What sort of synergies emerge when artists collaborate on a poetic project (e.g., James Weldon Johnson and Aaron Douglas; Langston Hughes and Aaron Douglas; Langston Hughes and Prentiss Taylor)? For this project, compare art and poetry projects from the Harlem Renaissance with the interrelationship between art and poetry today (e.g., through an analysis of album cover art for a particular rap artist or analysis of a music video as a means of interpreting a contemporary song). What difference does the art make to the words? You may want to make use of the resources in Special Collections for this project.

3. Politics: What makes artists, and their art, such a threat? For this project, examine the art of political protest. Compare modern art on a political topic (e.g., anti-war songs, poems, or paintings; art in support of social justice) with art from the Jazz Age and the Harlem Renaissance (e.g., Fitzgerald's short story "May Day"; poetry by Claude McKay or Langston Hughes; Willa Cather's

"Coming, Aphrodite!"; Ernest Hemingway's "On The Quai at Smyrna"). Examine how art moves people and why it is such an effective method for achieving political awareness and change.

4. **Sociology:** For this option, examine art as a social barometer. What do Hemingway's short stories or Langston Hughes's poems, for example, reveal about the psychological effects of war or racism? Compare Jazz Age and Harlem Renaissance art to modern art or films about war service (e.g., *Generation Kill* on Iraq) or racism (e.g., *Malcolm X*). How does art of the Jazz Age or Harlem Renaissance capture real and continuing social issues?

5. **Feminism:** Examine depictions of female characters by male and/or female artists. How does the gender of the artist influence the portrayal of female characters? What trends do modern portrayals of women have in common with portrayals of women from the 1920s and 1930s? What has changed? What has remained the same? You could, for example, compare portrayals of women in poetry or prose by Jazz Age artists (e.g., Hemingway, Cather, Parker, Hurston, Fitzgerald, Millay) with portrayals of female characters in modern novels, TV shows, or films (e.g., "Sex in the City").

6. **Folklife:** Explore any issue of your choice from *Their Eyes Were Watching God* in connection with the Casebook essays and/or Zora Neale Hurston's collection of folklife material at the Library of Congress.

7. **Open Discipline:** Design your own topic. Be sure that your topic is interdisciplinary in some way (i.e., that it combines the study of literature with some other academic discipline) and that it requires consideration of the material studied during this course. Discuss your topic with me to ensure it will fit the project parameters.

Grading: This assignment will count as 35 percent of your class grade. You will be given one mark out of five for each of the following categories:
- Interdisciplinary research methodology: You might read articles by scholars who conduct interdisciplinary work; read articles by, or interview, professors, musicians, art historians, curators, librarians, or other experts able to give you insights into your subject. I expect to see research on what scholars or other experts have to say on your topic.

- Innovation: You might listen to music or watch films from the 1920s, find early twentieth-century newspaper reviews, or examine historical documents. For contrasts, look at contemporary sources (through YouTube, Facebook, etc.) for recent trends in American art; use art galleries, special collections, or specialized databases. Incorporate innovation into your paper: append music, a video link, digital photographs, or a photocopy of a newspaper review.
- Close reading of the texts: Make effective use of quotes and employ extensive detail. Show that you have paid attention to the biographical, historical, and cultural contexts in which Jazz Age and Harlem Renaissance literature was written.
- Effective rhetoric: Use clear, correct prose.
- Effective ordering and presentation of material: Your paper should have a strong main idea, a title and introduction, a clear ordering of ideas, and a conclusion.
- Personal insights on the material under discussion: Explain why does the material affects you and why you think this material works so well as art.

Class Symposium

Your final assignment is to present a five- to eight-minute oral summary of your final research paper to the class. The presentation should give the essay's thesis (main idea) and a detailed description of one of your main points. Do not try to summarize your entire paper. In order to ensure all students have a chance to present, the time limit will be strictly enforced; any presentations exceeding the limit will be cut off.

I encourage the use of handouts, PowerPoint slides, film clips, or other audiovisual aids, especially for papers with a visual component.

Grading: All students will be given one mark out of ten for the content (quality of information, interest, specific details, good overview, Organization) and one mark out of ten for presentation (professional delivery, volume, clarity, eye contact, conformity to time limit).

Appendix Q

Self-Guided Field Trips and Reading Self-Assessment

Note to educators: For classes on the Jazz Age and the Harlem Renaissance, including the teaching of Hemingway's modernism, I usually design an assignment that will require the students to conduct two self-guided field trips throughout the semester. These can change every semester depending on what is available in the city where you teach. The nice thing about self-guided field trips is that you do not have to organize how the students will get there, or when they go. They are expected to conduct these field trips on their own time. For the self-guided field trips, I usually try to suggest things the students can do for free, or for very limited cost. I hand out the field trip assignment at the beginning of the course to give the students the maximum amount of time to work this activity into their semester planning. I also tend to use interactive course planning tools, such as Blackboard, to communicate with students if new field trip options come to my attention after the course has already started. Every community offers a widely available range of options for helping students to connect to the culture of the 1920s and 1930s. For example, look for local student jazz concerts (these are often available for free at high schools and university campuses); local museum exhibitions or the collections of a local historical society; community walking tours of art deco art and architecture; or community theater productions of plays from the era. Plays by Noel Coward tend to turn up with particular frequency.

This assignment has two parts, both of which involve your reflections on your class notes and your reading logs. Please note: you do not have to separate the two parts of the assignment if it makes more sense to you to roll them both into one. If you do decide to break your response into two parts, remember to use interesting subtitles instead of labeling them "part one" and "part two." Total length of assignment: 8 pages

Part 1: Legacy of the Jazz Age and the Harlem Renaissance (4 pages)

In keeping with our course theme—thinking about the historical continuity between our own times and the American Jazz Age—write a 4-page reflection based on any two self-directed field trips of your choice from the following list. (You may wish to make your own arrangements to go in groups.) In your response, reflect upon how experiencing an aspect of the Jazz Age or Harlem Renaissance today affected you as a viewer or listener. In what ways does the art and history of that period still speak to us? In what ways does the Jazz Age still matter?

- Attend a jazz concert: for example, "Take 5!" The Smithsonian Art Museum hosts free jazz concerts every third Thursday of the month (Metro stop: Gallery Place). See <http://americanart.si.edu/calendar/index.cfm?month=2&year=2009&date=2/1/2009>. There are also often free student jazz concerts on campus. Check the music department's website.
- Visit the Alexandria Black History Museum at 902 Wythe Street, Alexandria, Virginia (Metro stop: Braddock Road; admission: $2:00; hours: Tues–Sat. 10:00–4:00). See <http://alexandriava.gov/BlackHistory>. This museum tells the story of slavery in Alexandria. For Jazz Age history, be sure to watch the short video on the founding of the library. For specific directions see <http://oha.alexandriava.gov/plan-your-visit/bh-py-visit.html>.
- Take the two-hour walking tour "Before Harlem, There Was U Street" (meeting place: U Street/Cardozo Metro station, 13th Street exit; cost: $10.00; time: beginning 1 April 2009, Saturdays, 10:30 A.M.). See "Discover Washington's 'Black Broadway'" webpage, <http://www.washingtonwalks.com/tours/u-street.shtml>. Your guide will wear a blue and green Washington Walks badge. No reservations are necessary; walks are given rain or shine. .
- Attend a gospel service, at St. William's Chapel (place: Copley Hall, main campus, Georgetown University; time: every Sunday at 5:30 P.M.). Services are free, but it would be considerate to take an offering. See <http://campusministry.georgetown.edu/religious-services>.
- See "Paris/New York: Design Fashion Culture 1925–1940," at the Museum of the City of New York, New York, NY (3 Oct. through 22 Feb. 2009) (suggested admission as of 20 Feb. 2006, $5.00 for seniors and, students; free on Sundays, between 10:00 A.M. and 12 noon). See <http://www.mcny.org/exhibitions/current/paris-new-york-design-fashion-culture-1925-1940.html>.

Part 2: You, the Reader (4 pages)

For the second part of this assignment, use your past reading logs, your course notes, and your memory of class experiences to write a 4-page reflection on whether you are now a different kind of reader of Jazz Age literature than when you began this course. What kinds of things do you know now that you didn't know before you took this course—about the act of reading Jazz Age prose and poetry and about how those texts work?

Tell me stories about stories. How did literature end up surprising you in this class? I'm especially interested in hearing about any revelatory moments. In other words, tell me about any "AHA!" moments you've had as a result of this class. What kinds of insights did you have about a particular poem, a scene in a novel, or about a song as a result of something we did in class, or something you did as part of a field trip? How you structure this response is your choice (e.g., do you want to concentrate on a series of minor insights and link them to an overall thesis or theme about how your reading habits have changed? Or do you want to concentrate on one or two insights you had about how Jazz Age era poetry, music, and novels work?)

Grading: I will be looking for level of detail (specific examples from your class experiences, class notes, and quotes from your own reading logs); for clear, correct, accurate prose; and for your level of creativity, insight, and thoughtfulness in responding to the self-directed field trips and in thinking about your own in-class experiences.

Appendix R

Small-Group Activities and Writing Assignments

Small-Group Activities

1. To begin, I erase the notes from the lecture-board and write a list of places. The list would include San Juan, Mayagüez, New York, Hong Kong, Los Angeles, and Dubai, together with the settings of short stories or novels that we have studied previously in the course. The class is divided into groups of three or four students. Each group chooses a place from the list before I give the assignment. The assignment is for the groups to rewrite an episode of "Homage to Switzerland" set in a train station in the city they have chosen, paying close attention to the language, climate, and clientele (character demography) of the new location. To prime the process, I ask two questions: How is the station similar to and different from the original location? (I usually mention pretzels here, to cue our thinking beyond what has been set out in the instructions.) How do the distinct characteristics of the new city shape what occurs in the story?

2. I divide the class into groups of three or four students. After erasing the class notes, I make a list of the characters from the story on the board. Each group chooses a character. Their assignment is to draw/write a Facebook page for this person on a sheet of paper. Little prompting is needed on this task; students immerse themselves in the work, and questions emerge in each group. These may include: What is her/her status? Who would his/her friends be? What does he/she "like" and "follow"? What is his/her hometown? I take a moment to ask the students to be sure to rehash some concepts that we have touched on in the discussion, such as language, background, and markers of cultural orientation.

Writing Assignments

The small-group activity brings us to the last few minutes of class. The writing assignments below are posted on our class blog. I generally open the class webpage (<http://blogs.uprm.edu/huma3112>) at the end of the session in order to remind students about their next reading and the writing assignment. The latter usually includes several questions; the students each choose one and write a reflection (of approximately 250 words or one double-spaced page) in response:

1. Choose one of the three scenes in "Homage to Switzerland." Describe how the main characters in the scene (English-speaking man, waitress, porter, other waiting passenger) experience the episode; in one or two paragraphs per character, explain how the same reality would be slightly nuanced for each person. (In order to do this, you might consider how their perceptions depend on constructs like gender, cultural background, purpose of presence at station, economic status, age, and so on.)

2. What is the role of Einstein in "Homage to Switzerland?" Why do you think Hemingway wrote this story—and what links does its plot have with Einstein's work?

3. Compare "Homage to Switzerland" to a film, television show, novel, or song. Focus on the postmodern qualities that we have covered in class.

Appendix S

Student Prompts for Using Contemporary Reviews, Close Readings, and Primary Sources

I. Using Contemporary Reviews to Highlight Modernist Characteristics

In his 1933 review "A Letter to Mr. Hemingway," Clifton Fadiman points out Hemingway's use of "incongruous juxtaposition . . . placing two apparently unrelated aspects of life side by side so that each will unobtrusively bring out the horror of the other."

How are Madame Fontan and her husband, in "Wine of Wyoming," an example of Hemingway's "incongruous juxtaposition" in relation to the narrator, as well as to the locals, both whites and Indian, that come to their small establishment?

II. Close Readings of "Wine of Wyoming" and "A Long Christmas Dinner"

Although we have encountered these works through biographical research I ask that you change gears and apply a close reading without consideration for the biographical. We decided to explore these works in this activity because of their proximity in time with one another, both being written in 1930, but now I ask you to read them for their style, technique, and signature qualities we attribute to their modernism.

There are no other constraints on your written response, but try to find evidence that lends itself to a discussion of modernism. Your one-paragraph response could discuss the level to which dialogue carries the plot of "Wine of Wyoming," discuss the portrayal of time in "A Long Christmas Dinner," or compare another aspect of "Wine of Wyoming" to any of the plays from the collection.

III. Using Primary Sources to Guide Research

Your purpose is to determine what can be learned from the correspondence of the authors. Use the strategies for research that we practiced in class to gain insight about the authors or their work. Remember even if you don't make contact with an idea right way use the letters to guide your research toward something you haven't yet anticipated. The letters you read should determine what else you read: whether the letters lead you to the work of another author mentioned in a letter or to part of a biography referenced in a footnote, you should read all the relevant media surrounding the letters.

You could continue exploring the correspondence of those individuals we read in class, using your notes and short write-ups as a starting point for your research, or you could search the index of the collections of letters for titles, and for people you recognize from the excerpts of memoir and biography we read in class. Even better, you could just start reading and see what happens.

As you read, ask questions that require you to cross-reference another text to find the answers. The questions you pursue might be as simple as finding the title of a work left unnamed in a letter, or as complex as finding evidence of how a writer has evolved in his craft. In the first example, you could find the answer by reading the pertinent section of a biography to determine what the author was working on at that time. In the second example, you would have to read works that span the author's career, culling their titles and information about them from the letters. Of these two examples, one is only a starting point, whereas the other is a discovery worthy of scholarship.

Either way, keep a record of your readings in a bibliography that includes page numbers so you can return to them for evidence. Ultimately you will be writing an interpretive essay about an author's work that you encounter during your research of primary sources and other biographical texts. In class, we have been concerned primarily with how the authors view themselves and other prominent writers with regard to a modernist movement. In your essay you are not limited by such constraints. For example, you could search for evidence of how outside forces, such as world wars, monetary success, or the work of other writers, helped to determine the artist's new role in this era. The subject you choose is wide open for your original scholarship.

Works Cited

Adamson, Walter. "Fascinating Futurism: The Historiographical Politics of an Historical Avant garde." *Modern Italy* 13.1 (2008): 69–85.
Agathocleous, Tanya. *George Orwell: Battling Big Brother*. New York: Oxford UP, 2000.
Alfieri, Dino, and Luigi Freddi. *Mostra della Revoluzione Fascista*. Rome: Partito Nazional Fascista, 1933.
Baker, Carlos. *Ernest Hemingway: A Life Story*. New York: Scribner, 1969.
Barnard, Rita. "Modern American Fiction." In *The Cambridge Companion to American Modernism*. Ed. Walter Kalaidjian. Cambridge, UK: Cambridge UP, 2005. 39–67.
Berghaus, Günter. "The Postwar Reception of Futurism: Repression of Recuperation?" In *The History of Futurism: The Precursors, Protagonists, and Legacies*. Ed. Geert Buelens, Harald Hendrix, and Monica Jansen. Plymouth: Lexington Books, 2012. 377–403.
Bevis, William W. *Mind of Winter: Wallace Stevens, Meditation, and Literature*. Pittsburgh: U of Pittsburgh P, 1988.
Blum, Ralph. "A Play in Three Acts: I-Moscow." *The New Yorker* 16 Nov. 1963: 55.
Bowker, Gordon. *Inside George Orwell: A Biography*. New York: Palgrave/Macmillan, 2003.
Bridgman, Richard. *Gertrude Stein in Pieces*. New York: Oxford UP, 1971.
Brogan, Jacqueline V. "The 'Founding Mother': Gertrude Stein and the Cubist Phenomenon." In *Challenging Boundaries: Gender and Periodization*. Ed. Joyce W. Warren and Margaret Dickie. Athens: U of Georgia P, 2000. 248–64.
Brown, Mark. "British Library Buys Futurists' Metal Manifesto." *The Guardian* 19 Feb. 2009. Web. 18, 25 Apr. 2013. <http://www.guardian.co.uk/books/2009/feb/20/british-library-buys-futurists-manifesto?INTCMP=SRCH>.
Buzard, James. *The Beaten Track: European Tourism, Literature, and the Ways to "Culture," 1800–1918*. Oxford: Clarendon Press, 1993.
Campbell, Joseph. *The Hero with a Thousand Faces*. Princeton: Princeton UP, 1973.
Cavell, Stanley. *In Quest of the Ordinary: Lines of Skepticism and Romanticism*. Chicago: U of Chicago P, 1988.
Cohen, Milton A. *Hemingway's Laboratory: The Paris in our time*. Tuscaloosa: U of Alabama P, 2005.
———. "'There Was a Woman Having a Kid'—From Her Point of View: An Unpublished Draft of *In Our Time*'s Chapter II." *The Hemingway Review* 22.1 (2002): 105–8.
Cuddon, J. A. *Dictionary of Literary Terms and Literary Theory*. 4th ed. London: Penguin Books, 1999.

"The Effects of Absinthe—'Secondary Effects.'" Virtual Absinthe Museum. Oxygenee. Web. 12 Apr. 2012. <http://www.oxygenee.com/absinthe-effect/secondaries.html>.

1865 to the Present. Vol. 2 of *The Norton Anthology of American Literature*. Ed. Nina Baym et al. 8th shorter ed. New York: W. W. Norton, 2013.

"Ernest Hemingway: Wrestling with Life." *A & E Biography*. Narr. Mariel Hemingway. A & E Television Networks, New York, 1998. Television.

Fadiman, Clifton. "A Letter to Mr. Hemingway." *The New Yorker* 9.37 (28 Oct. 1933): 58–59.

Field, Allyson Nadia. "Expatriate Lifestyle as Tourist Destination: *The Sun Also Rises* and Experiential Travelogues of the Twenties." *The Hemingway Review* 25.2 (2006): 29–43.

Fitch, Noel Riley. *Walks in Hemingway's Paris*. New York: St. Martin's Press, 1989.

Fitzgerald, F. Scott. *The Crack-Up*. Ed. Edmund Wilson. New York: New Directions, 1945.

———. *The Great Gatsby*. Ed. Matthew J. Bruccoli. New York: Cambridge UP, 1991.

———. "Letter to Ernest Hemingway on *The Sun Also Rises*." *Antaeus* 33 (Spring 1979): 15–17.

———. "May Day." In his *Tales of the Jazz Age*. New York: Scribner, 1922. Digital Collections, University Libraries, University of South Carolina. Web. 19 Jan. 2013. <http://www.sc.edu/fitzgerald/mayday/mayday.html>.

Flynn, Catherine. "Joyce and Benjamin in Paris." *berfrois* 15 July 2011. Web. <http://www.berfrois.com/2011/07/exploration-of-paris/>.

"Foundations: Freud." Last modified 30 Sep. 2008. Yale Courses. *YouTube*. Web. <http://www.youtube.com/watch?v=7emS3ye3cVU>.

Gaillard, Theodore L., Jr. "Hemingway's Debt to Cezanne: New Perspectives." *Twentieth Century Literature* 45:1 (1999): 65–78.

Gajdusek, Robert E. "Dubliners in Michigan: Joyce's Presence in Hemingway's *In Our Time*." *Hemingway Review* 2:1 (1982): 48–61.

Gandal, Keith. "*The Great Gatsby* as Mobilization Fiction: Rethinking Modernist Prose." In *A Concise Companion to American Fiction: 1900–1950*. Ed. Peter Stoneley and Cindy Weinstein. Malden, MA: Blackwell, 2008. 132–57.

Gates, Henry Louis, Jr. *The Signifying Monkey: A Theory of African-American Literary Criticism*. New York: Oxford UP, 1988.

Gellhorn, Martha. *The Face of War*. 1959. New York: Atlantic Monthly Press, 1988.

Harris, M. A. "A Study of the Nature of Rhythm." *PMLA* 10, Appendixes 1 and 2. Proceedings 1895. xxi–xxv.

Haynes, John Earl, et al. *Spies: The Rise and Fall of the KGB in America*. New Haven: Yale UP, 2009.

Hemingway, Ernest. "The Art of the Short Story." *Paris Review* 23 (Spring 1981): 85–102.

———. *The Complete Short Stories of Ernest Hemingway: The Finca Vigía Edition*. New York: Scribner, 1987.

———. *Dateline: Toronto: The Complete "Toronto Star" Dispatches, 1920–1924*. Ed. William White. New York: Scribner, 1985.

———. *Death in the Afternoon*. New York: Scribner, 1932.

———. *Ernest Hemingway: Selected Letters 1917–1961*. Ed. Carlos Baker. New York: Charles Scribner's Sons, 1981.

———. *A Farewell to Arms*. 1929. New York: Scribner, 1995.

———. *Green Hills of Africa*. 1935. New York: Simon and Schuster, 1996.
———. *In Our Time*. 1925. Rev. ed., New York: Scribner, 1930.
———. Letter to Cyril Connolly. 15 Mar. 1948. Special Collections, University of Tulsa, Tulsa, OK.
———. Letter to Harvey Breit. 16 April to 1 May 1952. Special Collections, University of Tulsa, Tulsa, OK.
———. *The Letters of Ernest Hemingway*. Vol. 1: *1907–1922*. Ed. Sandra Spanier and Robert W. Trogdon. Cambridge, UK: Cambridge UP, 2011.
———. *Men at War*. 1942. Rpt., New York: Random House, 1982.
———. *A Moveable Feast: Sketches of the Author's Life in Paris in the Twenties*. New York: Charles Scribner's Sons, 1964.
———. *The Nick Adams Stories*. Ed. Philip Young. New York: Scribner, 1972.
———. "Nobel Prize Banquet Speech." 10 Dec. 1954. Read by John C. Cabot. Nobelprize.org. Web. <http://www.nobelprize.org/nobel_prizes/literature/laureates/1954/hemingway-speech.html>.
———. "Nobel Prize Banquet Speech," audiorecording. Read by Ernest Hemingway. Nobelprize.org. Web. <http://www.nobelprize.org/mediaplayer/index.php?id=1399>.
———. "Notes on the Next War: A Serious Topical Letter." *Esquire* Sept. 1935. Rpt. in *Hemingway on War*. Ed. Seán Hemingway. New York: Scribner, 2003. 301–6.
———. *The Old Man and the Sea*. New York: Scribner, 1952.
———. "On Writing." In *The Nick Adams Stories*. New York: Charles Scribner's Sons, 1972. 233–41.
The Short Stories: The First Forty-nine Stories with a Brief Preface by the Author. New York: Scribner, 1995.
———. "A Silent, Ghastly Procession." *The Toronto Daily Star* 20 Oct. 1922. Rpt. in *By-Line: Ernest Hemingway: Selected Articles and Dispatches of Four Decades*. By E. Hemingway. Ed. William White. Toronto: Bantam Books, 1968.
———. *The Sun Also Rises*. New York: Scribner Classic/Collier edition, 1986.
———. *The Sun Also Rises: A Facsimile Edition*. Ed Matthew J. Bruccoli. 2 vols. Detroit: Omnigraphics, Inc., 1990.
———. *To Have and Have Not*. New York: Scribner, 1937.
Herlihy-Mera, Jeffrey. *In Paris or Paname: Hemingway's Expatriate Nationalism*. Amsterdam: Rodopi, 2011.
Herman, Judith. *Trauma and Recovery*. New York: Basic Books, 1997.
Hitchens, Christopher. "On *Animal Farm*." In *Arguably: Essays*. New York: Twelve, 2011.
Holcomb, Gary Edward, and Charles Scruggs, eds. *Hemingway and the Black Renaissance*. Columbus: Ohio State UP, 2012.
Hollander, John. "Hemingway's Extraordinary Actuality." In *Modern Critical Views: Ernest Hemingway*. Ed. Harold Bloom. New York: Chelsea House Publishers, 1985.
Hotchner, A. E. *Papa Hemingway: A Personal Memoir*. New York: Random House, 1966.
Hurston, Zora Neale. *Their Eyes Were Watching God*. New York: Harper, 1994.
———. *Zora Neale Hurston: A Life in Letters*. Ed. Carla Kaplan. New York: Doubleday, 2002.

International Yearbook of Futurism Studies. Ed. Günter Berghaus. Vols. 1 and 2. Berlin: De Gruyter, 2011, 2012.
Jauss, Hans Robert, and Elizabeth Benzinger. "Literary History as a Challenge to Literary Theory." *New Literary History* 2.1 (1970): 7–37.
Jones, Jonathan. "Birds of Prey: Are Italy's 'Aeropaintings' Thrilling Celebrations of Flight—Or Just Barbaric Fascist Propaganda?" Rev. of Futurist Skies: Italian Aeropainting (art exhibit). Estorick Collection of Modern Italian Art, London. *The Guardian* 5 Jan. 2005. Web. 18, 25 April 2013. <http://www.guardian.co.uk/culture/2005/jan/05/1>.
Kant, Immanuel. *The Critique of Pure Reason*. Trans. J. M. D. Meiklejohn. Stillwell: Digireads, 2005.
Katz, Daniel. *American Modernism's Expatriate Scene*. Edinburgh: Edinburgh UP, 2007.
Kennedy, J. Gerald. *Imagining Paris: Exile, Writing, and American Identity*. New Haven: Yale UP, 1993.
LaCapra, Dominick. *Writing History, Writing Trauma*. Baltimore: Johns Hopkins UP, 2001.
Lagarde, Riana. "Hemingway's Steps Through Paris." Slow Travel France. Web. 18 Jan. 2013. <http://www.slowtrav.com/france/paris/rl_hemingway.htm>.
Laub, Dori. "Bearing Witness, or the Vicissitudes of Listening." In *Testimony: Crises of Witnessing in Literature, Psychoanalysis, and History*. Ed. Shoshana Felman and Dori Laub. New York: Routledge, 1992. 57–74.
Lehan, Richard. *Literary Modernism and Beyond: The Extended Vision and the Realms of the Text*. Baton Rouge: Louisiana State UP, 2012.
Levenson, Michael, ed. *The Cambridge Companion to Modernism*. 2nd ed. Cambridge, UK: Cambridge UP, 2011.
Lillios, Anna. "'The Monstropolous Beast': The Hurricane in Zora Neale Hurston's *Their Eyes Were Watching God*." *The Southern Quarterly* 36.3 (1998): 89–93.
Lyon, Janet. "Gender and Sexuality." *The Cambridge Companion to American Modernism*. Ed. Walter Kalaidjian. Cambridge, UK: Cambridge UP, 2005. 221–41.
MacCannell, Dean. *The Tourist: A New Theory of the Leisure Class*. Berkeley: U of California P, 1976.
Mao, Douglas, and Rebecca L. Walkowitz, eds. *Bad Modernisms*. Durham: Duke UP, 2006.
Marinetti, F. T. "Manifesto of Futurism." *Le Figaro* 20 Feb. 1909. Rpt. at Futurism. Web. 12 Apr. 2012. <http://www.unknown.nu/futurism/war.html>.
———. "War, the World's Only Hygiene." 1915. Futurism. Web. 12 Apr. 2012. <http://www.unknown.nu/futurism/war.html>.
McCann, Sean. "Teaching *In Our Time* in Our Time: An Online Professional Development Seminar." America in Class sponsored by the National Humanities Center. Web. Accessed 13 Dec. 2012. <http://americainclass.org/seminars/teaching-in-our-time-in-our-time/>.
McRae, John, and Malachi Edwin Vethamani. *Now Read On: A Course in Multicultural Reading*. London: Routledge, 1999.
Miró, Joan. Qtd. in "NGAKids, Inside Scoop: Miró" (Spring 2009): 1–4. Available as a downloadable PDF on National Gallery of Art website. 19 Jan. 2013. <http://www.nga.gov/kids/scoop-miro.pdf>.

Morris, Elizabeth. *The AA Essential Guide: Paris*. Hampshire: AA Publishing, 1998.

Morrison, Toni. *Playing in the Dark: Whiteness and the Literary Imagination*. Cambridge, MA: Harvard UP, 1992.

North, Michael. *Reading 1922: A Return to the Scene of the Modern*. New York: Oxford UP, 1999.

O'Donnell, George Marion. "Faulkner's Mythology." *The Kenyon Review* 1.3 (Summer 1939): 285–99.

Orwell, George. *Homage to Catalonia* [and] *Down and out in Paris and London*. Boston: Houghton Mifflin Harcourt, 2010. First published 1952 and 1933 respectively.

———. "Politics and the English Language." In *A Collection of Essays*. New York: Harcourt, 1981.

———. "War-Time Diary." In his *Facing Unpleasant Facts: Narrative Essays*. Ed. George Packer. New York: Houghton Mifflin Harcourt, 2009.

Österling, Anders. "Presentation Speech." Nobelprize.org. Web. 25 Apr. 2013. <http://nobelprize.org/nobel_prizes/literature/laureates/1954/press.html>.

Owen, Wilfred. *The Complete Poems and Fragments*. Ed. Jon Stallworthy. 2 vols. New York: W. W. Norton, 1984.

Paddock, Lisa. *Contrapuntal in Integration: A Study of Three Faulkner Short Story Volumes*. Lanham, MD: International Scholars Publications, 2000.

Penn Warren, Robert. "Hemingway [1947]." In *Literary Opinion in America*. Ed. Morton Dauwen Zabel. Vol. 2. 3rd ed. New York: Harper, 1962. 444–63.

Phelan, James. "Distance, Voice, and Temporal Perspective in Frederic Henry's Narration: Successes, Problems, and Paradox." In *New Essays on* A Farewell to Arms. Ed. Scott Donaldson. Cambridge, UK: Cambridge UP, 1990. 53–73.

Plimpton, George. "An Interview with Ernest Hemingway." In *Ernest Hemingway's* The Sun Also Rises: *A Casebook*. Ed. Linda Wagner-Martin. Oxford: Oxford UP, 2002. 15–32.

Poggi, Christine. *Inventing Futurism: The Art and Politics of Artificial Optimism*. Princeton: Princeton UP, 2008.

Potts, Paul. *Dante Called You Beatrice*. London: Eyre and Spottiswoode, 1960.

Pound, Ezra. *The Cantos*. London: Faber, 1987.

———. *Ezra Pound and Margaret Cravens: A Tragic Friendship, 1910–1912*. Ed. Omar Pound and Robert Spoo. Durham: Duke UP, 1988.

———. *Jefferson and/or Mussolini*. London: Stanley Nott, 1935.

Reynolds, Bruce. *Paris with the Lid Lifted*. New York: George Sully, 1927.

Reynolds, Michael. *Hemingway: The Homecoming*. New York: W. W. Norton, 1992.

———. *Hemingway: The 1930s Through the Final Years*. New York: W. W. Norton, 2012.

———. *Hemingway: The Paris Years*. New York: W. W. Norton, 1999.

———. "'Homage to Switzerland': Einstein's Train Stops at Hemingway's Station." In *Hemingway's Neglected Short Fiction: New Perspectives*. Ed. Susan Beegel. Tuscaloosa: U of Alabama P, 1992. 255–63.

Reynolds, Nicholas. "A Spy Who Made His Own Way: Ernest Hemingway, Wartime Spy." *Studies in Intelligence* 56.2 (2012): 1–11. CIA journal extract. Available online at <https://www.cia.gov/library/center-for-the-study-of-intelligence/csi-publications/csi-studies/studies/vol.-56-no.-2/pdfs/Reynolds-Hemingway%20A%20Dubious%20Spy.pdf>.

Ross, Lillian. "Portrait of Hemingway." In *The Art of Fact: A Historical Anthology of Literary Journalism*. Ed. Kevin Kerrane and Ben Yagoda. New York: Scribner, 1998.
Rubin, Andrew N. "Orwell's List of Crypto Communists." Against the Grain. Weblog. <http://andrewrubin.me/2011/10/02/orwells-list-of-crypto-communists/>.
Russell, Bill, and William Francis McSweeny. *Go Up for Glory*. New York: Coward-McCann, 1966.
Saint-Point, Valentine de. "The Futurist Manifesto of Lust." Futurism. Web. 12 Apr. 2012. <http://www.unknown.nu/futurism/lust.html>.
Shelden, Michael. *Orwell: The Authorized Biography*. New York: HarperPerennial, Harper Collins, 1992.
Simultaneity—Albert Einstein and the Theory of Relativity." Last modified 5 May 2007. Our World—from EarBot.com. *YouTube*. Web. <http://www.youtube.com/watch?v=wteiuxyqtoM>.
Singal, Daniel Joseph. "Towards a Definition of American Modernism." In *Background Readings for Teachers of American Literature*. Ed. Venetria K. Patton. Boston: Bedford/St. Martin's, 2006. 112–31.
———. *William Faulkner: The Making of a Modernist*. Chapel Hill, NC: U of North Carolina P, 1997.
Sontag, Susan. *Regarding the Pain of Others*. New York, Picador, 2003.
The Spanish Civil War. Nar. Mike Leighton. Allegro Corporation, 2009. DVD. History of Warfare Series.
The Spanish Earth. Screenplay by Ernest Hemingway and Joris Ivens. Dir. Joris Ivens. Photog. John Ferno. Film ed. Helen van Dongen. Nar. Ernest Hemingway. 1937; Video Yesteryear, 1983. DVD.
Stein, Gertrude. *The Autobiography of Alice B. Toklas*. In *Selected Writings of Gertrude Stein*. Ed. Carl Van Vechten. New York: Vintage, 1946. 3–237.
———. *Gertrude Stein: Selections*. Ed. Joan Retallack. Berkeley: U California P, 2008.
———. *The Making of Americans*. Normal, IL: Dalkey Archive Press, 1995.
———. "Picasso." In her *Selected Writings*. 293–95. Originally published as "Pablo Picasso" in *Camera Work* Aug. 1912 (Special Issue): 29–30.
———. *Three Lives* and *Q.E.D.* Ed. Marianne DeKoven. New York: W. W. Norton, 2006.
———. *Writings, 1932–1946*. New York: Library of America, 1998.
Stevens, Wallace. *Adagia*. In *Opus Posthumous*. Ed. Milton J. Bates. New York: Knopf, 1989.
———. *The Collected Poems*. New York: Knopf, 1955.
———. *Letters of Wallace Stevens*. Ed. Holly Stevens. Berkeley: U of California P, 1966.
Stoltzfus, Ben. *Hemingway and French Writers*. Kent, OH: Kent State UP, 2010.
Stoneback, H. R. *Hemingway's Paris: Our Paris?* Germantown, NY: Lines, 1990.
———. *Reading Hemingway's* The Sun Also Rises. Kent, OH: Kent State UP, 2007.
Svoboda, Frederic J. "The Great Themes in Hemingway: Love, War, Wilderness, and Loss." In *A Historical Guide to Ernest Hemingway*. Ed. Linda Wagner-Martin. New York: Oxford UP, 2000. 155–72.
———. *Hemingway and* The Sun Also Rises: *The Crafting of a Style*. Lawrence, KS: UP of Kansas, 1983.
Taylor, D. J. *Orwell: The Life*. New York: Henry Holt and Co., 2003.

Vernon, Alex. "Hemingway's War." In his *Hemingway's Second War*. Iowa City, IA: U of Iowa P, 2011.
Villard, Henry S., and James Nagel. *Hemingway in Love and War: The Lost Diary of Agnes von Kurowsky*. Boston: Northeastern UP, 1989.
Vincent, John. "How Hemingway Gored his Rivals." *London Observer*. 6 Mar. 2004. Web. 18, 25 Apr. 2013. <http://www.guardian.co.uk/world/2004/mar/07/usa.books>.
Wagner-Martin, Linda. *Ernest Hemingway: A Literary Life*. New York: Palgrave, 2007.
Wilder, Thornton. *The Selected Letters of Thornton Wilder*. Ed. Jackson Bryer and Robin Wilder. Ebook edition. New York: Harper Collins, 2008.
Williams, Raymond. "The Metropolis and the Emergence of Modernism." In *Modernism/Postmodernism*. Ed. Peter Booker. New York: Longman, 1992.
Williams, William Carlos. *Al Que Quiere*. Boston: Four Seas Company, 1917.
Wolkstein, Diane, and Samuel Noah Kramer. *Inanna: Queen of Heaven and Earth*. New York: Harper and Row, 1983.
Woolf, Virginia. *The Diary of Virginia Woolf*. Vol. 4: *1931–1935*. Ed. Anne Olivier Bell. New York: Harcourt Brace Jovanovich, 1982.
———. *Mrs. Dalloway*. New York: Harcourt Brace Jovanovich, 1981.
———. "Phases of Fiction." In her *Granite and Rainbow: Essays by Virginia Woolf*. New York: Harcourt Brace Jovanovich, 1958. 93–145.
———. *Three Guineas*. New York: Harcourt Brace Jovanovich, 1938.
Wordsworth, William. *Selected Poems and Prefaces*. Ed. Jack Stillinger. Boston: Houghton Mifflin, 1965.

Selected Bibliography

Anderson, Sherwood. "I Want to Know Why." *Smart Set* 60 (Nov. 1919): 35–40. Available online at The Literature Network. Web. 19 Jan. 2013. <http://www.online-literature.com/sherwood-anderson/1469/>.

Beisel, Nicola Kay. *Imperiled Innocents: Anthony Comstock and Family Reproduction in Victorian America*. Princeton: Princeton UP, 1998.

Bridgman, Richard. *The Colloquial Style in American Literature*. New York: Oxford UP, 1966.

Burns, Ken, dir. *Not For Ourselves Alone: The Story of Elizabeth Cady Stanton and Susan B. Anthony*. Florentine Films. WETA-TV, Hollywood, 1999. DVD. PBS Home Video, dist. Paramount Home Entertainment, 2004.

Cather, Willa. "Coming, Aphrodite!" In *Youth and the Bright Medusa*. New York: Alfred A. Knopf, 1920. 11–78. Available online at the Willa Cather Archive. Web. 19 Jan. 2013. <http://cather.unl.edu/0008.html#aphrodite>.

Comley, Nancy R., and Robert Scholes. "Reading 'Up in Michigan.'" In *New Essays on Hemingway's Short Fiction*. Ed. Paul Smith. New York: Cambridge UP, 1998. 19–46.

Conner, Marc C. "Fathers and Sons: Winesburg, Ohio, and the Revision of Modernism." *Studies in American Fiction* 29.2 (2001): 209–38.

Conrad, Joseph. Preface. *The Nigger of the "Narcissus": A Tale of the Sea*. First published as *The Children of the Sea*. New York: Dodd, Mead, and Co., 1897. Available online at the University of Missouri website. Web. 19 Jan. 2013. <http://web.missouri.edu/~materert/mod/Conrad.htm>.

de Grazia, Edward. *Girls Lean Back Everywhere: The Law of Obscenity and the Assault on Genius*. New York: Random House, 1992.

Douglas, Ann. *Terrible Honesty: Mongrel Manhattan in the 1920s*. New York: Farrar, Straus and Giroux, 1995.

Emerson, Ralph Waldo. *Essays and Lectures*. Ed. Joel Porte. New York: Library of America, 1983.

Ernest Hemingway: A Life in Michigan. WCMU-TV and Michigan Humanities Council, Mount Pleasant, MI, 2007. DVD.

Fantina, Richard. *Ernest Hemingway: Machismo and Masochism*. New York: Palgrave Macmillan, 2005.

Faulkner, William. *Absalom, Absalom!* New York: Random House, 1936.

———. *As I Lay Dying*. 1930. Rev. ed., New York: Random House, 1964.

———. *Collected Stories of William Faulkner.* 1950. New York: Vintage Books, 1977.
———. *Go Down, Moses.* New York: Random House, 1942.
———. *Light in August.* 1932. New York: Vintage, 1990.
———. *The Sound and the Fury.* 1929. New York: Random House, 1984.
———. *These 13.* New York: Jonathan Cape and Harrison Smith, 1931.
Fitzgerald, F. Scott. "Benediction." In *Flappers and Philosophers.* New York: Doubleday, 1920. Available online at Lit2Go. Web. 19 Jan. 2013. <http://etc.usf.edu/lit2go/84/flappers-and-philosophers/1410/benediction/>.
———. *The Great Gatsby.* New York: Scribner, 2004.
Fleming, Robert E., ed. *Hemingway and the Natural World.* Moscow, ID: U of Idaho P, 1999.
Flynn, Catherine. "'Circe' and Surrealism: Joyce and the Avant-Garde." *Journal of Modern Literature* 34:2 (2011): 121–38.
Freeman, Donald C., ed. *Linguistics and Literary Style.* New York: Holt, Rinehart, and Winston, 1970.
Goudsouzian, Aram. *King of the Court: Bill Russell and the Basketball Revolution.* Cincinnati: U of Cincinnati P, 2010.
Grebstein, Sheldon Norman. *Hemingway's Craft.* Carbondale: Southern Illinois UP, 1973.
Hassan, Ihab. *The Postmodern Turn: Essays in Postmodern Theory and Culture.* Columbus: Ohio State UP, 1987.
Hemingway, Ernest. "Conrad, Optimist and Moralist." *Transatlantic Review* (Oct. 1924); rpt. in his *By-Line, Hemingway: Selected Articles and Dispatches of Four Decades.* Ed. William White. New York: Scribner, 1967. 114–15.
———. *In Our Time.* 1925 Edition. American Studies at the University of Virginia. Web. 18 Jan. 2013. <http://xroads.virginia.edu/~hyper/HEMINGWAYX/contents.html>.
———. "The Unpublished Opening of *The Sun Also Rises.*" *Antaeus* 33 (Spring 1979): 7–14.
———. "Up in Michigan." In *Three Stories and Ten Poems.* Paris: Contact Publishing, 1923. Available online at *Three Stories and Ten Poems.* Wikisource. Web. 19 Jan. 2013. <http://en.wikisource.org/wiki/Three_Stories_and_Ten_Poems>.
Josephs, Allen. "Toreo: The Moral Axis of *The Sun Also Rises.*" *Hemingway Review* 6.1 (1986): 151–68.
Kalaidjian, Walter, ed. *The Cambridge Companion to American Modernism.* Cambridge, UK: Cambridge UP, 2005.
Klages, Mary. *Literary Theory: A Guide for the Perplexed.* New York: Continuum, 2006.
Lindsay, Clarence. "'I Belong in Little Towns:' Sherwood Anderson's Small Town Post-Modernism." *Midamerica: The Yearbook of the Society for the Study of Midwestern Literature* 26 (1999): 77–104.
Lucretius. *The Way Things Are.* Trans. Rolfe Humphries. Bloomington: Indiana UP, 1969.
Midnight in Paris. DVD. Dir. Woody Allen. Sony Pictures Classic, 2011. Film.
Owen, Wilfred. *The Complete Poems and Fragments.* Ed. Jon Stallworthy. New York: W. W. Norton, 1984.
Perloff, Majorie. "The Audacity of Hope." In *The History of Futurism: The Precursors, Protagonists, and Legacies.* Ed. Geert Buelens, Harald Hendrix, and Monica Jansen. Plymouth: Lexington Books, 2012. 9–30.

———. *Wittgenstein's Ladder: Poetic Language and the Strangeness of the Ordinary.* Chicago: U of Chicago P, 1996.

Scott, Fred Newton. "The Most Fundamental Differentia of Poetry and Prose." *PMLA* 19 (1904): 250–69.

———. "The Scansion of Prose Rhythm." *PMLA* 20 (1905): 707–28.

Skei, Hans. *William Faulkner, The Short Story Career: An Outline of Faulkner's Short Story Writing from 1919 to 1962.* Oslo: University Forl, 1981.

Stevens, Wallace. *Opus Posthumous.* Ed. Milton J. Bates. New York: Knopf, 1989.

Stewart, Matthew. "It Was All a Pleasant Business: The Historical Context of 'On the Quai at Smyrna.'" *The Hemingway Review* 23.1 (2003): 58–71.

Tanner, Tony. *The Reign of Wonder.* Cambridge, UK: Cambridge UP, 1965.

Toomer, Jean. *Cane.* 1923. Rpt., New York: W. W. Norton, 1988.

Wilder, Thornton. *Thornton Wilder: Collected Plays and Writings on Theater.* Ed. J. D. McClatchy. New York: Library of America, 2007.

Wittgenstein, Ludwig. *Tractatus Logico-Philosophicus.* Trans. C. K. Ogden. New York: Harcourt, Brace, and Co., 1922.

Woolf, Virginia. *The Essays of Virginia Woolf.* Vol. 5. Ed. Stuart Clarke. New York: Harcourt Brace Jovanovich, 1982. 40–89.

Young, Philip. *Ernest Hemingway: A Reconsideration.* University Park: Pennsylvania State UP, 1966.

Contributors

David Barnes is departmental lecturer in English literature at the University of Oxford, having previously worked as a lecturer at the University of Birmingham and as a visiting tutor at Somerville College, Oxford, and Emmanuel College, Cambridge. He has written widely on a range of British and American writers, and his work has appeared in the *Journal of Modern Literature, Comparative American Studies,* and *Comparative Literature.* His current project examines the political idea of Europe expressed by modernist American authors, including Hemingway, Pound, H. D., Fitzgerald, and Eliot, and he recently received an Ernest Hemingway Research Grant from the John F. Kennedy Presidential Library toward this research.

Phillip Beard teaches in the English Department at Auburn University in Auburn, Alabama. He has taught American literature as a Fulbright Scholar at Friedrich Alexander University in Erlangen, Germany. He specializes in twentieth-century American modernism and postmodernism, and has published articles on F. Scott Fitzgerald, Delmore Schwartz, and Thomas Pynchon. He also specializes in studying hybrid forms of American romanticism in twentieth-century literature.

Bradley Bowers is professor of English in the Department of English and Foreign Languages at Barry University in Miami Shores, Florida. After earning a PhD in English from the University of North Carolina at Chapel Hill, he served as a visiting scholar at Columbia University in New York, at the American Academy in Rome, and at the American University of Rome. He has published on such topics as Ernest Hemingway, Virginia Woolf, Italian futurism, and British and American modernism. In 2007, he edited an essay collection, *The Da Vinci Code in the Academy.*

James B. Carothers is professor of English at the University of Kansas and a founding editor of the *Faulkner Journal.* His primary research focus has been William Faulkner, approached through traditional scholarship grounded in the aim of adding to the collective understanding of particular texts and larger issues within Faulkner's oeuvre. While his most important work within Faulkner studies has been on the short stories, he has also sought to elucidate the comic and humorous elements of Faulkner's fiction and to explain and advocate for his often-neglected later fiction. Carothers has also studied and made presentations on Hemingway and Fitzgerald, and has tried to keep current in studies of modernism and of comedy and humor. He has presented on Hemingway's work at biennial international conferences in Kansas City, Spain, and Switzerland. Another area of interest is the literature of baseball, a voluminous popular culture subject to which he applies conventional methods of academic analysis.

Andrew Fletcher attended Fort Lewis College in Durango, Colorado, and has taught middle and high school English on Colorado's western slope. He is currently a graduate student at Bemidji State University in Minnesota, where he teaches courses in composition and argument.

Joseph Fruscione, who received his PhD in English from George Washington University in 2005, is a freelance editor, proofreader, and writing consultant. He is cofounder and communications director of PrecariCorps, a nonprofit designed to support adjuncts professionally and financially. From 1999 to 2014, he was an adjunct professor specializing in nineteenth- and twentieth-century American literature, culture, and adaptation, as well as in first-year writing. He taught at George Washington University, Georgetown University, and the University of Maryland, Baltimore County. In addition to his book, *Faulkner and Hemingway: Biography of a Literary Rivalry* (Ohio State, 2012), and an article on Ralph Ellison and Hemingway in *Hemingway and the Black Renaissance* (ed. Gary Holcomb and Charles Scruggs; Ohio State, 2012), he has focused extensively on F. Scott Fitzgerald in his teaching, research, and conference work. From 2010 to 2014, he wrote the annual bibliography on Fitzgerald and Hemingway studies for *American Literary Scholarship* (Duke UP). He is currently coediting an essay collection that will examine different aspects of academia, activism, and social media.

Meg Gillette, who received her PhD from the University of Illinois in Urbana-Champaign, is an associate professor of English at Augustana College in Rock Island, Illinois, where she teaches classes in American literature, directs the first-year writing program, and leads a summer study abroad program in Paris. Her research on reproduction in modern American literature has appeared in *Modern Fiction Studies, Studies in American Fiction,* and *Twentieth-Century Literature.*

Julie Goodspeed-Chadwick is an associate professor of English at Indiana University–Purdue University in Columbus, Indiana, specializing in twentieth-century American literature, transatlantic modernism, women and literature, literary theory, and American ethnic literature. Her research focuses on identity politics, namely the politics inherent in identity constructions, and responses to trauma in modern and contemporary literature. She works within various critical theory schools, and her scholarship is indebted to feminism and gender studies, trauma studies, embodiment theories, structuralism and semiotics, poststructuralism, Marxism, cultural studies, and ethnic studies. As a teacher-scholar, she aims to bring the work and ideas that invigorate her research into the classroom. Ultimately, her goals are to teach students how to approach, understand, and appreciate literary texts, difficult ideas and philosophies, and good writing; to invest students with the ability to think critically and thus to discern the significance, beauty, and cultural work of various types of literature;

and to demonstrate that students can engage in and contribute to the type of scholarly work expected in the university classroom and in the field of English studies at large.

Sharon Hamilton has fifteen years of teaching experience at universities in Canada, Italy, the United States, and Austria; she also served as academic dean at the International University of Vienna. Her work on modernist writers, such as Fitzgerald and Hemingway, appears regularly in scholarly journals. Her recent book chapters on H. L. Mencken's *Smart Set* (from which Hemingway learned important lessons about psychological realism) appear in *North America 1894-1960*, Volume 2 of *The Oxford Critical and Cultural History of Modernist Magazines* (Oxford UP, 2012), and *Literary Cultures and Middlebrow Matters* (Palgrave, 2011).

Jeffrey Herlihy-Mera, who earned his doctorate at the Universidad Pompeu Fabra in Barcelona, Spain, is a member of the Humanities Department at Universidad de Puerto Rico in Mayagüez, PR, and president of the Caribbean Chapter of the College English Association. He was awarded the chair of migrant/transnational studies by the National Endowment for the Humanities in 2012-13 and was a Fulbright Scholar at the Universidad del Azuay in Cuenca, Ecuador, in 2012. Herlihy-Mera is the author of *In Paris or Paname: Hemingway's Expatriate Nationalism* (2011) and coeditor with Vamsi K. Koneru of *Paris in American Literatures: On Distance as a Literary Resource* (2013). His work has appeared in *Modern Fiction Studies, Barcelona Review, European Journal of American Studies, Hemingway Review,* and other publications.

Jean Jespersen Bartholomew holds a BA in English from the University of Northern Iowa, an MA in English from Kansas State University, and is a candidate for an ALM from Harvard University. With more than fifteen years of educational experience, she teaches English at Carlbrook School in Halifax, Virginia. Earlier in her career, she worked as a freelance writer and editor and taught as an English instructor at both the College of DuPage in Glen Ellyn Illinois, and Kansas State University, in Manhattan, Kansas.

Anna Lillios is an associate professor of English at the University of Central Florida. Her research interests center on literature of place, particularly Mediterranean studies (focusing on the work of Lawrence Durrell) and Florida studies (focusing on the work of Zora Neale Hurston and Marjorie Kinnan Rawlings). She is the author of *Crossing the Creek: The Literary Friendship of Zora Neale Hurston and Marjorie Kinnan Rawlings* (UP of Florida, 2010), which received a 2011 Florida Book Award for nonfiction, and edited a collection of essays, *Lawrence Durrell and the Greek World* (2004). She directs the Zora Neale Hurston Electronic Archive at http://pegasus.cc.ucf.edu/~zoraneal and is the editor of *Deus Loci: The Lawrence Durrell Journal* and the *Marjorie Kinnan Rawlings Journal of Florida Literature*. She is a past president of the International Lawrence Durrell Society and currently serves on its executive board. She is also a past president of the Florida College English Association and received its 2008 Distinguished Colleague Award. She is currently the executive director and a trustee of the Marjorie Kinnan Rawlings Society.

Adam R. McKee is an assistant professor of English at CUNY–Queensborough Community College. He received his PhD in twentieth-century literature and culture from Florida State University in Tallahassee, Florida. His research focuses primarily on modernism, avant-garde movements, and urban studies. He has presented work at several conferences, including the Biennial Hemingway Conference, South Atlantic Modern Language Association, and the American Conference of Irish Studies. He received both his master's and bachelor's degrees from Kent State University in Kent, Ohio.

Mark P. Ott teaches at Deerfield Academy in Massachusetts. He is the author of *A Sea of Change: Ernest Hemingway and the Gulf Stream—a Contextual Biography* (Kent State UP, 2008). Ott has presented academic papers at international Hemingway conferences in Cuba, Oak Park, Bimini, Italy, Key West, and Spain, and his scholarship has been published in the *Hemingway Review*. He has been awarded grants from the Ernest Hemingway Society, the Ernest Hemingway Collection at the John F. Kennedy Library, and the Arts and Sciences Advisory Council of the University of Hawaii–Manoa.

Katie Owens-Murphy received her PhD from Penn State University and is now an assistant professor of English at the University of North Alabama. Her research interests include twentieth-century American literature, narrative and poetic theory, genre theory, and philosophy and literature. Her dissertation examined the impact of the lyric tradition on the twentieth-century American novel. Her work has appeared in the *Hemingway Review*, the *Arizona Quarterly*, and the *Journal of Modern Literature* and is forthcoming in the journal *Genre*. She has served as a full-time research assistant for the Hemingway Letters Project, which resulted in volume 1 of the Cambridge edition of *The Letters of Ernest Hemingway* (2012), and has taught courses on fantasy literature and the modern American novel.

Lauren Rule Maxwell specializes in contemporary literature from the Americas at the Citadel, the Military College of South Carolina, in Charleston, where she is an associate professor of English. A native of Richmond, Virginia, she graduated summa cum laude from Wake Forest University with a BA in English and a minor in biology. After writing professionally for health-care organizations in Washington, D.C., she earned her MA and PhD from Emory University. Her monograph, *Romantic Revisions in Novels from the Americas* (2013), is featured in the Comparative Cultural Studies Series of Purdue University Press. She has published articles in *Modern Fiction Studies*, the *F. Scott Fitzgerald Review*, and (most recently) *Margaret Atwood Studies*. She also has a chapter, "Consumer Culture and Advertising," in *F. Scott Fitzgerald in Context* (ed. Bryant Mangum, Cambridge UP, 2013). Maxwell teaches classes in American and contemporary literature and directs the M.A.T. Program in English Education. In addition to her literature courses, she teaches writing courses, including freshman composition, advanced composition, and professional writing. She also is involved with the Lowcountry Writing Project, a local site of the National Writing Project that provides professional development to teachers in the Charleston metro area and helps them use writing more effectively in their classrooms.

Margaret E. Wright-Cleveland directs the Office of Faculty Recognition at Florida State University. She serves as an adjunct instructor in the English Department and in the Women's Studies Program. Her work on race and modernism in American literature has been published in the journal *MidAmerica* and in *Hemingway and the Black Renaissance* (ed. Gary Holcomb and Charles Scruggs, Ohio State UP, 2012).

Index

alienation, 37, 39, 44, 47, 59, 63–64
Anderson, Sherwood, 106, 107, 110, 145; "I Want to Know Why," 144; "My Old Man," 144; "Unlighted Lamps," 145; *Winesburg, Ohio*, 107, 110, 111, 112
Anglophone modernism, 5
avant-garde, 2–4, 6, 28, 63, 72, 84, 106, 162, 167

Bad Modernisms, 3
Bevis, William, 32
boxing, 83–84
Braque, 78, 153

The Cambridge Companion to Modernism, 3
Campbell, Joseph, and *The Hero with a Thousand Faces*, 53
Cather, Willa, 140; "Coming, Aphrodite!," 140
Cézanne, Paul, 7, 67–68, 74, 77–79, 80, 120, 153
Conrad, Joseph, 144–45; *Heart of Darkness*, 144
correspondence: about Hemingway, 30–33, 52, 61; to Hemingway, 159, 162, 165–67; from Hemingway, 22, 83, 90–91, 101–2, 120, 159, 161–62, 165–67
Cubism and cubist style, 11–14
cummings, e. e., 79

D'Annunzio, Gabriele, 119
denotations, 12
dictatorship, 91, 97
disorientation, 5
Dos Passos, John, 98

Eliot, T. S., and *The Waste Land*, 35, 52–53, 55–56, 74
Ellison, Ralph, 59; *Invisible Man*, 133

fascism, 88, 89, 90–91, 96–98, 117–18, 120
Faulkner, William, 2, 4, 6, 7, 42–50, 105, 107–15, 128; *Absalom, Absalom!*, 48; *As I Lay Dying*, 47, 49; "Barn Burning," 52; *Go Down, Moses*, 48; *Light in August*, 128, 133; *The Reivers*, 49; "A Rose for Emily," 43, 52; *The Sound and the Fury*, 48; *These 13*, 114
femininity, 53
Fitzgerald, F. Scott, 2, 51–52, 82, 85, 87–88, 119, 125, 128, 132–34, 140–41, 160–61, 165; "Benediction," 140; "Echoes of the Jazz Age," 132; *The Great Gatsby*, 8, 51, 52, 125, 128–29, 132–36, 161
futurism, 7, 117–27
futurist movement, 7

gender, 45, 53, 107, 110, 111, 140, 141
The Great War. *See* World War I

Harlem Renaissance, 59, 106
Hays, Peter, 2
Hemingway, Ernest: bullfighting, 56, 90, 91, 120; code of behavior, 44; creative life, 5; early work, 10; in Europe, 4, 82–85, 88, 90, 118; iceberg theory, 79, 112; and Italy, 46; journalism, 22, 43, 84–86, 88, 92–93, 95, 100; and Key West or Florida, 52, 61; and KGB, 99; military, 8, 90; in newspapers, 21, 23, 84–85, 92, 93; Nobel Prize in Literature, 100–101, 129; postmodernism, 149–57; professional life, 5; proto-postmodernism, 2, 5; Pulitzer Prize for *The Old Man and the Sea*, 101; and Spain, 6, 58, 82, 89, 93, 95–100, 161; Spanish Civil War, 89, 93, 95–96, 99; and Switzerland, 8, 149–57; transatlantic, 4–5
Hemingway, Ernest, works by: *Across the River and into the Trees*, 154; "An African Story," 44; "American Bohemians in Paris," 86; "The Battler," 33–34, 37, 76; "Big Two-Hearted River," 5, 10–19, 31, 33–35, 37–39, 77, 78, 129, 131, 141, 144; "Cat in the Rain," 77, 129, 140; "A Clean, Well-Lighted

228

Place," 44, 48, 54, 123; *Death in the Afternoon*, 30, 79, 86; *A Farewell to Arms*, 2, 7, 29, 45, 46, 118–19, 123–24, 163; *The Fifth Column*, 162; *For Whom the Bell Tolls*, 46, 96, 99, 101, 154; "The Gambler, the Nun, and the Radio," 44; *Green Hills of Africa*, 21; "Hills Like White Elephants," 44, 48, 129; "Homage to Switzerland," 149, 150, 153–56; "In Another Country," 129–30; *In Our Time*, 3–5, 7, 10–11, 14, 17, 34–35, 37, 39, 43–44, 46, 72–80, 84, 85, 107, 112–14, 118, 121–22, 139, 141–43, 145; "Indian Camp," 33, 34, 76–79, 129, 139; *The Kansas City Star* (newspaper), 22, 93; *A Moveable Feast*, 21, 22, 85, 87, 93, 120, 139, 143; "Mr. and Mrs. Elliot," 25–26; "Nobody Ever Dies," 99; "Now I Lay Me," 129–30; *The Old Man and the Sea*, 46, 100–101; "On the Quai at Smyrna," 34, 122, 142; "On Writing," 7, 72, 74, 78, 79; "Paris 1922," 5, 7, 72, 73, 74; "The Short, Happy Life of Francis Macomber," 21, 43; "The Snows of Kilimanjaro," 44, 57, 95; "Soldier's Home," 6, 24, 33–35, 129–30, 139, 141, 143; *The Sun Also Rises*, 2, 4–7, 33, 45, 46, 48, 51, 52, 54, 56, 60, 64, 66–70, 85, 90–92, 118, 120, 122–124, 154, 162; "The Three-Day Blow," 76, 139; *To Have and To Have Not*, 5, 31, 33, 37, 38, 40; *Toronto (Daily) Star* (newspaper), 21, 84, 85, 88, 93, 142; "Up in Michigan," 7, 72, 74, 75, 140; "A Way You'll Never Be," 129, 131, 133; "Wine of Wyoming," 162–66
The History of Futurism: The Precursors, Protagonists, and Legacies, 118
Hurston, Zora Neale, 2, 4, 51–61; *Their Eyes Were Watching God*, 6, 51–54, 56, 58, 60

identity politics, 15, 16
irony, 5
Italy, 87–89, 94, 117, 118, 119, 131; Venice, 87, 89

Jazz Age, 93, 137, 138, 161
Joyce, James, 7, 48, 73, 74, 76, 77, 79, 94; *Dubliners*, 73, 77; *Ulysses*, 48, 76

Kale, Verna, 4
Kant, Immanuel, 32

LaCapra, Dominick, 15
late Victorian, 5
Laub, Dori, 18
Lawrence, D. H., 88
Levenson, Michael, 3

Lewis, Wyndham, 119
literary modernism, 3
lost generation, 2, 13, 65, 72, 83–85, 160–61
Lyon, Janet, 4, 5

MacCannell, Dean, 65–67; *The Tourist*, 65, 66, 67
Mao, Douglas, 3, 5, 9
masculinity, 5, 15, 19, 30, 53, 83, 161
McAlmon, Robert, 79
McKee, Adam, 4, 7
Metropolitan Museum of Art (New York), 117
Midnight in Paris (film), 62, 63, 82, 91, 160
Miró, Joan, 146
modernism: and America, 22, 29, 83–85, 105–11, 113, 115; cultural context, 8, 105, 106, 126, 137, 144, 145; cultural identity, 7; definitions of, 13, 44, 45, 52, 53, 105, 108, 109, 113, 118, 120, 151, 156; gender, 6, 110; Hemingway's writing style, 10, 22, 31–32, 36, 40, 69, 74, 92, 112; moral values, 6; national identity, 105, 108, 110; otherness, 6; race, 6, 7, 110; romanticism, 17, 53, 120; self-identity, 6, 110; stylistic repetition, 11, 12, 18, 22–29, 68, 142–43, 149, 155; techniques, 12, 45, 52, 92, 110–11, 160
modernity, 10
Monet, Claude, 78

narrative fluidity, 5
The Norton Anthology of American Literature, 52, 107

Orwell, George, 2, 5, 7, 88, 92–104; *1984*, 95, 97–101; *Animal Farm*, 92, 97, 100–101

Paris, 6, 21, 28–29, 43, 53, 54, 56, 62–72, 76–78, 80, 82–88, 98, 99, 101, 117, 119, 160–61; American expatriates in, 62, 83, 85–87, 92–94, 100, 117–18, 121, 125, 160, 166; cafés, 58, 62, 65–67, 70, 84, 85–87; Hemingway's apprenticeship of 1922, 21, 23, 27–29; Hemingway's Paris, 56, 66, 70, 72, 74, 77, 82–84, 119, 137, 139; Hemingway writing about, 51, 53–54, 56, 58, 64, 66, 78, 86–88, 95, 101, 155
Perkins, Maxwell, 52
Picasso, Pablo, 11–12, 23, 24, 78, 84, 95, 153
postmodernism, 149–57
postwar world, 18, 33
Pound, Ezra, 2, 74, 79, 83–86, 88–91, 119, 120, 160; *The Cantos*, 83, 86–87, 90
propaganda, 69, 97–99, 120

race, 7, 38–39, 45, 48, 58–59, 83, 107, 110–11, 113, 144
reception theory, 158

salon communities, 4
Scribner (publisher), 52
sentimentalism, 16
Sontag, Susan, 18
Southern Literary Renaissance, 106
The Spanish Earth (film), 95, 96
Stein, Gertrude, 2, 4, 5, 6, 7, 10–19, 21–29, 74–77, 79, 80, 82, 85, 143, 144; *The Autobiography of Alice B. Toklas*, 150; "Composition as Explanation," 75; influence on Hemingway's prose, 10–19, 21–29; *The Making of Americans*, 23, 26, 29; "Patriarchal Poetry," 21; "Picasso," 5, 6, 11, 16, 17; *Three Lives*, 6, 25–27, 75
Stevens, Wallace, 2, 6, 30–41; *Adagia*, 32; *Collected Poems*, 32–34, 36
stream of consciousness, 76
Svoboda, Frederic J., 14

Toomer, Jean, 4, 7, 73, 105–11, 115; *Cane*, 73, 106, 107, 111–15
totalitarianism, 97, 99, 101
transnational, 5

trauma, 91; in Hemingway's life, 90, 119, 128; in Hemingway's work, 5, 10, 13, 16, 17, 19, 54, 57; PTSD (or psychological trauma) or shell shock, 54, 57, 125, 128, 130, 135, 144
Twain, Mark, 121; *The Adventures of Huckleberry Finn*, 121
Tyler, Lisa, 2

Ur-modernists, 6, 8, 160
Ur-subjects, 56

Wagner-Martin, Linda, 14
Walkowitz, Rebecca, 3, 5, 9
Warren, Robert Penn, 13
Wilde, Oscar, 122
Wilder, Thornton, 2, 8, 160, 162, 165–66
Williams, William Carlos, 33, 150; *Yes, Mrs. Williams*, 150
Wilson, Robert Forrest, 86; *Paris on Parade*, 86
Woolf, Virginia, 73, 119, 124–25; *Monday or Tuesday*, 73; *Mrs. Dalloway*, 125
Wordsworth, William, 37
World War I, 8, 13, 33–35, 43, 44, 53, 54, 57, 60, 84, 85, 90, 93, 105, 108, 113, 114, 117, 119, 122, 128–29, 136, 138, 139, 143
World War II, 13, 89, 93, 94, 96, 99, 100–101, 117

www.ingramcontent.com/pod-product-compliance
Lightning Source LLC
Chambersburg PA
CBHW021825300426
44114CB00009BA/328